Books by Ralph Keyes

WE, THE LONELY PEOPLE: SEARCHING FOR COMMUNITY
IS THERE LIFE AFTER HIGH SCHOOL?
THE HEIGHT OF YOUR LIFE

The
Height
of Your Life

The
Height
of Your Life

RALPH KEYES

Little, Brown and Company — Boston – Toronto

FIRST EDITION

"The Height Report," an article adapted from this book, appeared in *Esquire,* November 1979; another version ran in *Reader's Digest,* March 1980.

The author is grateful to the following publishers for permission to quote material, as noted:

Bobbs-Merrill Company, Inc., for a quote from *Bubbles: A Self Portrait* by Beverly Sills, copyright © 1976 by The Bobbs-Merrill Company, Inc. Reprinted by permission of the publisher.

Mouton and Company, Publishers, The Hague, for a quote from William Stini's contribution to *Biosocial Interrelations in Population Adaptation* (1975), edited by Elizabeth Watts, Francis Johnston, and Gabriel Lasker.

MPL Communications, Inc., for lines from "Hello Twelve, Hello Thirteen, Hello Love" from *A Chorus Line* by Marvin Hamlisch and Edward Kleban, copyright © 1975 by Marvin Hamlisch and Edward Kleban. All rights controlled by American Compass Music Corp. and Wren Music Company, a division of MPL Communications, Inc. International copyright secured. All rights reserved. Used by permission.

Illustration credits appear on page 331.

LIBRARY OF CONGRESS CATALOGING IN PUBLICATION DATA

Keyes, Ralph.
  The height of your life.

  1. Stature. 2. Body image. I. Title.
GT495.K49   305   80-295
ISBN 0-316-49131-4

MV

Designed by Susan Windheim

Published simultaneously in Canada by Little, Brown & Company (Canada) Limited

PRINTED IN THE UNITED STATES OF AMERICA

For my mother,
whose writing has inspired my own

Contents

Acknowledgments

The help of many people has made *The Height of Your Life* a better book than it might have been otherwise. (Any defects remain the author's responsibility alone.) In particular I would like to thank those who follow.

Technical Assistance: Larry and Mary Ballen, Tom Coulson, Virginia Creeden, Eileen Creitz, Laura Evans, Susan Windheim.

Help with Research: Bim Angst, David Berry, Joan Scherer Brewer, Veronica Chapman, Donna Frabotta, Nancy Grunberg, Ava Plakins, and the staffs of the Libraries of Lehigh University, the Provident Mutual Insurance Company (Jean Denio, Tikvah Shulman), the Lincoln Center Theater Collection, and the Theater Collection of the Free Library of Philadelphia (Geri Duclow, Elaine Ebo, Laura Sims), who were all quite helpful.

Clipping Service: Bob Bahr, Joan Bigge, Michael Brandon, Juergen Haver, Lanny Jones, Pat Krauska, William Kruskal, Bob Lee, Marian Lee, Charlotte Keyes, Gene Keyes, Nicky Keyes, Scott Keyes, Nolan Miller, Nik Venet, John T. Wood. (Should anyone wish to consider this encouragement for sending me clips in the future, please do.)

Manuscript Criticism: Judith Appelbaum, Libby Blackman, Laurie Bloomfield, Bryce Britton, Craig Carnelia, Reba Gordon, Martha Johns, Charlotte Keyes, Jane Keyes, Scott Keyes, Julia Lawlor, Del Molarsky, Scot Morris, Hank and Mim Noordam, Charles O'Leary,

Jerry Parker, Philomène Resnikoff, Maureen Silliman, Robert Ellis and Terry Smith, Art Spikol, Brian Stabler, Bill and Anne Stillwell, Gay Swenson, Rod Townley, Louis Underwood, Jan and Marlene Van Meter, Stan Wood.

Literary Contributions: James H. Aldrich, Mary Alexander, Judith Appelbaum, George W. Arno, Phyllis Jean Aten, Pamela Ault, Laurie Becklund, Bennet Berger, Judie Black, Barbara Bodin, Danny J. Boggs, Dave Bowlus, Bill Bruff, Paul Buhle, Earl Burrows, Paul Cabbell, Bill Canby, Jane Canby, Eileen Maria Canzian, Bonnie Carine, Claudia Carlsen, Fred Cort, Jeannie Coulson, Gay Courter, Allan Cox, John Coyne, J. D. Dawson, Donna DeRose, Debbie Donahue, Roz Driscoll, Marie Edwards, Pat Edwards, Peggy Elder, Robin Lynn Emerson, Margot Ensign, Jeff Evans, Roy Fairfield, Francis J. Figlear, Laura Fillmore, Sara Finn, Sandy Forrest, Bob Friedman, May Garland, Sarah Leslie Gaylord, Tom Gillette, Harold Greenwald, Gary Grienke, Candace Hamilton, David Hamilton, Debra Handelman, Christopher Haring, Charlotte W. Harmon, Norma Harouny, Mary Hatch, Jonellen Heckler, Lou Heckler, John Herrmann, Pat Horn, Ellen D. Hughson, Ervin Jackson, Jr., Bill John, Paul G. John, Don Johnson, Margaret H. Johnson, Robert Johnston, Jennifer Joiner, Elizabeth Karnes, Richard A. Kauffman, Frances Keyes, Nancy Kinney, John Klein, Bev Kochard, Cheryl Kominski, Alice Koskella, Karen S. Kramer, John Krance, Patricia C. Krauska, David L. Kurtz, Elke Lambers, Norman J. Lass, Julia Lawlor, Doug Lea, Julie Lea, Richard A. LeBel, Tom Leech, Toni Logar, Margot McNeil, Francis P. McNiece, J. A. McQueeney, Kent Madin, Claire Mansfield, Sandra Martin, Jeff Mayer, Dave Mearns, Ed Menzel, Richard Menzies, Avrum Miller, Linda Mulligan, Mike Mulligan, Joe Murrey, Jr., Janet Nehrbass, Neil Nehrbass, Gail Newton, Adrian Noordam, Mim Noordam, Hanna Northway, Richard Northway, Lauren Ondra, Mike Ondra, Austin Mark Otis, Robin Paris, Beverly Parks, Jeanne Parr, Dick Peacock, Patricia Peacock, Steve Perry, Janna Susan Pitts, Lowell Ponte, Burt Prelutsky, Marvin Reichbach, Frank Rich, Eugene Richmond, John Robbins, Sue Robbins, Wayne R. Robbins, Hugh

Rohrer, Ed Salter, Jeff Salz, Carl Santangelo, George Sargent, Gil Schaffer, Patt Schwab, Joan Shaer, Leslie Shelton-Sargent, Pearl C. Sickles, Stephen Sivulich, Nozizwe Siwundhla, Byron Skinner, Barbara Sommer, Robert Sommer, Laura Spidle, Adrian Spidle, Julie Stewart, Anne Stillwell, Bill Stillwell, Orienne Strode, Linda Tatelbaum, Karen Taylor, Martin Thommes, Barbara Boyle Torrey, Fuller Torrey, Larry Trozzo, Marcello Truzzi, James Van Maanen, Terry Van Orshoven, David Walden, Pat Walden, Selma Wang, Mary Rose Ward, Gale Warren, Glenda Watters, Pat Watters, Neal Weiner, Sarah Wellen, Ray Wilkie, Sam Wilson, Kal Winer, John T. Wood, Don Wright, Edith B. Wright, Maria Zebrowski, Mark Zussman.

Special Thanks: are due my agent, Donald Cutler; my editor Bill Phillips, for his continued good support and editing; Michael Brandon, for extreme patience in copy editing; John Herrmann, for standing by when I needed it most; and especially my wife, Muriel, who continues to be my best source of support, help and good judgment.

Whoever I've missed — sorry; hope I'll pick you up next time.

The
Height
of Your Life

An Introductory Note
(incorporating a relatively
short comment about the author's height)

This book explores the effect of physical height on personal life. We're all so affected — even (as I discovered) those people whose height is so average as to make them wonder if they're invisible. If you've wondered how much your life's prospects depend on your height, rest assured. You are not alone. Though practically everyone has had such thoughts, they're hard to express openly. Height seems so, so — *childish* as a subject for adult concern. Should the relative length of grown bodies make any difference in the way they interact?

Perhaps it shouldn't, but it does. And that's what this book is about: the way relative height colors our feelings about each other — friends, colleagues, lovers, spouses, parents, and children — and our feelings about ourselves.

By way of illustration, I often write about the heights of public figures. This can be a touchy task. As I discovered repeatedly, the "official heights" of those in the public eye turned out to be nearly useless. (Alan Ladd, after all, was "officially" listed during most of his acting career as 5'10" — a 6-inch bonus.) Such unreliable statistics occur for a variety of reasons. For one thing, there's a certain generosity, a widely observed protocol that writers use in reporting the heights of celebrities — males especially. Men 5'6" to 5'9" are commonly called "5'10"." Those actually 5'10" or 5'11" can count on being rounded up to "6-foot." Even men shorter than 5'6" but taller than the small Paul Williams expect the courtesy of being called "5'6"." (For whatever reason, this etiquette of reporting height is one based on slots: 6-foot, 5'10", 5'6"; rarely is a public figure called 5'11", 5'9", or 5'5".)

As a hedge on protocol, like many of us, celebrities are prone to dissemble about their height. And as we all do, they're likely at least to grab a maximum height measurement — recorded at a peak of growth when young, stretched as tall as nature permits, ideally with shoes on — then hang on to this figure as their official "height" forever.

Anyone who doesn't feel quite tall enough (who does?) is subject to some such benefit of the doubt. Years ago a generous yardstick measured my own height at 5'8". After that I called myself 5'8" for years in perfectly good conscience. But when two former friends challenged this claim, I was forced back to the measuring rod. They were right. In truth I'm 5'7.62" — 1.38" below the 5'9" average for American men (women average 5'3.6").*

But all is not gloom. While researching this book I learned that after a full night's sleep the human body normally measures from one-half to a full inch taller before it once again compresses under the weight of the day. After discovering this good news, I arranged to spend the night with friends who have a doctor's scale in their guest room. And sure enough, although at midnight I was a boring 5'7½", by 8 A.M. I'd shot up to a thrilling 5'8"! So my moral dilemma has now reduced itself to a single question: When telling others I'm 5'8", need I add "at eight A.M."?

_____
* Sources for data and quotations throughout are cited in the notes that begin on page 306.

What's seldom realized is that human height is not a stable measurement. It changes during the course of a day and also over a lifetime. After age thirty we all shrink an inch or two. The "height" claimed by someone much beyond that age may in fact be accurate — as of several years before.

For such reasons, I've generally ignored the "official" heights of public figures in the absence of confirming evidence. The only 100 percent confirmation would be to measure such a person barefoot, or at least back-to-back. Next best would be an eyeball inspection. Since such evidence was seldom available, I'm able to report less often than I'd like the "actual heights" of those about whom I write. Instead, what I tried to do was train my eye to judge relative height accurately — in person, on television, in movies, or in photographs — then report these assessments. Even this technique is risky, because, as I point out in the text, so many of us are so very clever at camouflaging our actual size.

Eventually I reached the point of estimating heights as much by observing attitudes as by noting feet and inches. This is not as strange as it may sound. In subtle but basic ways our personal style is a product of our physical size, though we're rarely conscious of this fact. A speech professor in West Virginia has even found that his students can regularly guess within an inch the height of a speaker they've heard on tape but never seen.

Ultimately, determining "actual heights" proved less interesting than exploring the intuitive sense of each other we all develop based on our relative size. This sense lies at the heart of what I've tried to write about in *The Height of Your Life*. In the end it proved far more revealing than mere feet and inches.

1 Who's Bigger?

When two people come together in a face-to-face relationship, a conscious or unconscious sizing-up process ensues, that looks much like what we see in infra-human primates.

— ABRAHAM MASLOW

The main thing I wanted Jimmy Carter's aide to tell me was this: Is the President bigger than I am?

Carter's assistant rose from his desk and ran his eyes slowly up and down my frame. "Yes," he finally concluded. "I believe he is."

How much bigger?

"Oh, maybe an inch or two."

I must have looked skeptical (not to say disappointed), because the man then called out to his secretaries, "How tall would you say the President is?"

"Five-eight," a young voice replied.

"Five-ten," an older one quickly corrected.

The three huddled briefly and agreed on 5'10". Just a few days before, they recalled, Jimmy Carter had needed formal wear for a scheduled dinner. In order to rent some, they'd asked him his height. Carter had said he was 5'10".

But so do a lot of people, I suggested.

The President's assistant smiled slightly. "Are you suggesting that Jimmy Carter might tell a lie?"

While waiting to appear on "A.M. America" (later renamed "Good Morning America"), a guest watched in fascination as his fellow guest — a tall author — leaped to his feet when 6′5″ host David Hartman entered the room. "I wonder if I'm taller than you?" asked the author. To find out they stood back-to-back. Hartman proved to be an inch or so taller. The smaller man seemed disappointed.

Finding herself at the library without her card, a friend of mine asked if she could take a book out anyway. This woman is thirty-six and has bold streaks of gray in her hair. She is the mother of a three-year-old child. She also is 5 feet tall.

"I don't know, dear," said the librarian, looking dubious. There was an uncomfortable silence. Finally the librarian asked, "What school do you go to?"

"What school?" my friend replied. "What do you mean, what school? I'm thirty-six. I have a daughter. My hair's turning gray. How can you ask what school I go to?"

"But you're so short!" was the reply.

Andrew Tobias once made a passing reference in print to the fact that Robert Redford wasn't tall. Never, the journalist later reported, had he ever provoked a response like the one to this single "allegation."

"Write a story about war in the Middle East," Tobias explained, "and you get four, maybe five letters. Mention . . . that Robert Redford is short, and you *really* catch it." Some readers wrote to protest that the actor was in fact a 6-footer. Others thought he was average. A woman who had once shared an elevator with Redford claimed 5′7″, 5′8″ tops. "This is an issue," Tobias concluded, "I think it is becoming clear, the importance of which cannot be underestimated."

In what's since become a classic of height scholarship, Tobias then embarked on a thorough investigation of the matinee idol's size. Redford himself wasn't talking, and his friends covered up. So the inventive Tobias took to working from photographs — superimposing premeasured grids and comparing nearby objects (subtracting always for shoe heels, except in the case of a single prized picture of Redford "Barefoot in the Park"). At last the actor caved in and met his measurer. And at last Tobias revealed to us that Redford is 5'9¾" — "give or take."

Tobias's exposé created quite a stir at the time it appeared. Fellow journalists clucked sympathetically and reported their own frustrations when trying to write about a most sensitive subject. "You think people lie about their age?" commented one. "Ha! Height is worse."

For adults, height poses a paradoxical problem. The "mature" approach to this problem is to deny that it exists. Since the relative length of bodies *should* make no difference in the way people interact, therefore it doesn't. No one really believes this, of course. We're constantly making assessments of each other based on height alone. ("Well, that's the way little guys are." "She's a big woman and can take care of herself." "Little and feisty." "Big and strong.")

At some level we're all aware of each other's height — particularly when we must look way up or down to make eye contact. Such consciousness of relative size comes out in odd ways, many quite innocent. When a tall man sweeps a small woman off her feet in warm embrace for example — *he* may not consider that a statement about who's bigger, but *she* does (ask any little woman). When a smaller person backs off from a taller person, this could simply mean that the taller person doesn't use Dial. More likely it means that the shorter party is trying to make eye contact without developing a stiff neck. For the same reason, tall people tend to spend a lot of time seated when they're with smaller companions.

Our daily lives are made up of so many such micro height adjustments that we're normally not even aware they're taking place. Yet the life of each one of us is channeled into paths determined by the reactions of other people to our height and our own reaction to theirs.

Research has shown, for example, that the relative length of bodies can dictate choice of friends: like heights tend to cluster. When it comes to picking a marriage partner, height has been found near the top of the list of traits both parties try to match. The physical problems to which we're vulnerable vary with our body size, as do the sports we choose to play, the candidates for whom we vote — even the work we do and salary we're paid. Some jobs are considered more suited to smalls (astronaut, religious leader), others to talls (corporate vice-president, Miss America). Personnel officers in a number of fields so clearly prefer taller job applicants that they're willing to pay them a premium.

As the result of such subtle and not-so-subtle responses to our height, we're each a product of the feet and inches we've been granted. How we feel about ourselves, how we deal with others, and how we are dealt with all depend in some measure on how tall we are.

This is not true just of talls and smalls. A secretary of 5′3″ once complained to me that her average height resulted in very average treatment. "A tall woman walks in," the secretary explained, "and people say, 'Oh, she's nice and tall.' A short woman walks in and they go, 'Oh, she's nice and petite. A five-three woman walks in and they just go, 'She's nice.' You're nothing in particular."

During interviews conducted for this book I've heard in endless variety the ways in which people feel their lives have been influenced by their height. For actor Joel Grey, being short meant being limited to parts as a sidekick, a pal, or as Billy the Kid on TV's ''Maverick'' until relatively late in his career. The small size of race driver Mario Andretti made it difficult for him to get cars to race and spurred his determination to ''show'' taller nemeses. Julia Child found that being 6'2" kept her from being able to join the WACs during World War II. Joan Rivers, a foot shorter, found that height meant she ''got to be the 'girl' '' when practicing with other girls during dancing class.

For teacher Sarah Wellen, being 4'11" (Mrs. Wellen did *not* seem that small when teaching me two decades ago) made her feel the need for 4-inch heels to stay on top of things in the classroom. The junior-high-school teacher never realized how essential this boost was, she wrote me, until: ''One day I planned an afternoon softball game for my 8th graders, so I brought my sneakers to change into. I dismissed my class and sent them to the ballfield to await me while I changed and while I disciplined a boy whom I kept after. As I changed shoes behind the desk, I talked seriously and intensively and then stood up next to the boy. He very quickly put me in my place by looking down at me (now that I had lost my 4-inch heels) and saying as he looked at the top of my head, 'Yes, Mrs. Wellen. Yes, Mrs. Wellen.' My authority had vanished with the 4-inch heels!''

At the spectrum's other end, a 6'8" museum employee described what it was like to work for a 5-foot boss. ''He was so uptight about my height,'' said this man, ''that I began coming into his office slouched and would immediately go down to my knees and then explain the new project to him. This worked beautifully; he relaxed and we soon had a fine rapport and I was promoted after a very short time. Oddly, I didn't feel demeaned by this behavior on my part. It was his problem, and I felt badly for him and just tried to help. And it worked out for us both."

Obviously, the lives of those at the extremes of the height continuum are going to be colored by such dramatic episodes more often than the lives of those closer to the middle. But even from an average perspective, one's height can shape one's outlook. "I am 17¼ hands high," wrote an editor, "5'9" to you. You can't get any more average than that. My average height seems to have heightened a trait of mine. You see, people are either doers or watchers. Tall men and short men are doers. I'm a watcher. For many years I have been half-convinced that I am invisible, a bemused watcher of the doers. When a person, ten years later, says he remembers me, I don't believe him. He couldn't, because I was invisible."

As such reports suggest, to some degree we're all a product of height-related feelings — our own and others'. In response to such feelings, we commonly develop a "style" suited to our size. There are common elements to such styles. Based on reports from people up and down the spectrum, I've constructed the summary of size-suited styles on the next page.

To gather further information about how people of all sizes feel about their height, I distributed questionnaires on the subject. Among two hundred responses to my "Twenty Questions about Height" (see Appendix A) and in scores of interviews, I've found it rare for *anyone* of *any* height to state flatly, "I like my height." One 6'4" stockbroker did tell me unequivocally that he liked his tallness because he thought it had helped him get ahead in life, love, business, and basketball. But such pride of size was a rare exception. Others in the same elevated height range complained of problems finding clothes, friends, and a comfortable seat on the airplane. Those in the middle tended just to accept their height without really considering its pros and

Size-suited Styles

MEN			WOMEN
7'0"	Wilt Chamberlain	Life grim up here; concern about being a goon; privacy impossible; flashes of bitterness ("How's the weather down *there?*") In a word: *remote*	6'7"
6'11"			6'6"
6'10"			6'5"
6'9"			6'4"
6'8"	John Kenneth Galbraith		Veruschka 6'3"
6'7"		Aware of height, sensitive about tallness, but from a commanding position. ("We must be responsive to the feelings of smaller people.") In a word: *imperious*	6'2"
6'6"			6'1"
6'5"			Vanessa Redgrave 6'0"
6'4"			5'11"
6'3"			5'10"
6'2"			5'9"
6'1"			5'8"
6'0"	Gerald Ford	Hyper-normal; minimal height awareness; little consciousness of others' sensitivity on subject ("What's all the fuss about?") In a word: *oblivious*	5'7"
5'11"			Betty Ford 5'6"
5'10"			5'5"
5'9"	*U.S. av.*		5'4"
5'8"		Ultra–height conscious; sensitive about own size but more sensitive about others'; nervous humor common ("My height doesn't bother me; yours does.") In a word: *fidgety*	*U.S. av.* 5'3"
5'7"			Erma Bombeck 5'2"
5'6"	Woody Allen		5'1"
5'5"			5'0"
5'4"		On the charts, barely; hard to get the joke at this level; denial common ("I haven't got any height problem!") In a word: *feisty*	Judy Garland 4'11"
5'3"	Mickey Rooney		4'10"
5'2"			4'9"
5'1"			Edith Piaf 4'8"
5'0"	Paul Williams	Off the charts; resignation common; sometimes cheerful ("I was going to thank all the little people until I remembered — I *am* the little people.") In a word: *bittersweet*	4'7"
4'11"			4'6"
4'10"			4'5"
4'9"			4'4"

NOTE: Although this chart relates more to male than female styles, it has enough to do with the latter that points of reference for women are included.

cons. And below the average (5'9" for men in America, 5'3.6" for women), small people of both sexes invariably wished they were taller.

In fact, the majority of those who filled out my questionnaire said that at times they wished they were a different height. Oddly enough, more women said this than men. Out of 101 women responding, 60 said they wanted to be a different height, compared to 54 of the 99 men. Of the women who wanted to be a different height, only one wanted to be smaller — a woman 5'11½" who thought she might have an easier time finding clothes if she were 5'9". Another woman, 5'5", said she'd like to be either taller or smaller because "I *hate* being average."

With these few exceptions, the overwhelming wish of those who wanted a new height was to be taller. "I have stood on a stool to make me the height I would like to be," explained a 5'0" mother who would rather be 5'7". "It gives me a whole new perspective on things. I wouldn't always be looking up to people. I could more easily reach ordinary things. I'd be more comfortable at the countertop." Even a woman of 5'9" said she'd prefer being 6 feet because there seem to be "very real political and social advantages up there."

Among men who wanted to be taller that sort of rationale was most common. A 5'11" ex-priest thought he'd rather be 6'3" because "tall people are more successful at basketball, baseball, business, rafting, making love and writing books." Sociologist James Coleman, a 5'10½" consultant to major corporations and author of the "Coleman Report" that changed the shape of American education, said the reason he'd always wanted to be taller was because "height brings acknowledgement, deference and power."

On the whole, I wouldn't mind being taller myself. Not that I mind being 5'7.62". There are lots of advantages to that size of body. It costs less to feed, fits comfortably into all kinds of cars, and overall has a neat and tidy quality. It's just not 6-foot. Rarely am I the biggest. Practically speaking, I like the height of my body. But who's practical when it comes to height? (Even Elvis Presley, who was nearly 6 feet tall, but not quite, wore lifts at times to get over the hump.)

Since so few of us are happy with our final feet and inches, the height we report to the world tends to be a hodgepodge of fact, fantasy, and whatever we think we can get away with. Among a group of job seekers who were measured *after* they'd recorded their heights on an application, ten out of ten were found to have rounded upward by at least an inch. In another comparison of real versus stated height, this one among a group of Air Force women, the overstatement was found to average an inch. And it's doubtful such cases are simply matters of oversight: a third study found that one group of women who were warned in advance that they'd be measured reported their heights more accurately than a second group who weren't warned but were also measured.

Among my own "Twenty Questions about Height" was one asking if the respondent ever lied about his or her height, and if so, why. Out of 99 men, 35 admitted that they did, as did 28 out of 101 women. "I was applying for my first driver's license," explained a woman of 5'3½". "My best friend at the time had received hers a few months earlier and I wanted to have the same statistics on my credentials. P.S.: She lied too!"

Said a 5'10½" woman: "When men ask me I usually say 5'10" so as not to sound like I'm 'pushing it.' . . . I have often noticed that men with whom I see 'eye to eye' barefoot will tell me they are 6' tall or more."

I too have had subjects repeatedly tell me they are heights that my eye knows aren't accurate. But a measure of the sensitivity surrounding this subject is that I rarely say anything — to a man, especially. It would just be too insulting. Because for men, height is more than a mere statistic; for men it's a measure of manhood.

"*Men* are 6' tall and above," explained a 5'11" psychologist about the extra inch he generally awards himself. To justify the quarter-inch of padding he normally includes when reporting his height, a 5'11¾" college teacher turned his questionnaire over and wrote on the back:

When growing up the goal was to be a "six-footer." Everything over that was just gravy, but six feet — that was the magic number.

There was a time when I was younger that I thought I had made it. Then, during a Marine physical, I got the cold news. 5'11¾"! I've tested it out many times since and it's always the same.

So what other choice did I have? I lied! Again and again, each time trying to convince myself, as if the simple repetition of it would make it so. Get it on the driver's license! That makes it Official Truth. If I'm arrested it would then probably be sent to the sacred files of the FBI. And nobody seemed to question it. It was the perfect scam. I learned to say it with a straight face, with conviction even.

"Height?"

"Six feet."

"Even?"

"Even."

I still find it hard to accept. I'm haunted by the thought that the whole thing might be metaphorical, that it might be the story of my life.

The problem with an issue such as height is that it's so caught up with symbolic measurements that have little to do with actual ones. In the course of my research I've seen Julius Caesar listed among Short Men in History and also among Tall Men in History, depending on what point the lister was trying to make. For the same reason, although there is no known measurement of the man, we've debated for centuries whether Jesus was small and meek or tall and commanding. The sort of God we imagine him to be dictates the size we think he was. According to singer Teddy Pendergrass: "There's only one man who's a perfect six feet. Jesus Christ, right? Well I'm six feet, a half inch. Just half an inch from perfection."

By measuring heights with our values, we're prone to make mistakes. One of the more interesting results of my research was the finding that over half of those I polled around the time of Jimmy Carter's inauguration thought he was the same size as Richard Nixon or taller. In fact he's 2–3 inches shorter. But Carter is no fool and like most politicians (especially those of modest size) has been content to let the public eye measure him in symbolic rather than real inches.

"We had a great deal of trouble with Carter," reported Lady Katharine Ridley, head researcher for Madame Tussaud's Exhibition in London. "We wrote for an interview but didn't get one. The embassy sent 'round some pictures but we weren't satisfied with them at all. We finally just had to work from press photographs."

As she said this, Lady Katharine flipped through the meager contents of a folder labeled CARTER. Ideally, she explained, Tussaud's tries to arrange personal interviews with contemporary public figures so that its wax sculptors can work from precise measurements of every limb, made with calipers and a tape measure. This was the procedure followed for the entire Royal Family, Richard Burton, Alfred Hitchcock, Winston Churchill — even Benjamin Franklin, not long after the Exhibition opened in 1770. When such real-life measurements aren't available, Tussaud's turns to the next-best sources: tailors' records, actual suits of clothing, or tombs built to size. President Eisenhower's wax statue, for instance, is dressed in his actual uniform; and from tailors' measurements, Tussaud's researchers concluded that John Kennedy and Richard Nixon were both around 6 feet tall.

When all else fails, as was the case with Carter, Lady Katharine must turn to whatever information is available — photographs, paintings, biographies, or eyewitness accounts. But such sources pose problems. "I'm always dubious of 'eyewitness accounts,' " she explained. "You get such extraordinarily differing reactions to people's heights." Peter the Great, for example, was so tall that contemporary descriptions of him ranged from simply "big" to "gigantic," with all sorts of numbers cast about. After a field trip to Leningrad, where she examined statues, old paintings, and archival data, Lady Katharine concluded that the eighteenth-century Russian czar was in fact 6'6¾" tall.

Impressed by the care they took in getting heights right, my wife Muriel and I figured that as long as we were visiting Madame Tussaud's, we ought to measure not only Jimmy Carter but lots of people in the collection. This wasn't always easy. For one thing, the Exhibition is kind to its smaller subjects in a way by making them hard to measure. Liza Minnelli was folded up like an *N*. J. Paul Getty was seated, and so was Pablo Picasso. Elton John loomed down from a pedestal.

Then there was the Royal Family. Isolated on a raised platform and surrounded by a velvet rope, Queen Elizabeth et al. were particularly hard to get at. Worse yet, since all the Windsor women were wearing formal, floor-length gowns puffed out with crinolines, measuring the heels of their shoes (for the purpose of subtraction) could be seen as an insult to the crown. But if bystanders were perturbed by our fingering about beneath the royal underskirts, they said not a word. I suppose Britons have come to expect this sort of behavior from American tourists.

Based on our time with the Royal Family, I can report with

greatest confidence that Queen Elizabeth is 5'3¾"; Princess Margaret, 5'2½"; Prince Philip, 6'0"; Prince Charles, 5'9½"; and Princess Anne, 5'7".

Here are some other results of our day with a carpenter's ruler at Madame Tussaud's:

Mahatma Gandhi	5'3"
Elton John	5'3½"
Vladimir I. Lenin	5'5"
Alfred Hitchcock	5'5¾"
Pierre Trudeau	5'5¾"
Winston Churchill	5'6"
Martin Luther King, Jr.	5'6½"
Pelé	5'7½"
Pope Paul VI	5'8"
Adolf Hitler	5'8"
Humphrey Bogart	5'8¼"
Richard Burton	5'9¼"
Dwight D. Eisenhower	5'9¼"
Telly Savalas	5'10"
Benjamin Franklin	5'10¼"
Mao Tse-tung	5'11"
Henry VIII	6'1"

Finding little in Carter's folder, Lady Katharine phoned the Sculptor's Section. "Well, they came to the conclusion he's five feet ten-and-a-half inches," she reported back after a mumbled conversation. "But I wouldn't put too much weight in that."

On a television program subsequent to our Tussaud's visit, commentator Bill Moyers wrapped up a survey of Jimmy Carter's presidency by mentioning his observation to a member of the U.S. House of Representatives that physically the thirty-ninth President is a small man. "And that's the way we intend to keep him," responded the congressman.

On the questionnaire he filled out for this book, Moyers himself made a confession about the height he reports to the world. "I'm prone to add half an inch — to 6'0"," wrote Moyers.

Why?

"Sounds . . . sounds better," he explained. "More like a man."

Although he can credibly round up to 6 feet, Lyndon Johnson's former press secretary added that what he'd long wanted to be was 6'4".

Why?

"So I could look LBJ in the eye."

Moyers was only kidding, of course. And yet . . .

Height does matter. And in the back-to-back of our minds, bigger always will be better.

2 Is Bigger Better?

I don't want short grandchildren.

— A Minnesota woman, explaining
why she opposed Vietnamese refugees
settling in her town

When lesser-known Michael Medved (who is well over 6 feet tall) went about promoting *What Really Happened to the Class of '65?* with his better-known coauthor David Wallechinsky (who is well under 6 feet tall), television talk-show hosts would commonly stride right up to Medved, extend a hand, and say, "Happy you could be with us, Mr. Wallechinsky!"

A man of 5'9" waited patiently for popcorn at the movies. As his turn came up, the cashier bent down to put away some change. Another man, about 6'4", joined the first at the counter. When the cashier looked up from her change she turned immediately to the taller man and said, "May I help you?"

A newspaper once assigned two reporters — one 5'6" tall, the other 6'2" — to approach various workers who wait on the public and simultaneously ask for service. In every instance, the larger of the two men was helped first. "Your height seemed to demand that I speak to you first," explained a car-rental clerk to the taller newspaperman. Said a waitress: "I'd never thought about it before, but I must've been serving tall people first all the time when confronted with a situation like this.''

In the height sweepstakes, tall is ahead. Way ahead. You might say tallness stands head and shoulders above any other size in the competition for rewards social, sexual, financial, athletic, political, and practical (like being able to see in crowds). Big John Kenneth Galbraith, at 6'8" a beneficiary, calls the bias in favor of size one of society's ''most blatant and forgiven prejudices.''

Studies repeatedly have confirmed the status of stature. In one experiment a group of nursing students consistently overestimated the heights of two people introduced to their class as ''administrators'' and consistently underestimated the heights of two others then presented to them as ''fellow students.'' In another experiment a man was introduced variously to five random groups of college students as everything from a mere visiting student to a visiting lecturer to ''a Distinguished Professor from England.'' When asked to judge the man's height, the students' average estimate went up consistently with the rank they thought him to be.

Just to get a sense of who stands where in our society, I've made a hobby over the past few years of collecting press descriptions of public figures based on their size. Here are some samples:

Tall	*Small*
. . . tall, handsome, athletic . . .	. . . small, pallid, inexorably bland . . .
— *San Francisco Examiner* on then vice-presidential candidate Sargent Shriver	— *Newsweek* on U.S. Budget Director James McIntyre

Tall *(cont.)*

. . . a tall stalk of black-haired loveliness . . .

> — *Parade* on former Alabama first lady Cornelia Wallace

. . . a big, likeable bear of a man . . .

> — *Newsweek* on former New York Yankee pitcher Floyd Bevens

. . . tall, handsome and polished . . .

> — DAVID BRODER in *The Atlantic* on Texas politician John Connally

Mr. Gann is a tall, soft-spoken, polite man who prefers to play golf or visit his four children and 11 grandchildren . . .

> — *New York Times* on California Proposition 13 cosponsor Paul Gann

With his tall, powerful build, mane of blond hair and rugged features, the 29-year-old Godunov cuts an overwhelming figure onstage.

> — *Newsweek* on dancer Aleksandr Godunov

Small *(cont.)*

. . . a short, slightly chunky woman who wears white socks and loafers . . .

> — *Esquire* on umpire Bernice Gera

. . . a small, balding troll of a man . . .

> — *Time* on drag racer Bill Jenkins

. . . a tiny dandy who dangles his toes from his swivel chair . . .

> — DAVID BRODER in *The Atlantic* on Texas politician John Tower

Mr. Jarvis, short and stocky, is an abrasive, cocky campaigner with a booming voice who likes to relax by smoking cigars . . .

> — *New York Times* on California Proposition 13 cosponsor Howard Jarvis

With his short stature, hook nose, beady eyes, unkempt hair, he looks like a loser . . .

> — *Parade* on screen actor Dustin Hoffman

Tall (cont.)

. . . a handsome, imposing man who stands over six feet four inches tall . . .

> — *Current Biography* on Australian Prime Minister Malcolm Fraser

He is a tall, dark, handsome brute, 6 feet 5 inches in height with Hollywood looks and bearing.

> — *New York Times* on Boston Red Sox pitcher Mike Torrez

Small (cont.)

. . . tiny (4′11″), unimposing and charismatic as a bowl of rice . . .

> — *People* on Chinese Vice-Premier Deng Xiaoping (Teng Hsiao-ping)

. . . he is small and squat, a slug of a man, with large reptilian eyes blinking out from behind horn-rimmed glasses.

> — *Philadelphia Inquirer* on author Theodore White

Among thousands of clippings in my height files, I've found "diminutive" by far the media's favorite synonym for "short." Deng Xiaoping, for example, is called "diminutive" seven times in descriptions, "tiny" twice, "stubby" once — and "that sawed-off revisionist," by some American Maoists.

Even more revealing than the synonyms used for body size are the euphemisms — words that don't describe tallness or shortness so much as the qualities we associate with such heights. "Feisty" is the classic example, a word normally used in tandem with "little" — as in "Alabama's feisty little Governor George Wallace." "Distinguished," by contrast, may not be synonymous with "tall," but it rarely refers to any other size (for example, "the tall, distinguished secretary of state").

On the next page is a list I've compiled of adjectives commonly applied either to tall or to small people. Many are euphemistic "code words" that we use to suggest someone's size without being so crass as to mention it.

Tall	*Small*
aristocratic	bantam
awesome	boyish
awkward	brash
big	bumptious
bluff	Chaplinesque
Bunyanesque	cocky
burly	compact
commanding	diminutive
deaconlike	elfin
distinguished	feisty
formidable	gnomish
gallant	impish
gargantuan	jaunty
gawky	jockeylike
gigantic	Lilliputian
glacial	little
good-sized	molelike
Gulliverian	munchkinish
huge	Napoleonic
hulking	natty
imposing	peppery
impressive	pint-sized
king-sized	plucky
lanky	puckish
large	pugnacious
Lincolnesque	runty
lofty	sawed-off
looming	scrappy
lumbering	short
massive	slight
mountainous	sparky
overwhelming	spunky
rangy	squat

Tall *(cont.)*	Small *(cont.)*
regal	strutting
rugged	stubby
strapping	stumpy
striking	tiny
tall	wiry
towering	wizened

Americans in particular have always looked up to big men who sit tall in the saddle and won't stoop to anything so small as short-changing another man, belittling him, or giving him short shrift. But the big-bias is not just American, nor is it modern. Lest we forget, King Saul got his job because "from his shoulders and upward he was higher than any of the people."

Excavators of prehistoric tombs in different parts of the world commonly find taller skeletons in elegant crypts, smaller ones tossed together into common graves. In ancient Egyptian wall paintings, size is known to reflect status: the taller the figure, the more important the person.

After reviewing evidence from many cultures, sociologist Pitirim Sorokin earlier this century concluded that in all probability the "correlation of tall stature with the upper social classes and low stature with the low social classes which exists in present civilized societies has also existed in the past and in the most different societies."

Some sort of peak in the history of tall status was reached during the reign of Frederick William I in Prussia from 1713 to 1740. Not tall himself, Frederick displayed a reverence for tallness from earliest childhood. As a boy he loved to collect large peasants about him and drill them like soldiers. After assuming his father's crown, Frederick instituted height as the main criterion by which his soldiers would be judged. Officers could not be promoted without enough of it. Commanders of regiments whose members had the tallest average size were the most generously rewarded.

The result of this value system was a mad scouring not just of Prussia but of all Europe in search of recruits Frederick could look up to. Nearly a thousand Prussian agents engaged in such recruiting. When the promise of rewards failed to tempt a particularly tall specimen, he was shanghaied. Since Frederick suffered excuses from the recruiters badly, according to biographer Robert Ergang, "Whenever there was a young man whose head protruded above the crowd, there one of these agents would appear sooner or later." Knowing their colleague's weakness, his fellow emperors sent Frederick gifts — of tall men. From Moscow Peter the Great sent 80, then 150 more. Austria's envoy contributed 24.

After accumulating thousands of soldiers over 6 feet tall, Frederick made plans to breed them with women of comparable stature. It was said that in Berlin the emperor once spotted a well-proportioned woman towering over the rest and decided on the spot to mate her with one of the tallest of his soldiers. Giving the woman a scribbled message, Frederick told her to deliver it to the commandant at Berlin. The message read: "The bearer is to be married without delay to Macdoll, the big Irishman. Don't listen to objections." But this giantess proved not only big but smart. Rather than delivering the message herself, she passed it on to an old beggar woman, who upon presenting it as instructed was promptly married to Macdoll. (Frederick had compassion enough to annul the marriage.)

A shrewd, sensible ruler in other respects, Frederick William was not to be budged when it came to his love of tallness in his soldiers. His favorite pastime was drilling the tallest of them — the elite Potsdam Grenadiers, who ranged from 6 feet to well

*Frederick William
reviews his tall Grenadiers*

above 7 feet tall. Even when sick in bed, Frederick found relief by having the Grenadiers march around it.

Prussia's "walking colossi" became the talk of Europe and that country's leading tourist attraction. Unfortunately, the tall, uniformed bodies, which were beautiful to Frederick and fascinating to gawkers had serious drawbacks as soldiers. Many of the Grenadiers were none too agile. Few were very fast. Shortly after Frederick William's death, Prussia's new emperor, his son Frederick the Great, disbanded the Grenadiers and for a time, in the words of Nancy Mitford, "the roads of Europe were covered with huge weak-kneed loons trying to find their way back home."

Though exaggerated, the bind Frederick William got himself in with his love of tallness is one with which we still struggle. The dilemma is this: While man's aesthetic and social taste clearly prefers tallness, nature shows no such preference. Nature doesn't give a damn. Height is man's issue, not hers. In Nature's eyes the relative virtues of size are purely circumstantial. If anything she's given the nod over time to smaller bodies. Anthropologists estimate that for most of human history, selection pressures kept male heights within a range of 5'2" to 5'10". This was due partly to the stunting effects of malnutrition and disease and the fact that smaller bodies better resist such stress and have an improved chance of surviving. In times of famine, taller bodies are the first to go.

When you wander around in an old graveyard, two realities leap out at you: how much shorter the adults' graves are than those in modern cemeteries, and how many more of the graves belong to infants than is common today. Some experts think the two phenomena are related. "Until recently, both health and nutritional problems were more serious for the youngster destined to be large," anthropologist Ashley Montagu has written. "At least part of the recent increase in overall size visible in modern populations is due to the fact that improved standards of food and medical care have allowed genetic combinations to survive which would have been selected against in ages past.''

In countries such as the United States and Japan, which have experienced a rapid overall rise in human heights, a changing diet is probably the underlying cause. This dietary change is not one of quantity so much as quality, with more meat, eggs, and dairy products being set on the table. Such a diet seems to contribute not just to tallness, however, but to obesity, heart disease, tooth decay, hypertension, and other physical problems. Thus, whether or not tallness itself is ''good,'' serious questions can be raised about whether certain *sources* of the trait are, on balance, beneficial.

In a study of the heights of different groups of people around the world, anthropologists Thomas Landauer and John Whiting found unusual tallness to be correlated with two societal traits: to a lesser extent with the keeping of dairy herds, and to a greater extent with stressful child-rearing practices. These practices included the scarring of young bodies, piercing of the skin, and the molding of newborns' heads. The men of tribes that engage in such practices, the researchers found, average 2½″ taller than the men of tribes that don't. Closer to home, they discovered that American babies whose skin is pierced during vaccination before the age of two also average 2½″ taller as adults than unvaccinated children. In a separate study, Whiting and a colleague also found that babies who are born in hospitals and immediately separated from their mother in the American way tend to grow taller than babies who are not born in hospitals and who are left in their mother's arms after delivery. The anthropologists claim that all such evidence ''leaves little room for doubt that early stress leads to accelerated growth.''

I can't say whether or not Landauer and Whiting have proved a *causal* connection between infant traumas and mature height.

What interests me is that, conclusive or not, their data plausibly suggests that tallness is not necessarily a symptom of a benign upbringing. Their findings suggest the opposite. Needless to say, few of their colleagues have rushed forward to stand shoulder-to-shoulder with these anthropologists on this one. Nor have their findings been refuted. The reaction of British growth expert J. M. Tanner is typical. After reading Landauer and Whiting's report with great care, Dr. Tanner commented: "I have no substantial points of criticism to make of the article and I don't believe a word of it. . . . It needs checking up."

Dr. Tanner told me this in the cramped office of the Institute of Child Health in London, where he's spent the past three decades studying patterns of human growth. More than any other person, J. M. Tanner has been responsible for documenting in his books and articles the overall worldwide rise in heights over the past couple of centuries. Proving this trend has not been easy. Museums' suits of armor that look as though they'd be a tight fit on Mickey Rooney are not proof — they might have belonged to a small minority of knights who never saw combat. Nor can we conclude that because we must stoop to walk through the hold of Old Ironsides that everyone must have been short back then: small men have historically been selected as sailors for their better sea legs.

As Tanner has regularly pointed out in his writing, only since Belgian statistician Adolphe Quetelet stood his children up against a wall and meticulously recorded their rates of growth a century and a half ago have we had any reliable data on this subject. Scattered statistics collected since that time indicate a steady increase in average height, particularly in developed countries (although in the United States this trend has recently leveled off). But as Tanner emphasizes in his reports, we have yet to prove conclusively the cause of this rise — though improved nutrition and health care certainly contribute. Other plausible contributing factors that have been suggested include increased mobility (which leads to human crossbreeding), more leisure time and exercise, and even the looser modern clothing, which gives the body greater room to grow.

Surrounded by his books, papers, and stacks of research photographs of naked bodies marked limb by limb, centimeter by centimeter, the 6'½" British physician (who resembles actor Jack Palance) talked excitedly about a recently discovered treasure trove of American height data being analyzed for the first time: manifests of American slaves. Until the Civil War, as required by an 1807 law, heights of slaves were carefully recorded — to the quarter-inch — in such logs. For this reason, we have far better data on the height of slaves than we do on their owners (about whose size we know next to nothing). For comparison, however, there is some English census data on white working-class people of the time. To the horror of those who believe in both white and tall supremacy, preliminary analysis has shown that the overall heights of black slaves far outstrips that of the English Caucasians.

"They were a very small people by modern standards," said Tanner of his countrymen. "They worked in the factories for incredibly long hours, and under incredible conditions. And their food was adulterated to an unbelievable degree. They put arsenic in the beer to make it froth better, and the tea was mixed with aluminum sulfate or something. At that time the ordinary foods — even the food that rich people ate — were very adulterated indeed."

The living conditions in general of the British factory workers were "absolutely appalling," he noted. People of all ages worked long hours in foul air. Pregnant women stuck to the job until a couple of weeks before giving birth, then quickly returned, leaving infants at home, pacified by knockout solutions laced with morphine. There wasn't enough food to go around. "I bet that's the reason they were so small," Tanner concluded.

But the doctor was quick to add that smallness per se should not be associated with bad health, deprivation, or even weakness. Tanner once did work in the highlands of New Guinea, where he was most impressed with the physique of that region's natives. "They're *very* short," he observed, "but, my God, they're muscular! They are *all* muscular — that goes for the women as well as the men in the hill tribes there. It has to be an evolutionary thing. They were up against something which demanded really strong people and the others just got knocked off."

Working in underdeveloped countries, Tanner has found it common that the leaders want for their people every advantage enjoyed by more developed countries — including bigger bodies and the enriched diet to produce them. According to Tanner, the goal is mistaken. What's the point in producing larger bodies, he asked, until the land yields enough food to support them? "Certainly a small peasant is a much more efficient creature in terms of the calories he has to eat relative to the calories he can grow on the land," Tanner explained. "If you're a mum in the highlands of Peru and you're small, you tend to survive; if you're a bit larger, you don't."

Those who don't live in the Peruvian Andes or the highlands of New Guinea may still be wondering how this applies to their own body. Properly fed and cared for, isn't a tall body better off physically than a small one?

Not necessarily. Looking at the body simply as a piece of machinery, one finds a rather balanced spec sheet, with advantages at both ends of the scale. Based on the medical and physiological data I've been able to find on the relative virtues of body size, here are the specs:

Energy Efficiency

Fuel requirements are higher for tall bodies — directly so in terms of calories, indirectly in terms of fabric for clothing, leather for shoes, and more gas for bigger cars. However, since a tall body has proportionately less surface area exposed, it's able to retain body heat better.

Smaller bodies can generally function more efficiently with less fuel of all kinds. Since they dissipate heat better, small bodies tend to work more effectively in hot settings. Long-term expenditure of energy (as in marathon racing) is better sustained by a smaller body.

Strength

With larger muscle cells and more of them, tall bodies possess greater absolute strength. In addition, their longer limbs perform better as levers, adding mechanical strength — which makes tall bodies better able to wield a club or throw a javelin. Such strength is best suited to short bursts of activity.

Though weaker in the absolute, small bodies have more strength per pound of body weight. And the arms on small bodies can more easily lift the torso, as in chin-ups or gymnastic events.

External Structure

Their longer limbs and higher center of gravity give tall bodies an advantage in reaching, throwing, and jumping, a disadvantage in balance and stability. Tall people are more likely to fall (slipping on ice, say), and more vulnerable to the greater impact of such a fall. There's also more strain placed on the joints of tall bodies, especially on vertebrae.

The disadvantage in reach and jumping ability are offset by greater balance and agility in smaller bodies, with their shorter limbs and generally lower center of gravity. Since the consequences of falling are potentially not as great, at least one sports physician thinks smaller athletes are less injury-prone.

Internal Structure

The organs of tall people are under greater stress — lungs in particular. As a result, tall bodies are known to be more susceptible to lung-related diseases such as tuberculosis and emphysema. Tall bodies also are more vulnerable to stomach ulcers, diabetes, and some forms of headache.

Tallness can be symptomatic of an extra Y chromosome (XYY), giantism, acromegaly, and Marfan's syndrome (from which Lincoln may have suffered).

Smaller bodies per se, from what I can find, are not known to be vulnerable to any specific diseases, though stunted growth is itself a symptom of many ailments — especially those involving the heart. Relative to its weight, a smaller body has higher metabolism, larger blood vessels, and greater cardiac output (which could contribute to its greater endurance).

Reproductive Ability

In optimal settings, tall female bodies have been found more fertile and less subject to complications in childbirth (though one Japanese study found short couples slightly more fertile).

Among a group of Harvard graduates, the tall men were found to produce more children than small men. In stress settings (such as high mountain areas), small women are known to be more fertile and have greater reproductive efficiency overall.

Durability

Although talls are known to be more fragile in stress settings, no correlation has been established between height and longevity in an optimum environment. One study finds small bodies live longer, another finds tall bodies do. A third study finds no contrast in mortality rates as related to height. Take your pick.

Miscellany

• Based on research done for his novel *Burr,* Gore Vidal noted of former Vice-President Aaron Burr (who was sued for divorce at the age of eighty on grounds of adultery): ''Burr was a small, trim little man, and small, trim little men last longer sexually. In fact, they last longer in general than more corpulent, capon types, like George Washington, who seem to have no sexual vitality and a relatively short life.''

• In a study of 6,000 male business executives, Dr. Harry Johnson of the Life Extension Institute in Manhattan found that those who listed themselves as taller than 6 feet also tended to report a greater frequency of sexual intercourse than did subjects who listed themselves as shorter. Of those claiming to be over 6 feet, 21.5 percent reported having intercourse more than twice a week, compared to 19.0 percent who said they were 5′8″–6′0″, and 13.1 percent of those reporting in under 5′8″.

• Trichologist Betty Roney of London's Roney Clinic found

that among 2,000 of her hair-loss patients, the number over 6 feet tall was twice the national average. Roney speculated that this resulted from circulation problems and the added distance blood must travel to the scalp in tall people. (It could also have resulted from tall men having more money with which to pay for her services.)

As can be seen, evaluated like a car, the mechanical pros and cons of small and tall bodies are far more balanced than their relative social standing. In fact, when it comes to overall durability, smalls may even have the edge over talls. "In many ways, the smaller man is the more efficient as an organic mechanism," anthropologist Harry Shapiro of New York's American Museum of Natural History has suggested. "With increasing size and bulk the physiological processes of the body are placed under corresponding strains and disadvantages."

So if tall bodies function no better mechanically than small bodies and may indeed even have a worse service record, where did they get their good reputation? For the answer to that question we must look not to our bodies but to our minds.

3 In the Mind's Eye

Kaufman rose to his full height.

"Are you asking me to leave?" he demanded.

[Ernest] Martin, who was at least as tall as Kaufman, had lived with the misapprehension that Kaufman stood over everybody else. When he stood up, he was surprised to suddenly realize he was as big as Kaufman.

— HOWARD TEICHMANN in *George S. Kaufman*

We are used to fitting what we see into an intuitive system of reference which makes everything of "reasonable size," so that our mind "sees" things differently from our eye. Scientists call this a "constancy" effect.

— RALPH STEPHENSON and JEAN R. DEBRIX
in *The Cinema as Art*

Imagine my astonishment when I met the late Rod Serling. This guy, I figured, had to be huge. On "The Twilight Zone," Serling's presence was so commanding, his tone so authoritative, the voice so rich. On my television set, Rod Serling loomed very large. Probably he was in the John Wayne and Gary Cooper range.

In person he loomed a lot smaller. Smaller than I even. A splendid man — just about a foot shorter than I'd expected. As I reached down to shake hands with Mr. Serling it was all I could do to keep from bursting out, "You're so short!"

I'm glad I didn't. Serling must have heard that a lot. Every shorter public person does. Mario Andretti, for instance, says that he's been told "You're so short!" so often it surprises him when he isn't. Writer Erma Bombeck, after years of hearing how much shorter she was than expected, once told an audience, "Gosh, I thought you'd all be taller." ("I've been sick," one listener later explained.) And among three wishes he once listed for a magazine, comedian Jerry Stiller included the wistful hope that someday, sometime, just for the sake of variety, he'd be greeted by "You're so much taller than I thought!"

Some people *are* greeted that way. Frank Perdue of chicken

fame, for example — Elmer Fudd personified. Low fives, right? . . . Add a foot. Perdue stands over 6 feet tall and is constantly being told he's much taller than people had expected him to be. So is Julia Child, who's as tall as Perdue, though I'd never have anticipated it. Nor would a lot of people, if the frequent "You're so tall!" comments the cooking teacher hears are any indication. While shopping, Julia Child once overheard two women behind her whispering animatedly.

"It must be Julia," said one.

"It can't be," insisted the other. "She's too tall."

We see what our mind tells us to see. Sportscaster Joe Garagiola has impressed one interviewer as "a strapping six-footer," another as "a short, square fellow." *Playboy*'s Hugh Hefner has been "tall, dark and handsome" to one pair of eyes, "short, wiry and intense" to another.

Depending on its needs, wishes, and associations, the mind lies to the eye about height. This is one reason why eyewitness reports of criminals' size are so undependable; fear can be a great magnifier. Even under normal circumstances, our eyes generally are a poor judge of someone else's height. Someone may look tall because he or she reminds us of someone else who's tall. Another person may look small because we wish this upon them: our eyes can be influenced by our desire to "belittle" someone. Howard Cosell is an authentic 6-footer, but we commonly perceive him as smaller because our mind (if nothing else) cuts him down to size. Cosell is so mouthy. He doesn't *act* tall. By contrast, until he married a woman so much taller — at a time when he was one of the world's most powerful men — who had an inkling that Henry Kissinger was such a squirt?

Just to help cut down on the number of such gaffes, on the next page is a list of people in the public eye who regularly fool it — a little pocket guide that you can clip 'n' carry.

Smaller than You Might Imagine	*Taller than You Might Imagine*
Marlon Brando	Warren Beatty
Charles Bronson	Ingrid Bergman
Johnny Carson	H. Rap Brown
Geraldine Chaplin	Fidel Castro
Julie Christie	Howard Cosell
Robert Conrad	Jules Feiffer
Walter Cronkite	Bobby Fischer
Bette Davis	David Frost
Robert De Niro	Jerry Lewis
Kirk Douglas	Billy Martin
Peter Falk	Richard Nixon
Jane Fonda	Gilda Radner
Buckminster Fuller	Ronald Reagan
Steve Garvey	Cybill Shepherd
Patty Hearst	Tom Snyder
Katharine Hepburn	Lowell Weicker
Reggie Jackson	
Mick Jagger	
Paul Newman	
Jack Nicholson	*Go Both Ways*
Laurence Olivier	James Caan
Burt Reynolds	Farrah Fawcett
Suzanne Somers	Joe Garagiola
Sylvester Stallone	Hugh Hefner
Ringo Starr	
Elizabeth Taylor	
Andy Warhol	
Raquel Welch	
Henry Winkler	

Our perception of height is such a product of our feelings that even the same person can shoot up or down in our estimation depending on where we stand with that person. A 6'1" husband tells me his 5'4" wife sees him as huge, dark, and looming when they're not getting along but small, soft, and cuddly when they are.

Actors and actresses are well aware of their ability to fool our eyes about height. When I was just beginning to take notes for this book, Mae West stood high on my list of Tall Women. To me, she's always been a classic of the breed. Towering. Looming. A big mama.

In fact Mae West barely tops 5 feet.

I first got an inkling of this astonishing news when *Newsday*'s Jerry Parker returned from the set of Miss West's latest movie (*Sextette*) to tell me that the star was teetering — not due to her age so much as her unusually high heels. Rumor was rife on the set that only personal vanity about her size kept the elderly movie star so dangerously shod.

I then began to study her case further and discovered some interesting facts. First of all, Mae West is small and always has been (she hasn't just shrunk with age). Repeatedly those writing about this woman lead off with a remark about how much shorter the actress seems in person than on stage or screen. This is obviously what Mae West wants. Among hundreds of still photos of her, I've found only a handful that show her in anything other than a floor-length gown. The long, vertical sweep of those dresses carries the eye upward to her high pompadour. For a bonus, the actress made regular use of stairs and platforms when posing for her photographs.

Thus did Mae West fool our eyes. But every bit of this artifice would be transparent and ridiculous if she hadn't also fooled our mind's eye. The real reason this woman seems big is that she acts big. Mae West never gets pushed around; she does

THE GENIUS
OF MAE WEST

knee

foot (approx.)

unspecified
aid underfoot

the pushing — of men, in particular. "Mae's ability to over-power any surroundings was incredible," screenwriter Anita Loos once observed. That's why Loos, 4'11", was stunned when she first met the overpowering actress: "I found her to be as tiny as I, who couldn't have dominated an anthill."

If we take any pride at all in our ability to perceive the world accurately, the ease with which our eyes can be fooled has to be disturbing. What can you trust if not your own eyes? Be comforted. There are perfectly understandable reasons that our mind deceives our eyes about height, reasons that get to the heart of ways we size up and mis-size each other — especially those we see only on the screen.

Take the case of Rod Serling. Think back to how we used to see him as host on "The Twilight Zone." Alone. On an uncluttered set. No other bodies around to judge him against. That resonant voice fully in charge. Those eyes looking right at ours. With only such evidence before us, how could we judge Rod Serling as anything other than tall?

To begin to understand the role of our minds in interpreting human height, we must examine more closely how body size is perceived: (a) relatively, (b) by level of eye contact, and (c) in equation with power.

Height Is Relative

When we see her television program, the reason we don't normally realize that Julia Child tops 6 feet is both simple and deliberate. Everything in her kitchen was installed higher than normal: stove, sink, counters, and shelves. Not in on the secret, our eyes assume everything in this kitchen to be of "normal" size — including the cook.

Size is strictly a relative concept. Things are only small or large in relation to other things. This basic, easily forgotten principle is well-known to those who can take advantage of it. Realtors, for example, commonly decorate model homes with small furniture. The reason is very practical: such furniture makes rooms look relatively larger in the eyes of prospective buyers.

This principle of relative size has also long been exploited by moviemakers. Rooms on movie sets are normally built smaller than life-size. This not only makes them easier to fit within the film frame but also helps make the actors look larger than life. Even the late, large John Wayne was made to appear larger still with the aid of low doorways and tiny chairs that made him seem bigger by contrast.

For the opposite effect, extralarge furniture and rooms were designed to shrink 5-foot Mary Pickford for the little-girl roles she played well into her thirties. "If I touched a glass it would be a third larger than any actual glass," she explained in her autobiography. "Knobs of doors were both larger and higher, and of course the people I worked with were selected for their abnormal height. I believe the men averaged six feet three or four."

Lily Tomlin has used the Pickford approach to wonderful comic effect by sitting on a huge rocker to play a little girl. Even though the audience knows that it's really an adult perched up there in a pinafore with her feet dangling high off the floor, it's a constant struggle to convince the eyes.

Misjudging size relative to setting is not just something we do when watching entertainers. Our own bodies are also subject to such mental/visual distortion. Psychological experiments have demonstrated that the longer one spends in a sensory deprivation chamber, the more one loses the ability to accurately estimate the size of one's body. It's also been found that the more time subjects spend within specially designed "Lilliputian rooms" with lowered ceilings and miniaturized furniture, the bigger they judge themselves to be.

As psychologist Seymour Fisher has pointed out, the size we sense ourselves to be can vary greatly in the course of a single day depending on the setting. Standing before a skyscraper we feel dwarfed. Entering a small elevator we feel large. But if a tall person joins us in that elevator we feel small once again.

Comparing ourselves to others is the most common means by which we judge our own height. J. M. Tanner, the 6′½″ physician-researcher discussed in chapter 2, is average to tall. Tanner told me that on only two occasions in his adult life has he been acutely and uncomfortably aware of his size. The first time was when he attended services at a Russian cathedral. There, surrounded by "tiny little black-clad women," he began to feel so Gulliverian — "so very, very uncomfortable" — that he couldn't wait to flee the church. The second occasion occurred when he attended a meeting of research fundraisers and felt a similar anxiety without knowing why. Only gradually did it dawn on him: the meeting's chairman, a man of 6′7″ or so, had chosen the group in his own image. Tanner was the smallest man present. "Though for a lot of people this would be common," explained the doctor of feeling relatively short, "for me it was very odd."

When discussing relative height, it's important to keep in mind that what we're talking about is a difference measurable in *inches*. Merely four inches divide bodies considered "short" from those considered "tall" (5′8″–6′0″ is about the average range for Western men; 5′2″–5′6″ for women). Only relative to a contrasting body does one become short or tall. Alone in a room Willie Shoemaker might as well be Wilt Chamberlain. Warming up together on a gym floor, basketball players don't look especially tall — but they suddenly do when an average-sized trainer brings over some towels.

Thomas Wolfe, the 6'6" writer, used to say that he never felt tall when alone in his apartment; only when he stepped outside was he reminded (incessantly) by others of how big he was — relative to them. Most of us have had no such experience. Yet we are aware of how a tall man can make us feel like a little kid, or how a country populated with relatively short citizens can make us feel like Gulliver among the Lilliputians. Conversely, smaller visitors to this country (from countries where they may not be so small) are prone to comment on how "dwarfed" they feel by our jumbo-sized citizenry.

The most acute observation yet made about the relativity of human height is that of Dick Cavett. Asked if he was self-conscious about his height, the 5'6" Cavett replied: "No. But I'm self-conscious about other people's."

Height Perception Is Affected by Level of Eye Contact

A woman of 5'2" once told me that the only time she's really conscious of her 6'3" boyfriend's 13-inch height advantage is when they're standing in line for a movie. Unable to sit, lie down, or even back up to make eye contact easier, she has no choice but to crane her neck upward so they can converse. By the time they get into the movie, the strain both on her neck muscles and her morale lingers as a reminder that her boyfriend is quite a bit taller than she is.

No settings are more conducive to height consciousness than long waiting lines, crowded elevators, and milling cocktail parties. In such settings not only are there lots of other bodies with which to compare one's own, but such comparison can literally become a pain in the neck. This is due to a second influence on perception of height: the level at which our eyes meet others'.

Three very important phrases in the English language remind us regularly of the relationship between height and eye contact. These are:

- *look up to,*
- *look straight in the eye,* and
- *look down upon.*

Obviously such phrases have less to do with physical than with psychological interaction. Who looks up to whom, who deals eye to eye, and who gets looked down upon are very important issues in our society. For this reason uneven eye contact is the source of lots of humor, sort of. Nervous jokes are common about "eyeball-to-kneecap" confrontations between short men and tall ones. When the New York Giants drafted a 6'6" offensive tackle, fullback Larry Csonka remarked, "It's good to have a lineman you can look straight in the belly button."

Using level of eye contact as a means to judge height is much more important to grown-ups than to kids. Since circumstances usually prevent our standing back-to-back to size each other up, comparing the angle at which our eyes meet another person's is our only real adult means of doing so.

In an interview, Harvard biologist Stephen Jay Gould explained that "the difference between 5'8" [his own height] and 5'10" is the difference between an average and a tallish person." As he said this Gould spread his thumb and forefinger slightly apart. "It's *that* much. It's *nothing.* It's eye level that matters — whether you're looking up or whether you're looking down. So I wonder if the angle of the sight line may not function as a cue to inferred rank."

Among both men and animals, "gaze behavior" is an important means of sorting out who stands where. Those who are supposed to be above the rest of us have historically been given a boost in the form of thrones, platforms, or pulpits from which they look down; bowing, curtsying, and prostration provide insurance that the looked-down-upon will in fact be looking up.

When 6'10" basketball star Bill Russell was to meet Ethiopian Emperor Haile Selassie, the tiny monarch insisted that their encounter take place in the back of his limousine. It wouldn't do, the king explained, for such as himself to have to look up so far during an audience.

Since we do often judge rank according to level of eye contact, a throne, practically speaking, is far more potent a symbol of power than a crown. Thrones force subjects' eyes upward to establish eye contact, while crowns rest above this process. For the same reason, wearing high heels or lifts can effectively enhance stature by altering angles of eye contact, while hats are less effective for this purpose. (Isn't this why hats for women go in and out of style but heels are always with us?)

Gaze level has a lot to do with how women and men relate. The political clout of New York's Bess Myerson, for example, has not been hurt by the regularly noted fact that, being nearly 6 feet tall, she "looks men in the eye."

By contrast, a 6'4" businessman told me that on the rare occasions when he'd met a woman who didn't look up to him he experienced extreme discomfort. "I'm used to looking down at women," the man explained. "I like to have the psychological edge."

My wife and I once were fooling around with a pair of glitter platform shoes that had 4-inch heels — about equal to the difference in height between us. Her wearing them, we figured, would put us on equal footing. This sounded like fun. Sitting down, Muriel strapped them on. Then she stood up to look at me — straight in the eye. Do you think that after years of studying height I was prepared for this experience? I was stunned. Mortified. Looking directly at a pair of eyes I'd looked down at for fifteen years was unnerving beyond description. I still

Gaze Behavior

*Philippe de Gaulle
and René Lévesque*

*Dustin Hoffman and Harvard's
Hasty Pudding Club President*

*Senator Lowell Weicker
and constituent*

*Arthur Burns with Mr.
and Mrs. G. William Miller*

*Fidel Castro with U.S.
businessmen and wives*

*James Stewart, Helen Hayes,
and John Lindsay*

can't explain why. I just know I couldn't wait for her to get those platforms off.

In a reverse of my own experience, a man of 5′5″ told me of putting on a woman's wedgies as a goof at a dinner party with old friends. Sort of like lampshades for the feet. But once he stood up and began to walk around, the man was startled to discover how different the world looked. That little change in visual angle made even old friends' faces take on an entirely different cast. But even more important than the way such faces *looked* from on high was the way their owners *felt* — looking up at a man's eyes when before they'd always looked down upon them. The man said he enjoyed this experience immensely. He wasn't sure his friends did.

The world seen by talls is in many respects different from the world seen by smalls. Talls note whether we've dusted our refrigerator top; smalls know when we've spilled soup on our tie. Talls get the first word on whose hair is thinning; smalls are the last to know. Smalls are used to looking up; talls are used to looking down. To this extent, they live in dissimilar worlds.

Psychologist Robert Sommer once put the staff of a hospital in wheelchairs for a day to acquaint them with how it felt to be disabled. He found that this experience was much harder for some than for others, depending primarily on their height. ''Tall people,'' reported Sommer, ''were very uncomfortable at being looked down on, but this did not affect medium or short people.''

Because angle of vision controls our perception of the world, it is a common source of misperception. That's another reason why movie stars usually seem taller than they really are. In addition to the larger-than-life proportions the projector gives them, we see every one of them by looking up at the screen. Our eyes must rise as high to Richard Dreyfuss as to Clint Eastwood. Since we're so used to assuming that anyone we look up to is bigger than we are, how could we not assume Dreyfuss to be taller than he is? — or Burt Reynolds, or Marlon Brando, or any of the taller-seeming smaller actors?

There's another, final reason why our mind's eye magnifies celebrities. A basic tenet of the psychology of perception is that size is associated with value. Whatever our mind judges important our eye will judge large. And power is among our ultimate values.

Height Is Equated with Power

A few months after Jimmy Carter entered the White House, I asked 82 college students who they thought was taller, Carter or Richard Nixon. Forty-nine percent thought the current President, 46 percent the former President. Almost a year later I asked the same question of 47 students at a different college. Of this group, 66 percent thought Carter was taller; 30 percent Nixon. Jimmy Carter, remember, is in fact 2–3 inches shorter than Richard Nixon.

A number of explanations could be suggested for this misperception of Carter as relatively taller, but I think the most compelling reason is this: the principal value with which tallness correlates in our mind is power. Those with control over our lives must be big; those without such control, small.

While he was President, Lyndon Johnson had the power to appear even larger than his actual 6′3″ or 6′4″. On his first trip back to Washington after retiring, Johnson impressed one long-time LBJ observer as "looking less tall."

And it's not just Presidents. Anyone who looms large in our mind is liable to loom large in our eyes. Kids have been found to draw Santa Claus increasingly bigger as Christmas draws near. Voters regularly assume that their preferred candidate is taller than his opponents without evidence. And a 6'1" man I know has told me that although he's now nearly a foot taller than his mother, she remains so powerful in his life he cannot shake his mental picture of her as gigantic.

One group of people who get regular evidence of how we associate size with power are psychologists and psychiatrists. At the outset of treatment especially, patients are notorious for perceiving the therapist as taller than they are whether this is true or not. One 5-foot-tall clinical psychologist told me that it's become almost a routine in therapy for her patients to say that she seems larger than they, though this has rarely been the case.

Centuries ago, Magellan and other explorers returning from Patagonia with tales of its giant warriors variously said these Indians were 7, 7⅓, 8½, 10, or 11 feet tall. When finally measured, male Patagonians turned out to average 5'10". Not giants. But awfully good warriors. And therefore, by "logical" conclusion in the mind — huge.

The same is thought to be true of "Amazons." The Amazons of legend (and possible reality) were tribes of ferocious women warriors. Depending on the tribe, such groups were renowned for cutting off one breast the better to shoot arrows; for enslaving men or shunning them except during brief mating liaisons; and for killing off most male babies in favor of girls, who were potential warriors. Whether or not such women ever existed is beside my point. This point is that by reputation what all Amazons had in common was their ferocity, not their height. Rarely were they described as especially tall. Some legendary Amazons were even said to be small. But over the years we have mentally translated ferocity into exaggerated size. Today that translation is so complete that the word "Amazon" is nearly synonymous with feminine height. When we refer to "a real Amazon," or "a woman of Amazonian proportions," what we're describing is physique, not temperament. A big, meek woman could today be credibly called Amazonian; a ferocious, short one could not. To such a degree are size and strength one in our minds.

The connection actually isn't difficult to understand. During childhood, "big and strong" are nearly one word in our mouths. This, we are assured, is what we'll grow to be if only we eat our spinach. Once we are grown that association is hard to break. In particular, men will commonly scan upward in a roomful of other men to calculate who they could "take" should the need arise.

Even when relative physical strength isn't a factor, it's hard not to assume that a taller body wields greater clout. In an analysis of size relationships in magazine advertising, sociologist Erving Goffman has demonstrated that size is commonly used as a visual shorthand for authority. Reported Goffman: "So thoroughly is it assumed that differences in size will correlate with differences in social weight that relative size can be routinely used as a means of ensuring that the pictures' story will be understandable at a glance." Thus the dominant figure in an advertisement — a policeman, say, or an executive — is nearly always the tallest figure. On the rare occasions when a woman pictured in an ad is taller than the man she's beside, his social role is usually subordinate — a waiter, a chef, or a little old winemaker.

Knowing how strongly we associate size with power, when casting powerful legendary figures in history, moviemakers commonly cast them tall — even when this flies in the face of history. James Caan as Billy Rose. Paul Winfield as Martin Luther King, Jr. Anthony Quinn as Aristotle Onassis. Max Von Sydow as Jesus.

For a movie called *The Amazons,* a casting call went out for actresses 6 feet tall or more. "We had to have big girls to make this picture credible," explained director Terence Young. Young, who is credited with discovering Ursula Andress, didn't even consider her for one of his Amazons. The director said he would have loved to use the Swiss-born actress, but "she's far too small, simply not powerful enough."

Of all the distortions our mind's eye makes about height, equating tallness with power could be the most significant. Examples of this tendency and its consequences recur throughout this book. The assumption that bigger people are stronger people influences in fundamental ways how men deal with women, parents with children, employers with employees. Lovers, athletes, politicians — all of us — regularly make such assumptions. We constantly size each other up according to height and draw power conclusions that favor the tall.

Need I say this makes smalls none too happy? In fact, the assumption that smaller people are weaker people is enough to make some of them fighting mad — as taller people often discover. "Think back to your days on the beat," a Royal Canadian Mounted Police manual once instructed. "It was always the little guy who caused the trouble and caused the fight."

If truth be told, smalls and talls don't particularly care for each other. Usually this is just a matter of sullen discomfort, especially on the part of the smalls. But sometimes such smoldering resentment flares up into open attack. Some highlights of such warfare:

• *Spring 1970* — At California's Villa Park High School, Tony Horn and friends sit down on the gym floor to protest preference shown talls in choosing teams; Short Power Day is proclaimed.

• *Fall 1971* — 5′4″ sociologist Dr. Saul Feldman gives paper on "The Presentation of Shortness in Everyday Life — Height and Heightism in American Society" to American Sociological Association; charges "American society is a society with a heightist premise: to be tall is to be good and to be short is to be stigmatized."

• *Winter 1971* — At New College in Sarasota, Florida, 4'10½" sophomore Wendell Wagner posts a list of Short Demands; included are: lower library shelves, admissions quotas favoring small applicants, required courses on the history of tall oppression, a Mickey Rooney Film Festival.

• *Spring 1972* — 5'5" Assistant U.S. Treasury Secretary Edwin S. Cohen claims talls have unfair economic advantage; he proposes a tax break for those under 5'6".

• *Winter 1978* — 5'2" Edmund A. Szymczyk sues General Motors, his employer, for $600,000; he alleges jokes by coworkers about his shortness and Polishness have hurt his job performance, lost him promotions, and cost him peace of mind.

Such attacks by smalls upon talls dates back at least to David and Goliath. In London on June 25, 1713, *The Guardian* carried a notice announcing the formation of a club limited to men 5 feet and under. The members were to meet on December 10 (the shortest day of the year) at the Little Piazza for a meal of shrimp. "It is the unanimous opinion of our society," read their manifesto, "that since the race of mankind is granted to have decreased in stature from the beginning to this present [this once was a common belief], it is the intent of nature itself, that men should be little; and we believe that all human kind shall at last grow down to perfection — that is to say, be reduced to our own measure."

Three weeks later *The Guardian* announced the formation of a rival "Tall Club," all of whose members were to exceed 6 feet. Their public seal was to be a crane grasping a pygmy in its talons. Among this new group's goals was keeping in their place members of the club of little men, whom they threatened to carry off in baskets and imprison in a cupboard.

Such a tall response to small outrage is really rather unusual. Content with their psycho-physical edge, bigger people usually are rather gracious toward their smaller, feistier brethren — in public at least. Among themselves, things may be different. John Kenneth Galbraith has told of a conversation he had following John Kennedy's funeral with a fellow tall person — French President Charles de Gaulle. Galbraith had just finished chatting with Soviet envoy Anastas Mikoyan, he recalled, when "de Gaulle began by pointing to Mr. Mikoyan and asking why I had been conversing with such a short man. I said he [de Gaulle] obviously agreed with me that the world belongs to the tall man. They are more visible, therefore their behavior is better and accordingly they are to be trusted. He said that he agreed and added, 'It is important that we be merciless with those who are too small.' "

From such attitudes do chasms grow between the heights. This is not to say that bridges can't be built between them. It's just difficult. There's so much uneasiness all around. I know that my own discomfort when meeting a man who's much taller than I am is based on a simple awareness: at some level my physical well-being depends on him not losing his temper. This awareness makes me both very agreeable and quite uneasy. It is not a feeling conducive to friendship.

Psychologist William Berkowitz once studied friendship choice among college students relative to height. The results were clear-cut. Among 514 pairs of friends, the average height difference between the two parties was only 2.76 inches, a far smaller difference than would have occurred in random pairings of the subjects. "Similarity of height and friendship choices are related," Dr. Berkowitz concluded. In another study of how smalls and talls relate, researchers asked 84 students of both sexes at Virginia Commonwealth University to approach various standing men of different height until they felt uncomfortably close. On the average, the students stayed twice as far from a man of 6'3" than they did from one 5'4" tall.

In the opinion of psychologist Sidney Portnoy, a feeling of jeopardy makes smaller people wary of taller people. "I don't think it's a threat of bodily injury as such," he explained. "Just a general sense of [threat to] well-being." The psychologist's opinion is more than mere speculation. Sidney Portnoy is one of the few people ever to conduct a full-scale experimental study of how talls and smalls relate to each other.

For his Temple University Ph.D. thesis, Portnoy brought together people of different heights, grouped them variously by size, and observed how they interacted while performing a given task. His original hypothesis was that smaller men (5'2" to 5'7") would be likely to go along with the opinions of taller men (6'1" to 6'4") when they were grouped together. This did not prove to be the case. Among themselves, the smaller men had little trouble agreeing on the issues presented to them. But when taller men were added to their group, they grew noticeably ill at ease and argumentative. "It appears," Portnoy concluded, "that being with others of similar height boosts one's positive feelings about oneself and, conversely, being with others of a different height causes one to have doubts about himself. . . ."

In person, Dr. Sidney Portnoy was a man with whom I could get comfortable. When we met and shook hands in his office at the counseling center outside Philadelphia where he is head psychologist, neither of us had to reach up or down. We looked each other in the eye. Portnoy told me that he first started thinking about the effect of height on human relations while counseling children. "I found I had to get down on their own level," he explained. "Literally. I felt there was a lack of rapport when I was standing up above them and they were way down there because they were only three feet tall. When they had to look up at me there seemed to be a greater distance, both physically and emotionally."

So Portnoy began to alter his approach. First he squatted when talking with the children. Then he got down on his knees. At other times he sat on the floor, or in a little chair. Eventually Portnoy found that such equalizing of eye level made communication with the kids possible where little had existed before. That led him to consider height interaction as a thesis topic. Upon looking for existing research in this area he found that there was very little.

At about this time Portnoy and his wife went to see the film *They Shoot Horses, Don't They?* Since only first row seats were left when they got to the theater, they had to strain their necks to see the screen. The resulting physical tension, compounded by the movie's emotional tension, confirmed Portnoy's growing awareness of just how uncomfortable looking *up* can be. So he had his topic: "Height as a Personality Variable in a Conformity Situation."

After the experiment was completed and the smaller men had demonstrated how hard it was for them to develop rapport with taller ones, Portnoy queried some of the short subjects informally. Most confirmed that they immediately felt on edge when the big guys walked into their group. "I felt uneasy," they told the psychologist, or, "I felt uncomfortable." Since they did feel so threatened, observed Portnoy, the smalls' inability to get together with talls on a task at hand could be seen almost as an act of self-defense.

According to Portnoy, such feelings are understandable. In fact, they're not entirely foreign to him personally, he noted. Not long ago he taught a workshop that included a participant who was 6'9" tall. Standing next to this man, looking up more than a foot, the psychologist found himself quite uncomfortable. "It's like he was towering over me," he recalled. "I felt threatened." Taking note of his reaction, Portnoy made a point of discussing it with the taller man — while both were seated.

This eased the problem. But Portnoy told me he still would rather not stand directly next to someone so tall: psychological reactions aside, it's just too hard on the neck muscles.

Since completing his study Portnoy has kept tabs informally on the relative heights of bodies he sees clustered at parties. Invariably such clusters are limited to a certain range of heights. This doesn't surprise the psychologist. As he pointed out in his doctoral thesis, "if being with someone of a different height causes little self-acceptance, it is easy to see why persons would have a greater tendency to choose friends of the same height."

Citing research related to his own, Portnoy also suggested the possibility that "the perceived stereotype of power, superiority and threat are inherent in tallness." But this is not a hypothesis he's actually studied. In fact, little research of any kind has been devoted to the social role of tallness. What study has been done on height normally focuses on the more obvious problems of shortness. In general, tall people are seldom asked how they feel about their height-related role in society. Nor do they often volunteer such information. We know next to nothing about how tall people cope with reactions to their size. So I wondered — and tried to discover — just how does it feel to look down on a world of smaller bodies whose eyes are looking up at yours?

4 Talls

How's the weather up there?

— Author unknown

The only way I'll ever get any privacy is to cut off my legs.

— WILT CHAMBERLAIN

NOTE: Because tallness and smallness have historically been discussed most often in male terms ("Napoleonic," "Big Dumb Oaf," etc.), chapters 4 and 5 are male-oriented. Chapter 6 is on women alone. All the rest are "bisexual."

I have a friend named Rod Townley who is a poet. Rod is gentle, soft-spoken, and on the shy side. He's also 7 feet tall.

Rod's told me often what a literal pain in the neck his height can be, as have other tall men. The worst part is being out in public: the stares, the whistles, the gasps, the comments — especially the comments. If somebody ever said something original to him about his height now and then it might not be so bad. Nobody ever has. In fact Rod hears the same observations made about his size so regularly that he's been tempted to have a button made up reading "NO. FINE. 7 FEET" in response to the three most popular inquiries: "Do you play basketball?" "How's the weather up there?" and "How tall *are* you?"

From Rod and other talls I've heard often enough not to doubt that such comments grow wearisome. But I had missed the full flavor of the tall experience until I went to a Phillies baseball game with my 7-foot friend.

The subway was crowded and, with our wives and Rod's son Jesse along, we had to stand. With nothing better to pay attention to, the other passengers paid lots of attention to Rod. Their faces were a mixture of fascination, fear, and sheer wonderment. His long, sober head projecting a foot above the crowd was easily the most interesting thing present. Three teenage girls in particular would glance up at Rod open-mouthed, huddle over their giggles, then peek once again. Not used to this sort of attention, I found the whole ride mildly disconcerting. Perhaps because he's more calm in general, oblivious to the whole thing, or just resigned to it, Rod seemed at ease.

Entering the stadium wasn't a problem since the crowd was spread out, the fans intent on finding their seats. Watching the game was fine, too, since people seem more nearly the same size seated. But leaving the game was another story. Now the crowd was thicker, happier (the hometown Phillies won), and tipsier. As we joined a long, tightly packed stream of people filing out the exits, a gradual chorus of sucked-in breath began, followed by low whistles of surprise, and finally comments floating up and hanging like milkweed seeds in the air.

"Will ya look at that!"

"Hey — looka that guy!"

"How big ya suppose he is?"

"He must be a basketball player. Must play for the 76ers."

"Hey — you play for the 76ers?" asked a young voice at our side. We kept walking.

"No, hey, really — you a basketball player?" The voice was whiny, insistent. Its owner was a kid trying desperately to sprout a mustache. He fell in step with us. "Seriously, tell me, buddy — how tall are you? You gotta be a basketball player."

When Rod finally recognized his presence with a withering look, the kid fell behind, then disappeared into the crowd. But barely a minute later he was back, this time holding an imaginary microphone and howling into his hand. "Here we have at center for the Philadelphia 76ers, standing, standing — how tall did you say you stand?"

Though you could see that even to rebuke would be to join in the game, Rod finally muttered, "You know, you're really a very boring person," and at last his tormentor wandered off sullenly, without whatever it was he was looking for.

Waiting in line for the subway home meant once more becoming the unwilling target of startled looks, giggles, and muffled comments all around. "Hey, look at that," you could hear a father stage-whispering to his boy. "See how tall that guy is!"

In the train we once again were packed standing like prisoners off to Siberia. And once more Rod became a high totem of worship. "Hey, mister — how tall are you?" the blond-haired boy standing beside him asked. A good two feet shorter, the boy looked up persistently at the tall figure beside him.

Rod tried to ignore him, but as the stare continued, he finally mumbled, "Seven feet." Rod speaks softly and the boy, with his ear so far away, misunderstood.

"Six feet! Is that all?"

"Seven."

"Oh." The boy then turned to my wife, Muriel, and Rod's wife, Libby. Both are 5'4". "Which one of you is married to him?"

Muriel pointed to Libby. The kid turned to her.

"How do you reach up there to kiss him?"

"He can bend down, you know," Libby responded with uncharacteristic tartness.

"Whadda ya — carry around a milk crate to stand on or something?"

When we got home Rod said the evening's volume of comments was about par for a ball game. Depending on what's playing, he gets more stares than comments in movie theaters. In a more formal setting, like the opera, people usually confine themselves to stealing glances.

Sometimes the worst experiences occur when Rod's just walking down the street. There's a certain breed of person who accosts him regularly and demands to know how tall he is. "It's like they need to stop me from growing," Rod explained. "They're trying to pin me down, literally *down,* as opposed to letting me float in their imagination." Rod laughed.

"They'll accept any number I give them. Just for the hell of it I'll sometimes say eight feet. All they do is go, 'Wow!' I could probably say nine feet and they'd say the same thing.

"When people try to guess my height they always underestimate. They'll say six-foot-six or six-foot-nine. Never seven feet. It's like they don't *dare* go for the whole thing. They're just not used to exercising their imagination."

Somehow I felt the need to assure Rod that I hadn't set the evening up as part of my research for this book. I had thought we were just going to a ball game. Again Rod laughed. "When you're seven feet tall," he said, "you don't *just* do anything."

One doesn't have to be as tall as Rod to become a public spectacle. I've heard similar experiences reported by men as short as 6'2". But since talls seem to have it made (and are loath to admit otherwise), very little consideration has ever been given to the "problems" of being tall.

A rare attempt was made some thirty-five years ago by a man named Francis Riggs. Riggs was a school headmaster who grew to be 6'7" tall in a time when such height stood out even more than it does today. From 1898, when he was seventeen, until 1930, Riggs said he saw just one man taller than himself — in a circus. Based on notes he kept about his own experiences and using a survey of fellow tall men, Riggs in 1943 privately published a book called *Tall Men Have Their Problems Too.* Among the various case histories in this hard-to-find book, by far the most interesting is Case VIII, that of the author.

F.B. Riggs
Height Record

As far back as I can remember I always knew I was big. When I became 13, I began to realize that I was also very tall, not merely big. I began to feel "different," but as yet not uncomfortably so; for I was made to feel proud of my height. My mother gave me more responsibilities like buying railroad tickets and piloting her past the horses and carriages on New York streets. I had now reached the height my father was. I held my head up. . . .

I entered boarding school at 15. The Headmaster, Mr. Peabody, [who] realized that I was overgrown, clumsy and sensitive, told me that it would take me a year to catch up with myself. . . .

. . . I soon acquired the name "Biggs" which I regarded almost as a term of affection. Only a few thought of me as merely a good joke. One boy wrote a poem about me which went the rounds of the school before I saw it. It began with,

> *"Who is this new and dreadful monster*
> *A sun-burned mammoth or an Egyptian slave?"*

I pretended to think the poem funny. There was another boy who told me that my rapid growth was unhealthy. This I stoutly denied and proved my abundant health by showing him the hair on my chest. Yet I was afraid what he said might be true. . . .

One teacher had his unconscious share in the development of my height consciousness. An announcement had been made that all new boys should report for choir try-out and practice. I rather liked the idea. That evening I went to the practice room. I was late. Everybody had assembled. As I bowed my head to clear the doorway, the choir master caught sight of me and stopped me in my tracks with, "You're miles too big for the choir. Who could you walk with?" Everybody laughed. . . .

At college I was blessed with rare friends who really took me seriously and for whom I was never the butt of a height joke. My pride in their friendship prevented me from being too sorry for myself.

When in Boston, however, or in fact any city except, curiously enough, London, I was always reminded by someone of my height. There has never been any variation in the questions. It was the same in 1900 as it is today. The same in Seattle as in New York. In cities I became increasingly annoyed, sometimes enraged, and sometimes merely bored with those everlasting questions about "the weather up there," and "arguments" about me.

Once in a crowd when a short fat man began his inevitable introduction I cut him short with, "All right, I'll tell you if you'll give me a detail I can't *quite* figure out. Are you 5' or 5'6" around the waist?" I thought I was funny. The bystanders laughed. The fat one resented my query, but I was supposed to revel in his. I was young then.

Yet direct action was not always possible. I never knew what to *do* when people whispered or whistled in astonishment. Now I *do* nothing. . . .

I continued to be bothered in the cities. Sometimes I pretended not to know my height. For a period I used to give inquirers a printed card, tabulating my chief measurements. I was young then. . . .

As I grew older my height became something to use, not just to defend. Crossing the Atlantic a few years ago I used my height to good advantage when I saw a clergyman in his cups trying to dance with two bewildered girls at the same time. Several of us were watching the spectacle. Our remarks to him were of no avail. Finally, standing my full 6'7", I quietly observed, "I wonder if that young man knows that I am the Bishop from Alaska." The clergyman stopped dancing. The next day he cornered me and hoped that I would not report him. For five days he remained worried, but sober. On the sixth day I became a layman and we had a friendly and I believe fruitful conversation.

Based on interviews with other tall men and on their responses to his questionnaire, Riggs summed up the pluses and minuses they reported about being 6'5" or taller. Included among the advantages were self-confidence, easy entrée into conversations, periscopic vision in crowds, ability to reach high shelves, ease in changing light bulbs, fast walking, women's admiration, leadership, dominance, and being able to stay out of fights by keeping others respectful.

Among drawbacks to being tall Riggs included being more easily spotted by creditors, being the first noticed when things go wrong, and having problems finding a suitable bicycle. "Height is a disadvantage," he concluded, "when a tall man *thinks* that people notice him more than they really do, when he does not recognize the person who easily recognizes him, when boys and girls (especially young ones) whisper, laugh or jeer at him, when he must waste five minutes with each acquaintance to talk about his height, when the remark 'I feel so small' is coupled with a self-deprecating shrinking gesture."

This really is the heart of the issue. Like any odd-sized person, the tall man himself has no "problem." The problem is other people and their response to him. In private, tall men have told me, they don't feel odd; only in public, when others make them a spectacle. This constitutes their principle grievance. Heads bumped on doorways, knees pushed to mouth in airplane seats, coffinlike phone booths — these are all minor irritants to talls when compared with the lack of privacy in public.

Tall bodies for some reason are considered public property — much like the Statue of Liberty, the Washington Monument, or the Eiffel Tower — and are treated with about as much sensitivity. We generally keep our racial comments to ourselves. It's never been appropriate to comment on nose size. Whistling at women has declined over the years. But not commentary on tall bodies.

"No one ever made an interesting or amusing observation about his height," Thomas Wolfe once wrote of a fictional character in his story "Gulliver," "and ten thousand people had their fling about it."

But as a writer the 6'6" Wolfe saw some advantage in being a spectacle. By being forced daily into the pits of humanity, he explained, the tall man stayed in close touch with how little was on most minds. Such a man, Wolfe wrote, is "at once life's exile and life's prisoner; wherever he goes life reaches out and pulls him to it, will not let him go . . . And in the jibes the jests, the drolleries that are shouted after him a dozen times a day in the streets because of his great height, in the questions that are asked concerning it, and in the innumerable conversations that it provokes, he acquires a huge and damning accumulation of evidence concerning man's fatal unity, the barren paucity of his invention, the desolate consonance of his wit."

I've heard this sort of thing repeatedly from tall men. It's not the incessant commentary about their height that is so annoying, it's the stupefying boredom of it all. Were anyone to say something original or witty or different in any way, the constant chatter thrown their way might at least be entertaining. But soon after reaching their full height, tall people realize to their horror that the lifetime's commentary to which they've been sentenced comes mostly from those with least to say.

One of the few comments about his 7'1" size that ever surprised Wilt Chamberlain came from a drunk in San Francisco who took one terrified look up at the basketball player and mumbled, "Please don't fall this way." During nearly a decade at 6'7", twenty-four-year-old television actor Peter Isacksen told me, the only person ever to say anything out of the ordinary to him about his size was a nine-year-old boy who tugged at his pant leg and said, "Mister — you're the tallest white person I've ever seen."

Isacksen, late of "CPO Sharkey," has a broad, winning grin, which he flashed while telling me this story on the Twentieth Century–Fox lot where he was taking part in a "Love Boat" sequence. The smile faded quickly as I asked how he responded to all the rest of the comments — the ones about weather and basketball. Then Isacksen smiled again and told me that he just

Peter Isacksen meets Don Rickles

goes along, laughs at the unfunny remarks, tries to put people at ease. The actor said that he's noticed over the years that the comments come most often from guys among their pals, so he figures they're just uneasy and trying to impress each other. Isacksen's smile dwindled once again and finally died altogether as he thought the situation over. "Sometimes I wish I were more vicious," he concluded, "but I haven't gotten into a fight since the first grade." His smile then reappeared, but not full force. "I just try to make everyone feel comfortable."

In response to all the comments they hear, tall men have little alternative but to shuffle and grin. Experimenting with any other approach risks raising the anxiety level of shorter people, who are anxious enough as it is. John Kenneth Galbraith calls the ceaseless observations made about his height "passive admissions of inferiority." Intuitively recognizing them as such, he thinks the tall man has no need to respond, for the commentators are already handicapped enough.

Which isn't to say that a big man won't occasionally lose patience and respond with something like: "The weather's fine up here — how is it down around my ass?" Asked about the weather up there while in an elevator, one basketball player simply poured the Coke he was drinking onto the interrogator's head and replied, "Raining." The best response I've heard of to the "My, you're tall" comment is that of two tall brothers who always reply in unison, "Just that much nearer heaven!"

But even the perfect rejoinder never really works. Because what's at issue isn't the questions themselves, or the comments, but the anxiety that prompted them in the first place. Unable to say something direct, such as "You make me nervous" or "Please don't hurt me" (or even to know that that's what we're feeling), what we say instead is something such as "How's the weather up there?" — and hope tall people get the message.

The paradox in being tall is that precisely because everyone assumes them to be extra powerful, talls are never supposed to exercise any power directly. Short people can be as feisty as they like. Who cares? But if a tall person starts acting up, the existing trickle of fear in his presence may turn into a flood of terror. The tall man is painfully aware of this danger — because he's never allowed to forget it. From the time he first begins to shoot up over the heads of his playmates, a tall boy gets constant messages subtle and overt that he has to restrain himself; he must learn to hold things in and *never* lose control, because if he did he might hurt someone. Small people, the tall columnist Russell Baker once noted, are allowed all the malice they wish, but "malice toward none is the dreary birthright of the lengthy frame."

Beyond comments and questions, the most effective means we have to keep tall people at bay are stereotypes. Such stereotypes serve as pigeonholes for corralling big bodies in hopes they won't escape and wreak havoc. The classic tall stereotypes are "Big Dumb Oaf"; its modern corollary, "Basketball Player"; and, the most common, "Big Bully."

Big Bully is so pervasive a stereotype that Jimmy Cagney once said part of his fan appeal consisted of making sure any opponent he beat up on screen was bigger than he. Were his opponent cast smaller, Cagney would have looked bigger and therefore have been the bully. Similarly, when 6'5" Chuck Connors once played a villain opposite 6'7" James Arness, he had to wear 3-inch lifts in his boots so that he, not Arness, would look the bully.

Virtually any tall man who was a tall boy has some memory of the Big Bully tag being hung on him. George Mikan, the basketball star, has written about the time as a boy when he lashed out with his fists at a smaller kid who was taunting him for wanting to learn piano. The kid's head hit the pavement and he passed out. Mikan was panic-stricken at the thought the boy wouldn't come to, but he did. The school principal subsequently threatened to expel Mikan, scolding him as "a big bully taking advantage of somebody half your size." Soon after this incident Mikan gave up playing piano.

"Big kids are always pointed out as bullies," 6'2" National Football League coach Howard Mudd once told me. Tall at an early age, Mudd later used his size to his advantage as an All-Pro guard for the San Francisco 49ers. But he still remembers in particular the time as a 6-foot twelve-year-old when a fire was started in his neighborhood by another kid who had tipped over a kerosene lantern. Mudd kicked sand on the fire in an attempt to put it out. Before he succeeded, however, a neighbor lady came out and accused him of starting the fire himself. She'd known all along that he was a troublemaker, the woman screamed — a big bully. "I'll never forget that," said Mudd thirty years later. "Big kids are always being called bullies."

The stereotype of talls as troublemakers is not modern. Addressing the king of the huge Brobdingnagians two and a half centuries ago, Jonathan Swift's Gulliver commented that "human creatures are observed to be more savage and cruel in proportion to their bulk."

Gulliver subsequently suggested that "reason did not extend itself with the bulk of the body: on the contrary, we observed in our country that the tallest persons were usually least provided with it." Obviously tallness has been associated with stupidity for some time. It has yet to be determined exactly when or where the Big Dumb Oaf stereotype originated. We do know that long before Swift wrote *Gulliver's Travels,* essayist James Howell was comparing tall men to "houses of four stories, wherein commonly the uppermost room is worst furnished." (More recently a movie character played by Nick Nolte was described by one reviewer as "tall, blond, tanned and with obvious room to let upstairs.")

Such stereotyping is a potent means to remind talls of their place. Tall people are aware of this process and sensitive about it. Peter Isacksen said that in high school especially he didn't like the idea of being perceived as "just kind of a big, dumb oaf who probably always has a basketball in his hand." As a result, Isacksen did what he could to belie the stereotype. He took college prep courses, became a cutup (winning recognition as Class Clown), and tried out for plays rather than basketball — despite the pleadings of a coach. Ironically, now that he's out of school, the tall actor has discovered that he likes basketball and plays it often with his friend Ronnie Howard of TV's "Happy Days," who's a foot shorter and, says Isacksen, has yet to take him one-on-one.

Other talls make it a lifelong point not to get *near* a basketball if they can possibly help it. That's because in recent years Basketball Player has become the equivalent to Big Dumb Oaf as a pigeonhole for tall bodies. My friend Rod says this stereotype is so pervasive that even in his late thirties he still has to contend with people who actually get mad at him for not playing the game and tell him he *ought* to play basketball as if it were some kind of patriotic duty. Even tall men who make their living shooting balls through hoops can get so weary of this stereotype that they've been known to respond, "No, I'm a jockey," when asked if they're a basketball player.

Comments, questions, jokes, and the corral of stereotypes — these are the primary means by which we nontalls express anxiety about talls in hopes they'll go easy on us. Presumably tall people themselves are exempt from such feelings of anxiety. Being so used to the verbal crackle in their vicinity and so often reminded of the immaturity of it all, they themselves, one might assume, never resort to childish remarks in the face of someone taller. One could go further and speculate that tall men even *enjoy* the relief of a taller man's company.

Ha! In fact tall men can't stand meeting anyone taller. It drives them nuts. Long after the incident, a retired college professor of 6′1″ still marveled at his reaction to a 6′6″ visitor. Exaggerating their height difference was the fact that the smaller man was wearing only bedroom slippers. Even worse, they met in a basement apartment and the guest was standing on a step, above his host. The effect was to place the 6-footer at nearly a foot's disadvantage. "My first reaction," the professor recalled, "was instant antagonism to this monster. I wanted to punch him. Later I came to see why some short men tend to have a chip on their shoulder when faced with men of ordinary height."

Why should talls be so devastated by such a silly little thing as meeting somebody taller? Basically, I think, it's the sheer novelty of the experience. The rest of us look up to people every day, and though we may not like it, we have a lifetime's worth of experience in dealing with our reactions. The tall guy, on the other hand, has seldom had to look *up* at anyone: to feel strain at the back of his neck; to wonder, "Can this guy snap me like a toothpick?"; to . . .

When 6′2″ author Albert Payson Terhune met a giant two feet taller than himself, he found that after a mere five minutes of conversation "the muscles and nerves at the back of my neck were aching abominably from the unaccustomed strain. It is so on all the rare occasions when I have to talk for any length of time to a man considerably taller than I am. Many Big Guys tell me the same thing."

More revealing than Terhune's physical reaction to the giant was his emotional one:

I looked up at him, as we talked, I looked far, *far* up. And through my mind ran this idiotic line of thought:

"I'd like to have the gloves on with you, you lumbering man-mountain! You wouldn't last out one round against me, big as you are. I'd feint for the face, then send my left into your solar plexus. That would snap your head and shoulders forward and give me a chance to drive a right hook or an uppercut to your silly jaw. I could drop you, like a stunned ox.''

Then, all at once, with a sickish shock of shame, I realized what I had been thinking. This was the kind of thing I had been blaming the Little People for thinking about me and about all the other Big Guys!

Dazedly, I understood at last that it is a normal human complex, bred of sub-conscious envy at the greater size of the other fellow, a throwback to the ages when the Little People envied, openly and keenly, the Big Guy for the huge size which made him their master.

Movie director Michael Crichton, 6′10″, is quite familiar with the anxiety tall men experience when meeting a man who's taller. Since 99.99 percent of America's men are shorter than he is, Crichton is mostly familiar with the nervousness of those meeting him — the stammering, the sulking, the uneasy pawing of the floor. Crichton's reaction to such behavior had always been: How childish. How immature. What better evidence could one have of the refusal of some men to grow up?

Crichton's perspective changed, however. He was enjoying himself at a party one evening. Then 7′1″ Wilt Chamberlain showed up. Crichton soon realized he had started feeling very nervous — especially when Chamberlain drew near. ''Do you know,'' said Crichton, shaking his head at the memory, ''I did everything that everybody has done to me. I stood on my tiptoes. I made inane remarks to him. And finally I just thought, 'Oh hell, I can't stand it anymore. This party isn't fun anymore.' And I left.'' Crichton continued to shake his head, then looked up through his aviator glasses. ''It was very surprising, really. In fact, it wasn't until I left, until somebody talked to me the next day and said, 'Boy, as soon as he arrived you left, didn't you?' that I realized what had happened. It was only fifteen minutes before I just had to go.''

Crichton wanted to think this incident was just a fluke, but not long afterward 7'2" Kareem Abdul-Jabbar showed up on the studio lot where both of them were making movies. Crichton had the identical reaction. Until the Lakers' center left a few days later, all the filmmaker could think of, he recalled, was, "Get him out of here!"

"I think it threatens your narcissism," Crichton speculated about the presence of a taller man. "It ruins the fantasy that you are the biggest person in the world."

In Crichton's case, it's easy to understand such a fantasy. He is not just tall: he's huge. Although an inch or two shorter than my poet friend Rod, Crichton seemed bigger because he's bulkier. This bulk is ameliorated somewhat by his baby face and easy manner. Crichton was kind enough to stay seated during most of our conversation in his office at the MGM studios. The office — filled with tennis gear, a basketball, pop art, and one of those tall leather-sling director's chairs (which in his case seemed redundant) — was clearly not built with its current inhabitant in mind; when at one point he had to step out to consult with his secretary, Crichton bobbed his head way down to clear the doorway long before reaching it.

Discussing his life as a big guy, Crichton ticked off all the usual harassments: the looks, the comments, the stereotypes. Especially in his neck of the woods intellectually, the filmmaker said, "there is often the presumption that you are stupid, as a function of physical size." Crichton mentioned some other drawbacks to being tall that I hadn't yet heard about — such as the bad air that accumulates around his head as smoke drifts upward at cocktail parties. He also gets the feeling at such gatherings that he's missing a lot of the good gossip below.

Some of his dealings as a moviemaker, Crichton said, are complicated by people's reaction to his height. "It can be a particular problem with a certain category of male actor," the director explained. "Sometimes when I'm casting a role every guy that comes in for it says something about how tall I am. Every single one."

Other than making short actors nervous and feeling nervous himself around tall basketball players, Crichton said he doesn't mind his height or even feel that conscious of it. For one thing, the advantages of being tall are tempered by the fact that his chosen lines of work — medicine, writing, and moviemaking — are so prestigious already that tallness doesn't add much status. For another thing, Los Angeles, where he spends most of his time, tends to have lots of tall residents (at least in the parts he frequents) — but few elevators and lots of cars, which keep people seated and less height-conscious. In Los Angeles, Crichton said, there are extended periods of time when he altogether forgets about being 6'10" tall. Returning to New York can be a shock, because there "the heads seem to go down a bit." Leaving the country can be even more disconcerting, he added, though the nature of the shock varies from place to place. In Egypt, for some reason, people on the street call him "Lofty." In Malaysia, he's "watertower" — partly because of his height, partly because the heat and humidity make him drip onto people below.

But Crichton's strangest experience of all came during a trip to Kenya. He'd been in Nairobi just a short time when he began to feel on edge. Crichton wasn't sure why. Then, with a start, he realized: no one was commenting on his size! Not a single person! He'd acquired no nickname. The weather hadn't been asked about in days. He didn't even feel stared at. "It was like something was wrong with my hair," said Crichton, groping for a way to describe the eeriness of it all. "It was like my hair was dead. I had that kind of feeling — something awful. People didn't even turn as they walked by me in the street.

"I think maybe it was because there were so many different

tribes and because the people there had acquired a way of being extremely polite. But no one ever said anything. Never!''

Long after returning from Africa, Michael Crichton still seemed astonished by his invisibility in Kenya. I wasn't sure whether he enjoyed the feeling or not. Perhaps he wasn't sure himself.

5 Smalls

Let me tell you my theory of small men, Captain, then let me hear what you think. . . . Give me a guy less than five feet eight, Johnson, and I'll give you a real bastard nine times out of ten. It has been my experience that short men get a chip on their shoulders as big as an aircraft carrier. They're pissed off at life and God and everybody else just because they're midgets. They come into the Marine Corps just so they can be proud and tough once in their lives. They like to strut around in their uniforms, flashing their wings around and pretending their dicks are as long as anyone else's. I'm a blunt man, Johnson, and I'll tell you that I always keep my eye out for a little guy because I know he's down there low with his hands around my nuts waiting for a chance to give me the big squeeze. What do you have to say about my theory?

— COLONEL BULL MEECHAM in
Pat Conroy's *The Great Santini*

Perhaps you remember Randy Newman's song "Short People." This was the one about short people having grubby little fingers and dirty little minds, got to pick 'em up just to say hello, no reason to live, et cetera. Remember?

The song actually was a rather clever spoof of bigotry and had a catchy tune. By his own testimony, its author meant no offense. "It's just a joke," Newman explained when the song was released. "You don't think it'll bother anybody, do you?"

It did. After the song was banned by scores of radio stations, inspired three musical rejoinders (all titled "Tall People"), and was singled out for statewide prohibition by a 5'5" legislator in Maryland, Randy Newman realized that some people hadn't got the joke. Before retreating into sullen silence, the 5'11" songwriter had these further observations to make about his hit tune:

- I don't expect it to be a big commercial success in Japan.
- . . . outside of some kids with pituitary gland problems, I really don't think it offends anybody.
- There isn't any prejudice against short people.
- Of course no joke is worth hurting people's feelings, and some people are pretty angry about it. But I think it's only a tiny minority.
- I don't get why people are so offended by it.

Only someone so average-sized as Newman could have had such a problem. It wasn't Newman's song that bothered smaller people so much as the uses to which it was put. During the few weeks that this tune was among the tops of the pops, it was open season on short people. Anyone below 5′6″ who dared to enter a bar risked having the house start humming "Short People" in unison. Tall parents used the song as a lullaby for small kids, and small kids used it as a club against smaller kids. In one instance a short boy was surrounded by a circle of bigger ones serenading him with the song. And a 5′2″ college coed told me that her own father took to bursting into "Short People" as soon as she walked through the door. Whenever short people had the temerity to suggest that the humor was wearing thin, they were then subject to the real knockout punch: "What's the matter? Can't you take a joke?"

What really got to the smaller people wasn't Newman's song or even the very average perspective of the songwriter. What ground smaller teeth smooth was being faced once again with the historic choice confronting those of smaller stature: whether to laugh along at your own expense when jokes turn to your size, or not laugh and risk being labeled "touchy." Either way you're a loser. If not a funny little guy you're a feisty little guy. Always with the emphasis on "little."

Just as a tall person's body is public property, so is a short person's psyche. "Theories" abound about why little guys are the way they are. Rarely are such theories flattering. "[Henry] Winkler," observed a letter writer to *Playboy,* "truly suffers from the 5′6″ syndrome." "Mick Jagger," wrote a woman to *People,* "has . . . a short man's complex." By friend and foe alike, Robert Kennedy's personality was routinely explained with reference to his being the runt of the Kennedy litter — half a head shorter than John or Ted. Conservative author Ralph de Toledano even attributed Kennedy's compassion for the poor to his height, suggesting that "with the less privileged he did not need to compensate for his diminutive size."

The worst part about being short is that taller people claim the right to see right through a smaller person. Rarely do their "analyses" of short behavior show any imagination or insight. Most such theories are tautologies — pieces of circular logic suggesting that the reason short men act the way they do is because they're short, as if some behavioral hormone is released in direct proportion to height. Whatever the "theory," short people generally are held strictly accountable for their lapse of judgment in choosing not to grow up.

There were those around the courthouse who attributed the judge's snappishness to his height — barely 5 feet 4½ inches. Indeed, there was a small man's *machismo,* a feisty defiance about the man.

> — J. ANTHONY LUKAS in *The New York Times Magazine* on Judge Julius Hoffman

It is very queer that the unhappiness of the world is so often brought on by small men. They are so much more energetic and uncompromising than the big fellows. I have always taken good care to keep out of sections with small company commanders. They are mostly confounded little martinets.

> — PAUL BAÜMER in Erich Maria Remarque's *All Quiet on the Western Front*

Bond had always mistrusted short men. They grew up from childhood with an inferiority complex. All their lives they would strive to be big — bigger than the others who had teased them as a child. Napoleon had been short, and Hitler. It was the short men that caused all the trouble in the world.

> — IAN FLEMING in *Goldfinger*

"I wonder, sir, if you would indulge me in a rather unusual request?"

It is no matter for surprise that the pages of history are full of little men, the Napoleons and Hitlers, who have marched through rivers of blood seeking to prove to the world they were big ones.

> — PROFESSOR MARTIN ROTH in a letter to
> *British Medical Journal*

. . . if we think for a moment how many small men have become dictators: Napoleon, Mussolini, Hitler, Stalin. All were men of relatively small stature.

> — Royal Canadian Mounted Police training manual

Napoleon is the most popular explanation for why little guys are the way they are. "Well just look at Napoleon [nod, wink]" is the form this explanation usually takes. The regularity with which we fall back on a man dead well over a century to explain contemporary short behavior illustrates how little we actually know about this "issue." In a rare discussion of smaller-people's problems published over three decades ago, a research team commented that "no investigations of the behavior of persons with short stature have come to our attention. The absence of studies of short men is interesting in view of the fact that shortness in men is frequently mentioned as a liability." Some thirty years later, in 1975, two educators studying the relationship between height and self-esteem noted the earlier passage and pointed out that little additional research had been done in the intervening period on the consequences of shortness.

I think the whole "problem" makes everybody nervous all around — with short people themselves wishing the issue would just go away, normal-sized people often wishing short people would just go away. One of the few insightful observations I've heard about shortness was made by Dr. David Rimoin, who runs the Short Stature Clinic at Harbor Hospital outside Los Angeles. In an interview, the 6-foot endocrinologist told me that the dwarfs and midgets with whom he works seem to be better adjusted psychologically than "normal" short men. The former group, Rimoin speculated, are abnormal and know it; they feel a certain identity and a sense of camaraderie growing from their abnormality. Those in the latter group don't feel abnormal — just inadequate; there is no esprit involved in being a short man. But Rimoin emphasized that this was just speculation on his part. Neither he nor anyone he knew of had ever studied the issue scientifically. Rimoin does know that there's probably something out there worth studying. When *Time* ran an article on his clinic, the doctor was flooded with letters from desperate smaller men seeking his help. One full-grown man of 5′7″ said that if Rimoin couldn't get him to 5′10″ within the next few months, his wife was going to divorce him.

In several years of my own searching I've not only found little actual research on what it means psychologically to be short, but little serious consideration of any kind. Mostly what I've found are references to Napoleon. Even psychologist John Money — a world-renowned expert on psychological aspects of growth problems — when asked if he'd ever worked with short people, said: "No, I haven't worked with them. I've worked *under* them, but not with them." What was that like? I wondered. "Let me put it this way — I never really had a great admiration for Napoleon."

Before going any further, let's get one thing straight: Napoleon wasn't all that short. Napoleonic he may have been, but France's emperor was of rather average size for his time and place.

To pin down Napoleon's actual height I wrote to the Musée de l'Armée in Paris, which houses comprehensive information on Napoleon's physical appearance (including old uniforms). A Colonel MacCarthy of its staff replied:

> The height of Napoleon was 5 feet 7 inches. . . . This measurement is one given in the memoirs of Mr. Darling, carpenter of Saint-Helen who was appointed to construct Napoleon's coffin. I think that we can consider this measure as completely correct.

Colonel MacCarthy speculated that the French emperor may have been perceived as small because he was shorter than most of his aides and he dressed simply to contrast further with their feathers and braids. A second cause of the error, as pointed out in a modern biography of Napoleon by English physician R. Frank Richardson, is that an early mistranslation from French to English measurements gave the Frenchman's height as 5′2″. This mistake has been passed along in most subsequent writing about Napoleon. According to Richardson, Napoleon's fifty-two-year-old corpse was measured at 5′6″ and "was therefore slightly above the average height for Frenchmen." Since human bodies are known to shrink by an inch or so after the age of thirty, we can probably accept 5′7″ as Napoleon's height at the peak of his powers.

So how did Napoleon become history's quintessential little guy — the main man since Oedipus to have a complex named after him? To a large degree we have psychiatrist Alfred Adler to thank for this — and a lot of things. Not tall himself, Freud's disciple and subsequent rival invented the inferiority complex, overcompensation, and a range of other psychological concepts that we usually neglect to attribute to him. Overcompensation,

according to Adler, was a typical response to physical deficiency, including short stature. And in suggesting that politics
was a popular haven for overcompensators, Adler himself fell
back on "Napoleon being the favorite hero."

Even if we hadn't had Napoleon at hand to explain short behavior, we'd no doubt have come up with someone else —
Fiorello La Guardia perhaps (La Guardianic?), or maybe Richard Dreyfuss. Whether Napoleon was actually short or even
"acted short" is immaterial. His value to us is strictly as a symbol, a shorthand, a way to keep from considering seriously a
dimension of life that makes everyone uneasy.

Don't think smaller people aren't aware of how often they're
put in bed with Napoleon. Harvard University professor Mark
Moore, for example, at one point grew so weary of being called
Napoleonic that he began wearing a T-shirt with the French emperor's picture on it. Moore did so mostly for the fun of
it — his wife had had the shirt made as a gag. But the issue
hasn't always been a funny one for him, as he explained:

There was a stage when it used to make me furious — when people
would observe your accomplishments and have an easy and damaging
explanation for these accomplishments. It was never, "Gee, this person was talented and worked hard and had good judgment and did the
right things." It was always, "Well, you know, short people have inferiority complexes so they become compulsive and this forces them to
succeed." Sort of the Napoleonic idea. . . .

Large people's accomplishments are great works. Small people's
accomplishments are the result of a neurotic drive to succeed. That is a
problem. That really makes you mad.

In his early thirties, Mark Moore is a leading consultant on police practices, and one of the younger associate
professors on Harvard's faculty. The day we visited in his book-

cluttered office at the Kennedy School of Government, the curly-haired Dr. Moore had already been pondering what it means psychologically to grow up small. Married to a woman even shorter than his own 5'3", he's the father of two children destined genetically to be short. One of the children had just begun first grade. According to her father this six-year-old girl is intelligent, attractive, and mature for her age. Also, she's quite small. Watching his daughter trying to deal with her classmates' reactions to her size had revived Moore's own memories of himself at that age. "You get an awful lot of special attention," he said, "because you're adorable and because you look precocious. And a great deal of loyalty. But on a funny set of terms. The terms are that the other person is allowed on occasion to treat you like a baby or a child. This is part of their attraction to you." In the case of his daughter, her classmates were eager to defend her, but they also wanted to carry her around like a doll. "You can imagine," continued Moore, "that is quite gratifying to her, but at the same time it's humiliating. Seeing her go through all these things is rekindling a lot of my own anger about all this."

In elementary school, Moore remembered, he was always put first in line because he was shortest, got pushed around a lot, and, like his daughter, was fawned over as long as he was willing to play the mascot. Adults in particular were given to making comments like, "Gee, I'd like to put you in my pocket and take you home." Such experiences confront all short people from an early age with a choice between accepting other people's affection on their terms, or risking rejection on one's own.

Although a schoolboy athlete, Mark Moore found when he got to Yale that the only position he could fill was coxswain to the crew. The name tells the tale. Moore winces at the memory of his short-lived experience barking at tall rowers through a megaphone. "If that isn't an undignified position," he said, "thoroughly the most compromised position — a whiny little boss . . ."

So Moore left sports behind, concentrated on his studies, earned a Ph.D. from Harvard, served for a time as a consultant to the Justice Department, and ultimately found a bright future at the nation's leading university. Yet for all his success, Moore has remained puzzled about how to manage his size. Ignoring it is one option; but others don't. Those with whom he consults, especially, register all sorts of confusion in their faces when meeting this tyke — obviously wondering if he's up to the job. At a training program he conducted for senior government managers, Moore was asked by many where they could get their laundry done before they realized he was their teacher. Ignoring such a gaffe means letting others stew in their own subsequent embarrassment.

Defensiveness is a second possible approach ("Whatsa matter? You think I can't handle this job or something?"), though not a particularly attractive one.

Then there's the third option, to which Moore most often resorts: making light. One might call this the Paul Williams gambit. What it calls for is beating others to the punch line. On a platform in front of a new class Moore will often begin by observing that "although people are complaining about the amount of pressure they're under, I haven't noticed it." Then he adds: "Of course, I was six-foot-two before this program started." Not a real knee-slapper, he'll grant you. But Moore has found that his little routine does seem to accomplish something valuable. "It's a very successful joke," he explained.

There is something that gets done when you dispel the air, when you say, "Look, you're surprised I'm short. It's okay. I don't feel particularly bad about it. So you don't have to feel particularly bad about it.

Now let's go on and have a particular relationship.'' The strategy is usually chosen only as a device for getting over their awkwardness about the first meeting. In fact, it's not always true that you can do that, just as it's not always clear that my daughter can reconstitute the terms of her relationship with friends having once offered them the ''child relationship.''

It's a quandary. Kidding around about one's height can be taken two ways. Ideally, explained Moore, people get the message that he's not hung up about being short. But they may get the message that he's *very* hung up and has a neurotic need to raise the issue, which is expressed by his joking about it. This is the dilemma. ''If you don't raise it,'' Moore observed, ''it's a neurotic desire to keep it hidden. If you do raise it, maybe it's because you have a neurotic desire to get it out. It's always an issue.''

Of course other people have issues as well. Moore once taught a class that included a man 6'6" tall. When the participants went around the room introducing themselves, this man said, ''My name's Harry Taylor, I've come from Los Angeles, and I don't play basketball.''

So things could be worse. In fact, said Moore, of late he'd taken to calling shortness ''the ecologically sound shape.'' And he and his wife furnished their house to suit themselves — with small-scale furniture, and low chandeliers on which tall people might bump their heads if not careful. ''Of course, some of my best friends are tall,'' he added with a laugh. ''In fact, I've often thought of selling myself to be the middle seat on tight airplanes. I'll just say to some tall guy in the middle, 'If you want to be comfortable on this flight, all you have to do is pay for my ticket and I'll sit there.' ''

One question I often hear — usually from people of average size or taller — is: Why don't smaller people just ignore their height and be happy? Unfortunately, this is seldom a real option — at least not a good one. Because a smaller person who ignores his height is perceived in quite a different light from a larger one who does the same thing. What looks like quiet strength in the six-foot-plus body of a Gary Cooper or a Clint Eastwood can look like a coma in one shorter. Since we assume big people to be powerful, for them to just sit quietly is to be perceived as strong. Since we assume small people to be weak, for them to just sit quietly is to be perceived as impotent. And for a short person, ''just ignoring'' his height risks being literally overlooked. Like most people, a short person wants to have his presence noticed. The smalls' options for accomplishing this are fairly limited: be funny or be feisty.

Obviously, a lot of short people take the latter path, some rather successfully. Jimmy Cagney was pretty good at bristly strength, just as Robert Conrad is today. New York City Mayor Fiorello La Guardia was a classic case of a little guy capitalizing on feistiness. La Guardia's successor and size-mate Abe Beame was a less successful mayor and was less successful overall at managing his shortness — because he came across as neither feisty nor funny, just dull.

There are many short people who take the funny route. J. M. Tanner, the growth expert, recalled during our conversation being introduced to one of them — Ronnie Corbett, the smaller of ''The Two Ronnies'' who star in Britain's leading televised comedy show. Corbett in fact makes a living off his smallness. Besides performing, he is also the model for London's antilitter campaign, which is based on posters that show the tiny comedian buried in waste paper and saying, ''Litter's no laughing matter when you're only 5' tall.'' When Tanner met Corbett, he immediately suspected the man had a rare case of growth-hormone deficiency. Had the comedian come to doctors when young, he could have received shots of pituitary extract to bring him up to nearly average height. "Of course you realize, doctor," Corbett told Tanner once he'd had time to ponder this lost opportunity, "that every night I go down on my knees and thank God that I didn't have any contact with you when I was young!"

The same day I visited with one of America's tallest comic actors, Peter Isacksen, I also visited with one of its smallest — 5'2" David Landsberg. Landsberg, who also does standup comedy, for a time was a sidekick of Isacksen's as the character Skulnick on "CPO Sharkey." Together on camera the pair didn't need to say very much to get a laugh. All they had to do was "face" each other.

Landsberg is an energetic man. On the afternoon we visited in the lobby of the Century Plaza Hotel in Beverly Hills, the comedian was even more fidgety than usual, because he was about to audition for a role as a television character named Rodent. I wondered if this weren't demeaning.

"No, not at all," said Landsberg in his fast patter. "Not if they pay you five thousand dollars a week. They pay you five thousand dollars a week, I'd mate a mule in Macy's window."

With his glasses, thinning hair, and slight frame, David Landsberg, then thirty-one, looked and acted like a younger and smaller Woody Allen. He's grateful for being the size he is. If it weren't for his shortness, the comedian explained, he wouldn't be able to use half the routines in his act. With much of his conversation echoing these bits, Landsberg threw out such quips as:

• I went up to Raquel Welch the other day and I told her, "I swear to God, one of these days I'm going to screw you." She says, "If you do and I find out about it I'm going to be pissed."

• When I got married our wedding picture was taken *on* the cake.

• My wife's four-foot-ten. We have two kids. I'm not saying they're small, but we do keep them on key chains.

• I got in a lot of fights when I was a kid, only because I had to show, "No, you cannot push me around." The unfortunate part was they *can* push me around. I just didn't realize it. For which I received a tremendous amount of lumps. There's an old expression — "The bigger they are, the harder they smack you in the face."

• The bigger they are, the bigger they are.

So David Landsberg stopped fighting and started being funny. He learned how to make people laugh. He also learned how to play the guitar. This all made him popular, in a way.

"There wasn't a party I wasn't invited to," he recalled. "People always wanted to have Dave around. Funny, cute, played the guitar. Cute. Girls always said I was cute."

Did they go out with you?

"No. Cute guys do not get laid. That is a rule. A rule of thumb. The tides go out twice a day and cute guys do not get laid. Newton, I think. Newton was one of the people who said that."

Not all of David Landsberg's stories about growing up have a punch line, however. Here's one he tells about being fourteen and 4'3" and going to a doctor to see if there were any shots he could get to help him grow:

I had begged my parents, I begged them — *please* get me the shots. So my father took me to this doctor and he explained that it was too late for me to get the shots, and it wouldn't have helped anyway because I was developing naturally. He *wouldn't* give me the shots. And I mean I wanted — "I don't *care* — I just want to be tall. *Please*. Do something!"

Landsberg's voice rose, reflecting how he must have felt at the time. Then it dropped once again.

So he did the worst thing possible. He told me a story about a short surgeon who operated while standing on a box. I said, "I don't give a shit. When he leaves that operation he's got to walk out in the street, and people aren't going to say, 'What a surgeon!' All they're going to say is, 'Christ, is he short!' ''

There is an alternative to feistiness or funniness for coping with shortness that I haven't mentioned. This alternative is for the short man to pretend that he isn't. Denying shortness involves tactics ranging from herringbone suits to bald-faced lies and elaborate visual artifice.

J. Edgar Hoover was a classic practitioner of this approach. No more than 5'7" (and a stout defender of that height as a minimum for his agents), the late FBI director gave strict instructions to employees within the Bureau that if asked they were to say that Hoover was "just under 6-feet." Hoover also paid careful attention to how his physical surroundings made him appear. Toilets were selected carefully so the director's feet wouldn't dangle when he sat on them. The couch facing his desk was cut extra low so that visitors would sit beneath him. Adding further to Hoover's eye-level advantage was a riser under his chair that was hidden behind his massive desk. Agents visiting the director's office were warned not to go behind the desk lest they notice the riser.

The problem with the J. Edgar Hoover approach to coping with shortness is that it stems from self-contempt. A smaller person needn't love his height to reject the alternative of denying and camouflaging it. Those who do take this path normally don't want it known. For this reason the whole subject of trying to look taller is shrouded in mystery, trauma, and elaborate deception.

Seeking a sympathetic defense of this method, I went to a primary source — the Richlee Shoe Company in Brockton, Massachusetts. Richlee is the country's only mass-producer of elevator shoes. (Adler, the name mostly widely associated with elevators, is actually just a single retailer.) Visiting the manufacturer proved more difficult than I had anticipated. For one thing, company president Jim Richlee was always "out." Ultimately I discovered that he doesn't exist: Jim Richlee is the Betty Crocker of the shoe business. For another thing, the firm wasn't really located in Brockton — that's just the mailing address. The company itself operates out of a tattered former American Legion post in Avon, Massachusetts, south of Brockton. No external markings on this building betray what's going on inside.

Elevator shoe customers value discretion above all else. For this reason the company concentrates on direct mail orders to supply its eighteen thousand customers with shoes in sizes 5 to 12. Not tall himself, the head of this mail order operation had some interesting stories to tell about these customers. One needed a rush shipment of elevators so he could take vows eye to eye with his fiancée later in the week. Another man pleaded for elevated bedroom slippers so it wouldn't be obvious before they got in bed how much shorter he was than his girlfriend. Richlee couldn't fill this order but did like the spirit. "We're trying to get across the idea that you need to wear elevators all the time," explained Richlee's man in charge of mail order, "not just occasionally."

Do you wear them?

"Sometimes."

"We want him to wear them all the time," his assistant chimed in, "but he won't."

At Richlee's parent firm, Foot-Joy in Brockton, the 5'7" sales vice-president told me *he* hadn't worn a pair of elevators since test-marketing the firm's first line as a high school kid in the thirties. He thought one of the factory foremen might wear them, but he wasn't sure. "I suppose that's not a good advertisement," the sales manager conceded. "But a lot of people who work for Ford drive Cadillacs."

When promoted to his position five years before, one of the vice-president's stickiest problems had been dealing with the uproar among seventy-five retailers that was created by his predecessor's enlarging the size of the lettering on Richlee shoe boxes. This label still reads ELEVATORS, HEIGHT INCREASING SHOES, but today it's once again printed in discreet letters the size of typewriter characters. "Elevator wearers are funny people," the sales manager explained. "They don't want other people to know they're wearing them. Even Adler in New York mails in plain wrappers."

Though the actual number of elevator wearers is really quite low (especially since higher heels became acceptable for men), the use of such footwear plays an important symbolic role in American culture. Cartoons, gags, and songs about lifts are common, since the shoes are so symbolic of short anguish.

Perhaps that's why smaller people often feel constrained to take a stand on (if not in) elevators. Mario Andretti, for example, said elevators are something he'd never worn and never intended to wear. "I'll always stay the natural way," explained the Italian-born Andretti in his light accent. "I'll never camouflage what I am. I figure this is the way it is. That's all mama gave me."

What Mrs. Andretti gave her son is 5'4" of height. During our conversation on a rare day off between races, the driver seemed fairly calm about being well below the national average. But, then, he's calm about a lot of things. The man's ice-cold nerves have carried him to worldwide racing renown. That he's movie-star handsome with a thick head of dark, wavy hair, even features, and a strong, trim physique also helps. Such factors are conducive to calmness about shortness.

"There were times when I thought it'd be nice to be six-foot-four," Andretti conceded. "Especially when you see a 'long drink of water' go by and you figure, 'Gee . . .'

"On the other hand, I can't just go to the store and buy myself another trunk. I've got to do the best in life with what I've got and not really dwell on it. The way I feel is that my size is my size — that's all I have. It's nothing that I've ever been happy or unhappy about."

Which isn't to say Andretti *likes* the size he is. Accepting his height and liking it are two different things. "If I had a choice," he said, "if I could go to a store and they'd say, 'Well when you grow up what do you want to be?' I'd know exactly what I'd want to be. I'd pick five-foot-ten."

Not 6 feet?

"Not six feet or six-foot-five."

Why 5'10"?

"I think the beautiful people are about that height for a man. And some of the ones that are a little bit shorter have been shortchanged a little bit. That doesn't mean the guy should crawl into a hole for the rest of his life.

"I'm looking at my kids. My oldest is fifteen and he's as tall as I am now. I hope very hard that he'd be at least five-foot-ten."

Wouldn't it make you nervous to have a son looking down on you?

"No. That would make me beautiful. I'd love it. Here I could come up with a product a little better than me."

But, as he said, even with half a foot less height than he might like, Andretti was just making the best of it (including winning the 1978 world driver's championship, first ever won by an American), and not trying to flee from his height.

It is true that the race driver wore inch-high heels the day we visited in the study of his home in Nazareth, Pennsylvania. But Andretti claimed he's always avoided anything more radical, including platform shoes when they were stylish. This was for a practical reason. "When fashion would change," he explained, spreading his arms, "shit, I'd be down from the clouds again."

Early in our conversation, Joel Grey, like Mario Andretti, assured me that he'd never resorted to lifts. "I never wore elevator shoes," explained the Oscar-winning actor, shaking his head from side to side. "Never. Obstinate, perverse creature."

Indeed, when we chatted in his sunny apartment overlooking Central Park in Manhattan's Upper East Side, Grey was wearing ultraflat Capezio rehearsal shoes. Widely known for his performance as the MC in *Cabaret,* Grey is both short and slight — fragile almost — but with powerful dark eyes and a manner so imposing that any question about his strength quickly vanishes. Since he's in the public eye, Joel Grey has no choice but to deal with reactions to his size. He constantly is told, "You're so short!" by people who have before only seen him on screen. They usually follow with, "How tall are you?" Depending on his mood, Grey can be agreeable or not so agreeable in response. The lifelong entertainer has become so sick of being asked this question that he's taken to responding tersely, "Under six. Between five and six." At other times he resorts to humor. "Before I go any further," Grey at times has opened his nightclub act, "I want to clear up the two questions about me that are on everybody's mind. The answer to the first question is five feet five inches. The answer to the second is April eleventh, 1932, and one hundred nineteen pounds."

While performing at the Empire Room in New York City a few years ago, Grey's monologue included: "Can I help it if I find Woody Allen hilarious — five feet six? I have never missed a book by Truman Capote, five feet four. If I'm up late at night, I wouldn't dream of missing Dick Cavett, five feet seven. And it's so good to be in New York with a mayor like Abe Beame, five feet two."

Grey is ambivalent about this humorous sort of approach to his size. When I talked of being "mascotish," he immediately picked up the concept. "Mascotish," Grey said, nodding. "That's a good word. Boy, that's a trap. It's almost like playing the court jester, and it's hard to get out of it. But I'm doing it. Slowly."

The problem, he explained, is that such a style is learned early in life, when it can seem a means of survival. "That's how I used to get out of fights with guys who were a lot bigger," Grey recalled. "I'd use my wit, my humor." He smiled, but the smile slowly dissolved and finally disappeared. Grey shook his head, adding, "Not good."

What's not good about humor for survival, he continued, is that "you end up not really saying what you feel to that person because they're a danger. And you don't feel good about yourself because you've copped out, so to speak, when actually what you've done is be practical."

And the alternative?

Grey shrugged. "I don't know what the alternative is. The alternative is for people not to feel they have to bully other people — though sometimes small people can be very provocative, I'm sure."

The actor explained that abusing power, overexerting it — simply not knowing how to be graceful with power — is a potential problem for someone his size. "I have to watch out for that," he said. "I tend to say no too often, to come down too heavy just out of defense." But such self-defense can still seem necessary at times. Even today Grey finds that after a performance some big guy at times will reach to shake his hand and squeeze "just a *little* too hard — like he's looking to prove something. And you wonder, 'God almighty, what is that? What is he thinking? What kind of a childhood did he have? How does he feel about his size? His self?' " The actor shook his head. "I'm always amazed at the hostility of big people — certain big people. It almost makes you feel like you really do have some power or that there's something to be afraid of in you."

From his vantage point, Grey is painfully aware of the psychological distance separating bigger people from smaller people. Partly he's aware because bigger people tell him that in his trim presence they feel clumsy, ungraceful. But Grey is aware too of his own discomfort around people much taller than he is. One choreographer he's worked with is the 6'6" Texan Tommy Tune. When the two first met, Grey wondered how they could possibly work together. "I really didn't like it," he recalled of their early collaboration. "I didn't feel good about it. I had to really look up to him. And I felt that when we walked down the street I really looked tiny, smaller than I am, and that made me feel that both of us looked exaggerated — he looked taller and I looked shorter." But the more the two discussed this problem, the more Grey found they had in common — "so much to share and to understand about each other, so many shared views of life."

Paradoxically, although Grey had no idea what it's like to be Tune's size, Tune knew very well what it's like to be Grey's size. He was once. According to Grey, the tall choreographer reached into his memory one day and recalled that as a child he and his friends liked to pretend they were tall by playing on fruit-juice cans. Joel Grey grinned, then laughed aloud as he described the routine Tune subsequently devised for him — one in which the small singer clomped about the stage on a pair of foot-high cans with strings attached, while looking down on the audience from on high and singing . . . "Short People."

6 Petites and Amazons

Suddenly, the world seems infested with Napoleonic little girls . . .

— GEORGE WILL

A solo sung by the shortest cast member of Broadway's *A Chorus Line* goes:

Four foot ten,
Four foot ten.
That's the story of my life.
I remember when ev'rybody was my size.
Boy, was that great!
But then everybody started moving up, and . . . there I was
stuck at
Four foot ten!
Four foot ten.
(But I kept hoping and praying.)
I used to hang from a parallel bar by the hour, hoping I'd
stretch just an inch more.
'Cause I was into dancing then and I was good and I wanted
so much to grow up to be a prima ballerina.
Then I went out for cheerleader!
And they told me:
"No dice.
You'd get lost on the football field.
The pompoms are bigger than you."

There are a couple of differences between the inspiration for this song and the woman who sang it on stage. For one thing, actress Janet Wong is closer to 5 feet than 4'10". For another thing, she can't recall ever being the same size as anyone else. "I remember always being the smallest," Wong said one afternoon in her dressing room backstage at New York's Shubert Theater. "I was a terrible tagalong, with my brother and all his friends. I remember always going, 'Wait for me!' " — she waved frantically — " 'Wait for me!' They were always trying to get rid of me."

In high school Janet Wong took up smoking in hopes of looking older. The actual effect, she now realizes, was probably just the opposite. Probably it made her look like a little girl with candy cigarettes. "I remember once I went into a store for cigarettes," she recalled with something between a smile and a scowl, "and they said they were giving me the 'junior price.' "

That hurt. But so do a lot of things when you're always the littlest, always the youngest-looking. Soon after arriving in New York from Berkeley in her early twenties, Wong had her hair cut unusually short. Dressed in jeans and a parka she went into a pastry shop on Seventy-second Street one day for an éclair. When her turn came, the woman behind the counter leaned down and said sweetly, "Can I help you, little boy?"

The actress giggled while telling this story, then quickly shielded her mouth with her hand. "That was a mortifying experience," she said, shaking her head. Then she looked off and muttered almost to herself, " 'Can I help you, little boy?' I walked out without the éclair."

The day we met, Janet Wong was wearing her hair in a long pageboy, not short. Her face was small and delicate, like her whole frame. She wore Levi's stuck into high leather boots, and a maroon velour pullover. Finding clothes can be difficult for a short woman, I learned. "Ready to wear" for her, Wong said, means "ready to alter — ready to shorten. There were times when I felt if I had to alter one more pair of pants I'd kill." More important is the symbolic role clothes play in this woman's life. "I find that the kinds of clothes I like are 'little-girl clothes,' " she explained, "and I have to consciously force myself not to buy them because I don't need to reinforce that image."

Though many of the humiliations of being small cross sexual lines, looking young and "cute" seems the smaller woman's particular burden. Even in *A Chorus Line,* said the actress, where she's supposed to be little, the dance captain once asked if she could do something about her makeup; "You look about sixteen," he complained.

To get her part in the hit musical, Wong said, she had to be very pushy — calling constantly and pestering the director until the role finally was offered her. She'd first heard about the part when a friend told her they were looking for " 'a short, pushy Oriental girl' — and I thought of you immediately, Janet." She laughed at the thought and continued: "My family's always surprised at how aggressive and pushy I can be. I alternate between being very aggressive and very shy. Like with salespeople I can scream and yell and push my way to the front of the line or be quiet and let myself get pushed back. I'm always getting passed over by salespeople unless I assert myself. They think you're younger, and kids have all the time in the world anyway.

"But it is easier to get through crowds at my size, or get to the head of the bus line. And looking young and short means you can get away with things — faux pas and whatnot. 'Oh, she's so cute,' they'll say. 'She couldn't have done that.' It works. But it's real demeaning. I've made a conscious effort not to get away with things because I look cute. It's so easy.

"I would love to look glamorous. You know — real sophisticated and glamorous." Putting her hand behind her head, she mugged, then laughed at the idea. "I guess height is part of that. Part of my image of sophistication and glamour has to do with height. When you're asked to conjure up an image of somebody beautiful, you don't normally think of somebody five feet. You think of someone more normal."

Not long ago Janet Wong went to India for five weeks with a dance company and experienced what she calls "a gut reaction of relief" at being surrounded for once in her life by people similar to her in both size and skin tone. "At one point there was a hubbub behind me, and I looked back and this big crowd had surrounded a member of our company, a very tall woman with a big Afro which made her look even taller. They were reaching up to touch her hair and making a big commotion. I thought it was funny." She chuckled at the memory. "I thought: At last, she's getting hers."

This book might not have been written at all were it not for little women. The ones who work for my publisher have made it clear to their taller coworkers over the years that head pats, lap pulls, huglifts, and being called "honey," "dear," and "sweetie" are not their idea of a good time. When the suggestion circulated for a book on height, Little, Brown's little women were among its most enthusiastic backers.

My 6'1" male editor was as surprised by this as I was. Height, I'd always assumed, was primarily a man's issue — one that was dealt with on different terms by women when dealt with by them at all. I couldn't have been more mistaken. As became clear repeatedly during the course of this project, women are painfully aware of who's biggest and are every bit as concerned as men when they're not the tallest. Rock singer Suzi

Quatro, for example, has said that her hunger for recognition originates with her shortness. "I'm small," she explained. "I grew up small. When you're small, you *feel* small. If a beautiful girl walks into this room now and she is tall, I'm dead." Similarly, writer Joan Didion (who's near the 5-foot mark) has cited her diminutive body as underlying her passion for order. "If I were 5 feet 10 and had a clear gaze and a good strong frame," said Didion, "I would not have such a maniacal desire for control because I would have it."

Among those who answered my "Twenty Questions about Height" was author Lyn Tornabene (*Long Live the King; I Passed as a Teenager*). Tornabene listed herself at 5'⅝". Among the nicknames bestowed upon her have been "Shrimp," "Tiny," and "Little Manny" (which is what "a sadistic editor" called her). Her parents "joked" about her size, Tornabene recalled, telling others their daughter set out to be a 6-footer but never made it. As an adult, the successful writer said, she compares her size to others' in every setting I asked about (elevators, lines, parties, and so on) and many I didn't. "I *always* compare my height," she wrote, "and find it lacking."

Do people ever make comments to you about your size?

"Not as many as I make. But John Lindsay [New York City's 6'3" former mayor], when I met him for an interview, asked me if I was standing in a hole. Son of a bitch."

Is there a height other than your own you've always wanted to be?

"Yes. 5'8"."

Why?

"Because everyone likes tall people better than short people, because clothes would fit me better, because I wouldn't have to use step ladders in my kitchen — because I would be gorgeous, respected, and rich."

What do you especially like about being the height you are?

"Nothing."

Tornabene's reaction to life so far below American women's 5'3.6" norm is a bit more vitriolic than most. But not much. Women in her range generally had far more grievances than boasts to report on the questionnaires.

This isn't to say that no advantages to "petiteness" were suggested. Comedienne Joan Rivers, who is 5'2", said that as a smaller preteen she liked getting to be "the girl" in her all-female dancing class. "A friend of mine to this day wants to lead," she reported, "because she had to be 'the boy' when we danced." But other advantages to Rivers's size proved illusory. Being a short teenager at first looked like it was going to be "terrific," she said, because "I could go out with tall *and* short boys. The only hang-up was that neither *tall* OR *short* boys asked me to go out."

Given her druthers, the comedienne concluded, she'd rather be half a foot taller, for two reasons in particular: "All fashions are designed for TALL, skinny ladies (when I put on the layered look I look like a stump)"; and "I could *eat* more and it wouldn't show."

The latter issue is one raised constantly by smaller women — the grim injustice that an extra pound on their frame can resemble five on a taller one. For this and other reasons, among the vast majority of women who on the questionnaire expressed a wish to be taller, 5'6¾" was the average preferred height. Explanations offered ran the gamut from fashion ("willowy" seemed to be a popular look), to greater ease in reaching for things, to an overall desire to look more "impressive."

What ever happened to five-foot-two, eyes of blue? If that ever was our feminine ideal, it's obviously gone the way of June Allyson and Mary Pickford.

The perils of petiteness

The trouble with tallness

Earlier I listed male-oriented words used to characterize talls and smalls, as well as a mostly male comparison of the two groups as portrayed by the media. Here's a similar list and set of comparisons for women alone:

Tall		Small	
Amazonian	majestic	bouncy	impish
elegant	queenly	cuddly	mousy
gangling	rangy	cute	peppy
glamorous	regal	dainty	perky
goddesslike	stately	delicate	pert
gorgeous	statuesque	demure	petite
Junoesque	stunning	fragile	pixieish
lissome	svelte	frail	spritelike
lovely	willowy	gaminelike	waiflike

. . . this formidable, big boned, 5-foot, 8-inch actress . . .

> — *Us* on actress Colleen Dewhurst

. . . the tiny if sometimes turbulent Miss Fonda . . .

> — JACK ANDERSON on actress Jane Fonda

. . . tall, lithe, supple . . .

> — *Philadelphia Inquirer* on Veronica Porche (Mrs. Muhammad Ali)

. . . short, wiry, frenetic . . .

> — *The New Yorker* on singer Judith Cohen

. . . a tall blonde certain to win a second look from any man-about-town . . .

> — *The New York Times Book Review* on cartoonist Claire Bretécher

. . . for such a little girl (5'1", 95 pounds), she has a big mouth . . .

> — *Life* on gossip reporter Rona Barrett

Tall (cont.)

Small (cont.)

. . . a six-footer with a square handsome face and powerful legs . . .

> — *New Times* on volleyball player Mary Jo Peppler

. . . a "pushy little broad" with a quick tongue . . .

> — *People* on former presidential adviser Midge Constanza

. . . a tall, vivid girl with fine legs . . .

> — *Newsweek* on entertainer Lucie Arnaz

. . . a tiny, birdlike woman with skinny legs . . .

> — *Philadelphia Inquirer* on author Françoise Sagan

Standing five feet ten inches, [banker] Madeline H. McWhinney is an attractive woman with stylishly coiffed gray hair and brown eyes.

> — *Current Biography*

It was very difficult for me to believe that the small, gracious and modest lady pouring me tea was the woman whose every word was reputed to be taken as a command at the *Times.*

> — LALLY WEYMOUTH in *New York* on Iphigene Sulzberger

As this comparison suggests, women are increasingly judged on male terms, and shortness is no less a negative part of these terms than it's always been for men. Smaller men have had a lifetime to resign themselves, however bitterly, to the injustice of being judged by height. Smaller women haven't. On the contrary, until quite recently such women had every assurance of being the cultural ideal: petite, dainty, delicate. Having played by the rules and thought they'd won, short women are now being called out at home plate. One forlorn twenty-year-old of 5′2″ told me her favorite movies are thirties musicals. "All those chorus girls look just like me," she explained. "Five foot two and curvy. *They* were the fashionable ones then."

But it isn't the style of body that's changed for women so much as the style of being. It's no longer fashionable to be a small woman for the same reason it's never been fashionable to be a small man: lack of size implies lack of clout. When it was in vogue for women to be weak, fragile, and dependent — or at least to look that way — small size was the physical expression of that vogue. "I love the dainty little woman," said Rudolph Valentino in defining this ideal. "I adore her bird-like ways, her sweet pretenses, her delicious prettiness. I love her almost as one loves a cunning child."

The short woman who doesn't wish to be Valentino's little girl confronts a problem, for even more than a small man — and more than a taller woman — she is "infantilized." This diminution takes many forms. One is simply verbal: being constantly called "honey," "dear," and "you cute little thing." Another form involves actually being mistaken for a child — her husband's daughter, say, or her daughter's playmate. A twenty-five-year-old woman who's 5′1″ told me she had recently been the object of a pickup attempt by a sixteen-year-old boy with inflamed pustules. The worst part was that she was tempted to let him succeed, because she finds that too many men her own age avoid her — for fear of being charged with statutory rape.

But the most humiliating forms of infantilization that smaller women described are physical ones. These range from being elaborately pulled into men's laps to simple pats on the head. A 5-foot-tall actress said she's sure that her head by now has a "permanent flat spot" because it's been patted so often. A petite colleague of hers added that "the attitude is there even when the 'pat' isn't." Then there's the repeated experience of being lifted off the floor in "friendly" hugs. One forty-eight-year-old woman, 5′2″, compared the impotent rage she feels when so swept off her feet to the times as a child when her brother clamped her hands together and would not let go. An older

woman of 4'11" reported that after four decades of being invol-
untarily lifted off the ground she's resigned herself to the fact
that some men just can't seem to resist this temptation. One
longtime friend of hers in particular, she wrote, a man of 6'2",
has "always found a situation where he could lift me off the
floor. I hated it, but didn't want to scold. His wife was too big
to kid around with."

The overall effect of such repeated experiences, smaller
women complain, is to make them feel childish and insignificant.
"You never grow up if you're short" is the way sub-five-foot
humorist Judith Wax put it in her autobiography. "You may
grow old, wise, distinguished, accomplished . . . no matter;
people will go on treating you like a not-too-bright child. On
your way to get the Nobel, somebody will offer to hold your
hand crossing the street. Somebody *else* will probably ask you if
you hadn't better use the bathroom, honey, before you leave for
Sweden."

The ultimate put-down for women her size, the late writer
concluded, is "trial-by-physician." One male doctor in particular, a gynecologist, lost her business forever by responding to
Wax's inquiry about how long an operation would take by pat-
ting her bangs and saying: "Why worry your pretty head about
it, little girl? You'll be asleep."

For men in particular, a woman's shortness can be a most effective tool for trying to keep her in her place. But it's not only
men who use this tool. A twenty-five-year-old journalist of
5'1½" told me of a tough interview with a taller woman who
began by saying, "Why you're just a baby!" then said little
thereafter. Similarly a 5'2" college professor in her late thirties
reported that colleagues of both sexes frequently observe that
she seems too "small" to be teaching college. A taller student
of hers, an older woman who later became a friend, to this day

introduces her teacher by saying, "And this little girl here is a university professor."

From personal experience I know that men constantly lay such height numbers on each other. But I had no idea women were doing the same thing. If anything, I've found that women's size-based competition is more imaginative, detailed, precise, and anguished than any I know of going on among men. "I start with the other women and try to analyze why they're taller than me," wrote a 5'4" twenty-one-year-old about how she passes time in crowded elevators. "Do they have their hair piled on their head? Are they wearing wedgies? How about platforms? If all of these are 'no,' then I hit the heart of the matter — their legs. If they're long (ooohh, that hurts), I know they're legit. No getting around it. Nothing I can do about long legs. (I tried stretching exercises for about 10 months, every night. No dice.) I always try to justify why God gave them long legs and not me. He just made a mistake."

I've found that women, far more than men, admit feeling uncomfortable with smaller or taller members of the same sex — especially taller. Joan Rivers, for example, said that being in the presence of women much taller than she is made her feel "intimidated." This was a word used often by women under 5'4" to describe their reaction to the presence of a taller woman. Other feelings mentioned included "cowed," "like a kid sister," and just overall "on edge."

"I've long noticed," wrote a 5-foot psychologist, "that I have few tall female friends (tall = more than 5'5") but only recently have realized why. The 'awkwardness' and 'feeling young' that I experience around many women is because they are tall and 'grown up' and I am not."

While collecting information for this book in La Jolla, California, I found myself refereeing a conversation about height between two disparately sized women — Marilee, twenty-seven, a 5'2" unemployed restaurant manager, and Harriet, a 6'0" teacher, aged thirty-five.

"The biggest thing I feel is just inferior," said Marilee, a pretty brunette who wore monster platform shoes. "I sort of assume anyone taller than me is better than me. With women especially, I assume they're more competent, more intelligent, more mature and better in bed just because they're bigger."

From her vantage point, Marilee felt some of her worst problems were in relating to men. As a smaller woman Marilee said she feels constantly treated like a cutie-pie and put in the position of "a little girl cooing up to daddy." With unusually taller men the problem is exaggerated. "Psychologically it's bad to look up that much," she explained. "It's also physically painful; your neck gets *so sore*. It's also really hard when I want to be powerful with a man, when I want to be the aggressor."

Standing next to a tall woman, said Marilee, the feeling is more like Mutt and Jeff: "There's just a lot more of them than me."

Do you feel that way around Harriet? I asked. (You can ask this sort of thing in certain parts of California.)

"Very," Marilee replied without hesitation. "When I first met her I really freaked out. I came home and told my roommate all about her."

Harriet — slim, soft-spoken, with light eyes and streaks of gray in her brown hair — had listened attentively to Marilee's story. The ending surprised her. It always came as a surprise, she said, when smaller women seemed wary of her. "People tend to see me as more together, stronger, more powerful than I really am," Harriet said in her low voice.

Harriet's name had come up not long before as a possible participant in a women's rap group, a friend who was present had told her. Another member of the existing group turned thumbs down. "I find Harriet very threatening," this woman said.

Harriet has another friend, similar to herself in size, who she'll sometimes observe entering a crowded room. Others' reactions to this woman can be striking: often visceral, almost physical shock — as if startled by a bear. Probably, Harriet speculated, people have a similar reaction to her. Harriet's reserved manner also worries people, she had noticed. This too has something to do with being 6 feet tall. That height since her early teens, Harriet said she's always been subject to "a lot of nonverbal pressure to act older, more mature. To this day I have trouble being very playful." She still remembers her anguish when little Harold Marzoni slow-danced with her in the eighth grade and spent the whole time staring straight ahead — right at her newly developing breasts. Harriet is modestly endowed in that area and she pins the blame squarely on Harold Marzoni. "I'm convinced my small breasts evolve from that experience," she concluded with just the hint of a smile. "I think I decided to stop right there."

Having so many boys' eyes at chest level is just one among many horrors tall women recall about the time of life when they first spurted above everyone else. Early adolescence is generally the severest time of tall-girl trauma. Just when such a young teen wants most not to stand out in any way, her body betrays her. "I remember a country walk, with my first love," wrote an Australian woman (on her questionnaire) of how it felt to be tall nearly half a century ago, "and trying to walk in the ruts of the grass-grown road, so that I would be shorter than he was. My dearest ambition was to be 'little and clinging.' "

Carson McCullers suffered terribly from reaching 5'8½" by the age of thirteen. From an early age the writer was always tallest in her class, looking down on boys and girls alike, at times by as much as a foot. McCullers's biographer Virginia Spencer Carr calls excess height "the characteristic that Carson was most self-conscious about . . . each time she viewed the freaks at the Chattahoochee Valley Fair she feared that she might never stop growing."

In *The Heart Is a Lonely Hunter,* McCullers herself wrote of what it was like to be a tall girl of thirteen at a party: "Every kid at the party was a runt beside her, except Harry, who was only a couple of inches shorter. No boy wanted to prom with a girl so much taller than him. But maybe cigarettes would help stunt the rest of her growth."

Like her heroine, the author started smoking early in a desperate attempt to put a lid on her height. McCullers's mother also smoked, and she raised no objection when her fourteen-year-old daughter announced she'd taken up the habit. Soon after this a mission visited their house from the First Baptist Church, urging mother and daughter to resume active membership. To the Baptist ladies' horror, midway through their visit the mother pulled out her cigarettes and offered one to her daughter. Before the church delegation retreated in despair the woman explained matter-of-factly, "Oh, yes, my daughter Lula Carson and I have such a good time smoking together. We do almost everything together, you know."

Such compassion for the fears of a tall daughter is all too rare. Too often a tall mother who remembers her own growing pains will subtly encourage such a girl to slouch, or worse yet take her to an endocrinologist for risky estrogen shots that can speed maturation and stunt growth. But even with understanding at home, the junior-high years are tough for anyone sticking out as much as a tall girl must.

Among the women I interviewed while researching this chapter was a lanky, dark-haired actress named Lynnie Greene.

Early in our conversation Greene recalled of the sixth and seventh grades: "Can we put down that those were the worst two years of my life?" Early adolescence, she explained, was a time of daily consternation for her, a time of thinking, "Oh, my God, I'm going to be a giant. I am going to be the single tallest person alive."

She isn't. Lynnie Greene stopped growing just short of 6 feet. And today her reflections on what it means to grow up tall have mellowed. Bad as junior high was socially, she thinks standing out physically helped her win the student body presidency (she ran as "The Jolly Greene Giant"). Better yet, she felt up to the job. "I assumed along with the height of myself was strength and leadership quality," Greene explained. "So in terms of becoming a strong, centered, self-willed person, my height was helpful. But for becoming a secure, feminine woman comfortable with her own body, it was an enormous detriment."

The day she told me this Greene's CBS series "On Our Own" had just entered the top ten in TV ratings (it later was cancelled) and the actress was feeling flush. Not only were big little girls writing her from around the country in support, but so were men of all sizes. "Now is the best tall I've ever had," she explained with a smile.

But there are still slips back to earlier feelings about being tall. Just after we met (standing), I had told Lynnie Greene that she didn't appear to be as tall as her advertised 5'11". For that she gave me her biggest smile of the day. "Bless your heart," grinned Lynnie Greene at my observation. "Thank you very much."

Tall women are caught in a chink in American values. On the one hand femininity has traditionally been associated with daintiness. On the other hand the culture at large says bigger is better. "So much emphasis is placed on the virtue of anything that

is large-scale,'' Seymour Fisher has suggested, ''that a woman has to work hard conceptually to discern why the same principle should not apply to her body.''

Less and less is there any need to do so. In fact, the rewards for being a tall woman today are remarkably similar to those for being a tall man. So are the penalties. Like tall men, tall women generate in others mixed feelings of respect and anxiety, feelings that are expressed in terms much like those dealt with by tall men. No less than her male counterpart, a tall woman is subject to inquiries about her height and the weather up there (although one 5′11″ woman informed me that instead of being tagged as a basketball player herself, she was once told, ''You sure must have kept the basketball team busy!'').

Like a tall man, a tall woman can find herself both irritated by the extra attention she gets and appreciative of it. Increasingly, appreciation has transcended irritation. Among other reasons for this is the fact that contemporary fashions of all kinds endorse a taller look for women. At 5′7″ today's ''perfect-size'' model is 3.4 inches above the norm. The average Miss America contestant currently stands 5′6.6″. And looking ahead, perhaps, the White Rock soda company portrays the lady on their current label as 5′8″ (compared to 5′6″ in 1947, and 5′4″ in 1894).

In cities such as New York or Los Angeles especially, it seems that women are walking very tall indeed. Many are not reluctant to add 2 or 3 extra inches with heels for the sheer brazenness of it. In my conversations with women about their height, it was the tall ones whose morale clearly was highest. "I didn't used to like being so tall," went the most common refrain, "but now I do."

Obviously the changing role of women in general has a lot to do with tall women's esprit. Not since the time of Greek goddesses has feminine tallness been so stylish. But in the course of studying this issue I've come to wonder whether pride in size might not have characterized tall women long before fashion endorsed their look.

Our society's traditional assumption has been that height issues for women were the mirror opposite of men's — that tall women miserably suffered Satan's wrath while little women blissfully ate bonbons in Eden. Certainly women are aware of this assumption. There is evidence that it's learned at quite an early age. One study found that as early as age four or five girls drew themselves smaller than they drew boys, even though size differences between the sexes at this age are negligible. In another study, schoolgirls in grades five through eight were found to underestimate their own height relative to adults far more than did male classmates. Apparently women understand from an early age that society expects them to be small, smaller even than Nature expects.

But to say that women are *aware* of cultural size expectations doesn't mean they buy them. On the contrary, when child psychologist Jerome Kagan asked a group of third-grade girls to choose from among three otherwise identical silhouettes the one they'd most *like* to resemble, 64 percent chose the tallest one, 28 percent the medium-sized one, and only 8 percent the smallest silhouette. In a similar experiment, Canadian graduate student Avrum Miller found that college coeds consistently chose tall silhouettes as the ones they most wanted to resemble. Among other mature women as well, such as separate groups of

Japanese-Americans and Caucasian Americans studied over a decade ago, the majority expressed a wish to be taller — the shorter, Japanese-American group in particular. Such bits of data can't *prove* that women have always valued height, but they do call into question the stereotype of the miserable tall woman sitting dateless at home, pining to be petite and protected.

As Lynnie Greene, Harriet, Carson McCullers, or any tall woman can confirm, there is excruciating pain involved in being tall at too young an age. Nature's bit of sadism in making some preadolescent girls taller than nearly all boys at such a sensitive age needs more than the combined weight of *Ms.* magazine, Vanessa Redgrave, and the increasing popularity of women's basketball to be counterbalanced.

Recently I spoke to a group of sixth-graders about writing. One girl present towered over her classmates. Later I commented that she seemed tall for her age. The girl nodded glumly. I added that this certainly made her a standout. She nodded glumly again. Tall women are getting lots of strokes these days, I plowed on (studying height doesn't necessarily make you sensitive on the topic); lots of people are looking up to tall women. The girl didn't even bother acknowledging this thought. She just looked miserable. Well, you know, I suggested finally, girls who grow fast while young often slow down sooner than others; sometimes they end up average-sized, or even short. At this suggestion the girl's face lit up like a flashbulb. "Gee!" she exclaimed with a huge smile. "Do you think that might be true of me?"

Obviously, today as always, being too tall too young poses severe problems for a girl. But is the issue here height as such, or simply standing out at a time when a person would rather blend in? In other words, is the misery of a tall girl any more pronounced than that of her smaller sister who has a bad case of acne or a boy who thinks his penis too small? Or a boy who's too tall, for that matter? (Peter Isacksen said he can think of no worse time in his life to have shot up in size than at fifteen, which physiologically is comparable to thirteen for a girl.)

Our mistake all along may have been in assuming that the pain suffered by tall junior high school girls continues throughout their life. Some interesting research along this line has been done on a group of women first studied between the ages of eleven and seventeen. Observers first determined that girls who matured early physically (including, but not only by growing tall) were less well adjusted than those who matured later. The researchers hypothesized that this correlation would continue throughout high school.

Contrary to expectations, the early-maturing group — who at first seemed more maladjusted — proved over time to develop ''more favorable self-concepts.'' By contrast, the women who had taken more time to mature during adolescence were found later to have less-favorable self-concepts and greater social problems.

To illustrate the two trends, comparative case histories have been reported for two such women followed up in later years. The first had always been the tallest person in her class and had reached 6 feet by her first menstruation at ten years, eight months. The second woman had always been small, and did not menstruate until fifteen years, ten months, when she topped out at 5'5".

The shorter of the two girls was quite popular during junior high school. She later recalled this period as her ''absolute tops of happiness.'' But by late high school this girl's popularity had begun to wane, and in college she was crushed by receiving no bid from a major sorority. As a woman she married at nineteen, gave birth to three children, and at age twenty-nine was still complaining to a visiting researcher about her ''bad luck in sororities'' ten years earlier. The researcher's observation was that this woman "has not regained the high satisfactions of her junior high school years. In spite of forced good cheer and housekeeping competence, she is still almost as callow as a junior high school girl.''

The taller woman, by contrast, was miserable for most of her early years. Her tall mother fretted constantly over the daughter's height, in the self-defeating hope that "she not be tall and have to suffer as I did.'' This girl's classmates told the researchers that she was shy, withdrawn, and not much fun to be with. Such a style characterized the 6-foot woman through her early years of college. But after transferring to another college she began to emerge from her shell, make friends, date, and develop intellectual interests. At twenty-nine this unusually tall woman was on the verge of getting a Ph.D., had published two articles, and was engaged to be married to a 6'4'' graduate student. "For the first time in my life I feel like the person I've always wanted to be,'' she told a visiting researcher. "Life is good, exciting, full. I hope I can help my tall daughters in avoiding some of the unnecessary strains of my life. But, then, maybe we all have to grow up the hard way. Most of the really nice people I know have faced and surmounted tough times. I'm kind of pleased with myself now, but it took so very, very long.''

This finding reflects what tall women themselves have told me repeatedly: once past junior high school, pride is what they feel in their size — pride and potency. At first I assumed this pride just reflected changing times. Now I'm not so sure. Could it be that tall women since Juno have always felt inner pride but outwardly have gone along with the stereotype of a miserable giantess just to flatter society's conceit? Could five-feet-two and eyes of blue have been just the figment of a male songwriter's imagination all along?

For a thought or two on this subject, I went to a woman who's been over 6 feet tall for nearly half a century: Julia Child.

"Well, I've always found it very useful to be six-foot-two," she told me. "Restaurateurs have always remembered me — even before I got into television. And all the people who interviewed me for jobs always seemed to remember me. I guess most think, 'Here comes that tall girl!' "

Julia Child leaned back in her seat and laughed in her hearty way at this thought. From across the kitchen table her husband, Paul, joined in. Paul Child is good-humored, balding, and shorter than his wife, who herself is about as she appears on television (or perhaps a tad more relaxed, if that's possible). Together the two of them sit over a pot of tea most mornings, reading the newspapers and answering a white telephone that rings regularly from where it sits before them on the kitchen table.

Thinking back, Julia Child said that the only occasion in her adult life when her height was a nuisance occurred just before World War II near her home in Los Angeles. "There was a Navy visit and they corralled a lot of girls to go out on one of the ships," she recalled. "And as we got off the [tender] boat, we were each met by a Navy chap. So, inevitably, I was met by someone five-foot-two, which I felt was unfair." She pursed her lips at the memory. "I don't think he liked it any better than I did."

"There's something I always thought to ask you," said Paul Child after his wife described this episode. "I'm not six-two, I'm five-eleven. As you attained your height . . . were you particularly attracted to tall men?"

His wife smiled beatifically and replied, "No, I was usually *not* attracted to tall men — I don't know why that was. I like people just your height. I never met a really tall man that turned me on."

They both laughed in unison.

"I think that's very strange," she continued. "I'm very fond of Galbraith [John Kenneth Galbraith, their neighbor in Cambridge, Massachusetts], I must say."

"Too late now, Julia! You got me."

She kept smiling. "You're just the size and shape I like."

In fact, Julia and Paul Child might never have met at all had she not been 6'2". At that height the WACs during World War II turned her down as too tall. So instead she joined the OSS and was sent to Burma. There Julia Child met her husband-to-be. As it turned out, being a spy proved far more exciting than whatever it was the WACs would have had her doing. So even what at first seemed a penalty for being tall in the end proved a bonus.

In fact, the only current drawback to her size that Child could think of was in the clothing department — or rather *not* in the clothing department: she has to order everything by mail, including shoes. Luckily, she and Paul wear the same size and can sometimes share.

I wondered if working with smaller men ever posed a problem. To the contrary, said Child, she often finds that little men like big women such as her. Certainly she's always enjoyed little men. "I was madly in love with a small man at one point," she confided, "but we decided we were too much of a discrepancy. He was about five-foot-five — just a darling. He was adorable."

She laughed and winked, then turned to Paul, who was muttering, "I should have gone around on my knees." Both laughed.

"No," said Julia. "You're just the way I like you."

Turning back to me she continued with the thought that perhaps because opposites attract, a lot of her friends seem to be small. Moreover, not unlike a tall man meeting one taller, she finds it most disconcerting to have someone's eyes suddenly gazing directly into hers. "I am so used to seeing people at the top of their heads," she explained, "that I notice something seems odd if I see them higher."

"You think," suggested Paul, " 'What right have they to be as tall as I am?' "

Smiling from across the table, his wife didn't take issue. "I rarely look up to another woman," she continued, "although I am often conscious — 'Heavens! There's a nice tall man!' "

The two laughed together at that.

Whether because her whole family is tall (including a sister taller than she), because she grew up among California's out-sized people, or just because she's Julia Child, Julia Child seemed remarkably at ease and good-natured about her height so far above the national mean. "I think I've gotten a great deal of advantage in being tall," was her parting thought. "I think it's contributed a lot to my success."

"Julia," said Paul, "you'd be outstanding if you were six-foot-two or two-foot-six."

7 Height between the Sexes, Sex between the Heights

You are woman, I am man
You are smaller, so I can be taller than

> — From *Funny Girl,* music by Jules Styne,
> lyrics by Bob Merrill

[The man] must be . . . taller than the woman . . . for he must give the impression of being his woman's superior (mentally and physically).

> — HUGH MORRIS in *The Art of Kissing* (1936)

In recent years a number of studies found that infants responded differently when approached by men as opposed to women. In general, they exhibited greater anxiety when men drew near. This finding has been taken as evidence that gender differences are apparent even to babies.

But after surveying several such studies, psychologists Jeanne Brooks and Michael Lewis wondered if gender differences were really what was being tested. Poring back over the data of such experiments, they made a significant discovery: in most cases the male experimenter used to approach infants was between 5′10″ and 6′0″, the female between 5′3″ and 5′6″. Might not the infants be responding to size difference rather than sex difference?

To test this hypothesis the psychologists devised their own test of infants' response to approaching men and women — using men and women more equal in height. And this time there was no apparent difference in the way infants responded to men and women approaching their cribs. "These findings," the psychologists concluded, "suggest that height needs to be considered when exploring gender differences."

One of the least appreciated but most basic differences between men and women is that men, on the average, are taller than women. In the United States today the average difference is 5.4 inches. The fact that most men are taller than most women seems so obvious we don't often consider its consequences. In discussions of gender differences, the size disparity is generally noted only in passing, on the way to more basic issues. But what could be more basic than the difference in size between men and women? Or to put the question a bit differently, couldn't much of what we assume to be a difference between the sexes merely be a difference between the sizes?

I began researching this book with the assumption that height attitudes would be basically different for men and for women. I ended by concluding that such attitudes were basically the same — but there's one fundamental difference. Most women are shorter than most men. Over 90 percent of all American women are under 5'7", but only 25 percent of American men are that short.

The average woman is therefore equivalent in height to the short man. In many ways the social profiles of women in general and of smaller men are also equivalent. Both tend to:

- test low in self-esteem;
- be subject to vocational discrimination — sometimes in the form of "height requirements" that eliminate most women and short men (see chapter 9);
- be discounted when assertive — one as "bitchy," the other as "Napoleonic";
- be rewarded for submissive behavior — whether "feminine" or "mascotish"; and
- sit on a *whole lot* of unexpressed rage.

Disparity in height often creates real differences in how the world is perceived by men and women. No one knows this better than an average-sized woman straining to reach cupboards designed by an average-sized man.

But the real gap has to do with power. A husband who concludes arguments by saying, even in jest, "And don't forget — I'm bigger than you," is making sure this point is not forgotten. Size doesn't necessarily equal power, but it looks that way, and appearances matter. Sylvester "Rocky" Stallone once said that his wife's "greatest wish is to be 6'6" for one hour and knock the stuffing out of me." (Instead she filed for divorce the following year.)

In one imaginative psychological experiment, subjects of both sexes were asked to manipulate flexible manikins to symbolize relationships between men and women. Though both sexes tended to manipulate the figures into positions of male physical superiority, women relied more often on making the male doll taller to do so. "Men," the experimenters concluded, "it would seem, produce what they believe are more powerful male manikins without resorting to superiority in height, but women portray the aggressive male as aggressive partly by virtue of his height."

When the tables are turned and a woman is as tall or taller than a man, tallness and power remain linked in the mind. As a London social worker remarked about the increasing competence of female criminals in that city, "when you are hit by a 5'9" girl you stay hit whatever your size."

Tall women quickly discover that smaller people of both sexes assume them strong. This can pose something of a dilemma. A big woman may not want to be seen as a potential match for Muhammad Ali. On the other hand, she's not unappreciative of the advantages involved in people's fear of her size. The temptation is to work both sides of this street. "I can't understand why men are so afraid of tall women," actress-singer Sally Kellerman once complained. "They get scared off for some reason." But on another occasion the 5'10½" entertainer squelched a heckler by warning, "Hey, I once laid out a boyfriend with a left hook, so play it loose, huh?"

Most of the tall women I interviewed for this book had less confidence in their left hook than Sally Kellerman. But most also recognized the simple deterrent value of their size. A 6-foot-tall New York businesswoman told me she was sure her height explained why she's the only woman she knows in that city who has never been robbed, assaulted, or molested in any way. Added a 6'2" secretary from Philadelphia: "On the street at twelve or one o'clock in the morning walking to my car I've never had any fear because I know people think, 'Hey I'm not gonna mess with her.' If anyone ever hit me I'd probably die. I'm really a weakling. But people are always snickering and making remarks like, 'Do you want to fight?' or 'Don't hit me — hit him!' "

From the Amazons to Wonder Woman, our sense of the tall woman as man's physical equal is culturally reinforced constantly. In Carson McCullers's story "The Ballad of the Sad Cafe," the 6'2" heroine is a "dark, tall woman with bones and muscles like a man" who bosses the town in which she lives. The story's climax features the heroine wrestling her 6'1" husband for the affections of a dwarf. Having physically won the upper hand, the woman realizes that the dwarf wanted her husband/opponent to win; so she gives up her advantage and concedes the match. But it's clear who's biggest and strongest. More recently, Australian novelist Barbara Jefferis gave us *The Tall One,* featuring a big medieval woman of lusty self-assertion who is brought into line only after she meets and falls for a man taller than she. When this man deserts her, she is forced to join the circus as half of a sideshow attraction with a dwarf "husband."

Pairings of tall women and smaller men have always been a

source of public curiosity. Equating size with strength as we do, it's impossible to see such a couple and *not* wonder who dominates whom. When a cartoonist wants to suggest a henpecked, childish husband, the obvious shorthand is to make the man smaller than his wife. From Maggie and Jiggs, through Thurber's couples, to Andy Capp, relative size is basic for suggesting where men and women stand with each other on the funny page.

The case of Andy Capp is particularly revealing. In early panels of London's working-class hero and his rugged wife Florence, the two were of comparable size. But over the years Andy's shrunk quite a bit. Today he's considerably shorter than Flo. This height disparity has much to do with the charm of their relationship — he all feisty bluster, she strong and stolid. Responding to my inquiry about why he reduced Andy to this fate, the cartoon's creator, Reg Smythe, wrote:

When I first did the cartoon I did them both the same size but as you can see now they have changed. I began to realise that the childless couple has a special relationship, the man is inclined to become the boy and the wife the mother. So it seemed right to make Andy Capp smaller and Flo to become a rounded figure. This works quite well for me because if Andy was the same size as Florrie, and they had children, he couldn't do half the things he does without getting a tremendous amount of criticism. As Florrie and the readers say, ''Well, you know what kids are.''

If Andy Capp's childishness is best suggested by his smallness, mightn't the same size-maturity equation also be the source of our woman-as-child model of femininity? In other words, doesn't this traditional woman's role grow inevitably from her relative shortness?

Though the extent of the difference varies, on the average — everywhere — men have been bigger than women for all of recorded history. Anthropologist William Stini compiled the following statistics (abridged here) to compare modern men's stature as a percentage of women's in different parts of the world.

Sweden	109.0%
Yugoslavia	108.5
United States	108.5
Bulgaria	108.4
Portugal	108.2
India	108.2
Wales	108.2
Uruguay	108.1
Peru (highland)	108.0
Ecuador	107.8
Czechoslovakia	107.6
Japan	107.4
Chile	107.2
Burma	107.2
Bolivia	106.8
Brazil	106.8
Vietnam	106.8
Germany (north)	106.7
Thailand	106.6
Germany (south)	106.4
Costa Rica (rural)	106.3
Norway	106.2
Ukraine	106.2
Switzerland (Geneva)	106.1
Poland	105.8

Presumably men have been taller than women since the very beginning. But we can't be sure, because basically we are ignorant about the cause of the disparity. The process itself is clear. From birth until prepuberty boys overall are slightly taller than girls (though girls tend to be more mature skeletally). Beginning at age nine, on the average, girls start to pull ahead and stay ahead for up to three years due to this earlier growth spurt. For perhaps a year toward the end of her spurt a girl's muscles may also be bigger than those of most boys her age.

By age thirteen boys have begun to catch up, and they continue growing into the late teens or even early twenties. Most girls stop growing by fifteen. Because his growth spurt lasts longer and is more pronounced, the average full-grown male ends up taller and stronger (with greater muscle mass) than the average female. This all results from a complex difference in growth processes controlled hormonally in ways we don't fully understand. Here, as in so many areas, it seems as though the more experts know, the less they can conclude. Dr. John Money, who has coauthored two books on gender differences, told me he considers the question of why men are taller than women "foolishly teleological."

"Ask God," advised Money. "He designed it."

The origin and evolution of sexual size differences is a complex issue benefiting from too little concrete data. There is no apparent physiological *need* for men to be taller than women. The reason most men are taller than most women almost certainly involves selection over time. Conceivably both sexes started out equal or close in size, though fossil skeleton samples are too scarce for generalization (and the Bible is mum on Eve's height relative to Adam). We do know that there is little size difference between the sexes among primates such as gibbons, who dwell in trees as our earliest ancestors may have. By contrast, among primates such as baboons, who forage on open land, males tend to have a significant height advantage. Female baboons average only 81 percent of the male size, compared with a 99 percent figure for their gibbon cousins. A plausible explanation for this difference is that among branches and leaves there is simply no advantage to extra size for either sex of gibbon. Threatened by predators, the best defense is to hide. Largeness only makes a tree dweller more visible and less able to perch on weak branches. Up in the trees, therefore, extra size has no immediate and no evolutionary value.

Down below, the opposite is true. If they are tall, those living on open land can spot predators more easily and are better equipped to stand and fight when necessary. "In larger-sized primates with multi-male troops and offensive anti-predator mechanisms," anthropologists Walter Leutenneger and James T. Kelly have written, "the large size of males has been selected, at least in part, as a predator deterrent."

With so much to gain from extra size, males among big, land-dwelling primates such as baboons almost certainly have been selected for this trait over time — eventually outstripping females. Perhaps the same has been true of humans in their life far from the safety of branches and leaves. Among those who have studied this issue, it is widely believed that in common with other large, terrestrial primates, the difference in physical size between men and women can be traced partly to the early protective role assigned big men. J. M. Tanner has added that such an evolutionary process could explain the fact that the human male's size advantage over females doesn't become pronounced until late in adolescence, the age when extra size would have been most useful in the males' "primitive primate role of dominating, fighting, and foraging."

But such an explanation of why men have grown relatively large over time doesn't explain why women haven't followed suit. Couldn't both sexes have been selected equally for bigness?

To understand not just the absolute but the relative difference in size between men and women, the influence of *sexual* selection must be added to that of *natural* selection. Among most land-dwelling primates, mating takes place after contests between males. The victorious male wins his pick of females, and is not usually limited to one. Presumably this approach to mating also characterized early humans. Equal mating for all (in theory at least) is a relatively modern phenomenon.

It is well established that physical competition for females by males results in an exaggerated size gap between the sexes of a species. Among many species of primates studied by Leutenneger and Kelly, the degree of difference in body size between the sexes is determined, in their words, ''primarily by female availability.'' This relationship between the sexual size difference and mating by contest is by now so generally accepted that archeologist Richard Leakey thinks a substantial male-female size difference in the prehistoric human fossil skeletons he's finding in East Africa will itself constitute evidence of ''sharp social competition between the males.'' In such contests for women, size gives big men an advantage. This advantage doesn't even have to be exercised physically; the simple threat value of a bigger body alone can be sufficient. Leakey (with collaborator Roger Lewin) has written that the huge male leader commonly found among silverback gorilla packs ''achieves his position because of his magnificent stature and overt masculinity, features that attract the females to him and make his would-be successors think very carefully before trying to oust him.'' Finding a significant sexual size difference in his humanoid fossil skeletons, Leakey has concluded, will indicate that like today's silverbacks, yesterday's humans lived in tribes with harems dominated by men selected for their exaggerated size.

For women the size-selection process over time has quite likely been just the opposite of that for men. As taller men were being selected for better deterrence and dalliance, for various reasons smaller women probably were favored as their mates. Practically speaking, there simply would be no reason for early man to choose a bigger, sturdier woman until he settled into farming rather late in the game and could use more muscle behind (or in front of) the plow. Until that time a larger female mate would simply consume more food.

Additionally, it's been found that in demanding settings, where food is scarce and living conditions hard (as has been true for most of man's history), shorter women are more prolific and successful bearers of children than taller ones. Dr. A. M. Thomson has reported that in Scotland he and others have found that unwed and childless women tend to be taller on the average than their married, child-producing counterparts. Thomson thinks this suggests either an ongoing male preference for "a 'bonny wee thing,' or that tall women are more 'choosy' about the men they marry."

Anthropologist Marvin Harris has speculated further that man's tendency to engage in war has favored both bigger men and smaller women. Bigger men, said Harris, presumably were considered better warriors, just as smaller women presumably were more willing to serve as a reward back home for such warriors. In Harris's opinion, such women probably were less likely to want to join the battle or the hunt than their larger sisters. Even today taller women have been found more independent than smaller ones. According to Dr. Thomson, tall women not only are less likely to marry but are more likely to migrate from a home setting.

Over time, of course, social institutions developed to endorse the trend to larger men and smaller women — traditions that ratified the results of natural selection. "It is conceivable that once patriarchy was instituted," wrote sociologist Janet Saltzman Chafetz, "culturally defined notions of beauty came to favor strength and large size in males, and weakness and petite structure in females. Such definitions of beauty, marvelously supportive of patriarchal social institutions, would lead to selective reproduction favoring small, weak females, and big, strong males.''

Has woman had any say in this matter? Assuming her body size declined over time even as man's increased, was woman a willing or a coerced participant in the process of sexual selection? Some have contended that far from being reluctant, woman was an enthusiastic collaborator in her own decline in physique. ''If the male appears to excel in size and strength,'' suggested naturalist Frank Ward more than a century ago, ''it's because female preference has weeded out the little weak males in favor of superior sires.'' More recently, anthropologist Weston La Barre argued that man's advantage in body size overall ''is certainly the final result of sexual selection by the female.''

In other words, a basic influence in the greater height of men relative to women may be women's preference that this be so. Such a preference is not noted only by males. Two centuries ago feminist Mary Wollstonecraft scolded her sisters for embracing the ideal of feminine frailty as if ''proud of a defect.'' A modern counterpart, Elizabeth Gould Davis — one of the few commentators of either sex to consider seriously the effect relative size has on male and female roles — acknowledged fully and bitterly the responsibility of her gender for its own diminution. Davis was convinced, on the basis of existing evidence (which is scant), that women originally were the same size as men but ''brought on their own downfall by selecting the phallic wild man over the more civilized men of their own pacific and gentle world.''

Now that wars are fought by push button and meat is hunted mostly in supermarkets, one might conclude that height no longer matters in mating — that since all men are supposed to have equal crack at all women and vice versa, the competitive advantage of male tallness has gone the way of the club and spear.

Nothing could be further from the truth. Our minds may realize that size shouldn't matter in modern man's nonphysical jousting for women, but our instincts are something else. No adult is more painfully aware of who's bigger than a smaller man competing with a larger one for the attention of a woman. "If a small guy walks somewhere with one of the big beautiful ones," says the 5'6" hero in an Irwin Shaw story, "he knows that every cat in the place who's two inches taller than he is thinking to himself, 'I can take that big mother away from that shrimp any time,' and they're just waiting for the small guy to go to the john or turn his head to talk to the headwaiter, to give his date the signal."

A group of psychologists studying adult "body image" were surprised to discover how much less comfortable and more dissatisfied with their bodies men were when among themselves than they were in the presence of women. The researchers had assumed it would be the other way around. Not knowing quite what conclusion to draw from this finding, they speculated that "men may need to feel that they look big and powerful in order to impress other men."

That's it. Even though today's man may live and die without ever going *mano a mano* over a woman, some part of him is always aware of the odds should he have to. Knowing the odds are in his favor puts a tall man more at ease. And this ease adds to his advantage. Some say this is changing, that in today's world a tall body is no more useful than a greasy pompadour in the contest for attention from women. In our large coastal cities one can even see signs of a little "Annie Hall syndrome," as tall women rest their arms on the shoulders of small lovers. But you needn't travel very far inland to find that the taboo against woman being taller than man is alive, well, and flourishing.

Just two-hours' drive from New York, at Cedar Crest College for women in Allentown, Pennsylvania, I was once told by a professor that as a test of prejudice he'd polled a class about whom they would or wouldn't date. Most said they'd go out with a man of another religion. Some said they'd date a man of a different race. But none — not one — said she'd be seen with a man shorter than herself.

To find out if the height preferences in men expressed by this class were unique, I circulated a questionnaire among all of Cedar Crest's students (who for the most part are sophisticated but not avant-garde and are probably representative of American college women in general). Out of 79 women who responded, only 2 — both of them 5'11" by their own report — said they would go out with a man shorter than themselves. A single respondent said that she set no height limit at all for prospective dates. The rest said they'd only consider dating a man at least 1.7 inches taller than themselves on the average.

After completing this poll, I heard of a similar survey taken among college students of both sexes, titled "Height and Attraction: Do Men and Women See Eye-to-Eye?" In this psychological study, three researchers found that when shown photographs of men labeled "tall," "medium," or "short," a majority of 100 college coeds of all heights chose the ones tagged "medium" as most attractive. In contrast to the findings of myself and others, they found further that height per se was reported to be of little consequence in hypothetical date selection among these women and a sample of college men as well. But the study's authors speculated that while they may not *report* height to be a significant factor in choosing dates, in practice such subjects (men especially) may still adhere to this "cardinal principle." In the authors' words: "While men may report no awareness of the cardinal principle on a questionnaire, they may show behavioral conformity to it. Thus, men may not *report* height as an important factor in women's attraction to men, but in their daily lives, they may never ask out a woman taller than themselves.''

This ongoing taboo against women dating men shorter than themselves is among the strictest of this society. In a study of dating attractiveness, a team of social scientists once assigned University of Minnesota freshmen dates by computer on a purely random basis, with a single exception. Whenever a taller woman was randomly assigned to a shorter man, her IBM card was deliberately shuffled back into the deck. Though the researchers gave no explanation for their only departure from chance, the taller woman–smaller man taboo obviously was too big to buck.

Repeatedly during interviews I've heard stories illustrating this taboo. My favorite is that of a woman who as a teenager made marks on the front doorjamb indicating her height in different pairs of shoes. As her date walked in the door she made a quick visual check of which mark he reached, then scurried upstairs to choose shoes accordingly.

The taboo goes back a long way. In the mid-eighteenth century, the small poet Christopher Smart wrote his classic (to some) poem ''The Author Apologizes to a Lady for His Being a Little Man.'' This poem included the lines:

> YES, *contumelious fair, you scorn*
> *The amorous dwarf that courts you to his arms,*
> *But ere you leave him quite forlorn,*
> *And to some youth gigantic yield your charms,*
> *Hear him — oh hear him, if you will not try,*
> *And let your judgment check th' ambition of your eye.*

Say, is it carnage makes the man?
Is to be monstrous really to be great?
Say, is it wise or just to scan
Your lover's worth by quantity or weight? . . .

Does thy young bosom pant for fame:
Woud'st thou be of posterity the toast?
The poets shall ensure thy name
Who magnitude of mind *not* body *boast.*
Laurels on bulky bards as rarely grow,
As on the sturdy oak the virtuous mistletoe.

Look in the grass, survey that cheek —
Where FLORA *has with all her roses blush'd;*
The shape so tender, — look so meek —
The breasts made to be press'd, not to be crush'd —
Then turn to me, — turn with obliging eyes,
Nor longer nature's works, in miniature despise. . . .

Time has not eased Smart's complaint. Even in the state of
Kerala, in India's tropical south, I'm told, it's still considered
appropriate for the groom to be a coconut taller than his bride.
Although some societies are more bound by the smaller man–
taller woman taboo than others, even within such societies there
are couples who flout it. Such pairings in recent years have included:

> Paul and Anne Anka
> Richard Ben-Veniste and Mary Travers
> Billy and Sybil Carter
> Lynda ("Wonder Woman") Carter and Ron Samuels
> Altovise and Sammy Davis, Jr.
> Robert De Niro and Diahann Abbott

Dustin and Anne Byrne Hoffman
King Hussein and Lisa Halaby
Mick Jagger and Jerry Hall
Arte and Gisela Johnson
Henry and Nancy Kissinger
Sophia Loren and Carlo Ponti
Guru Maharaj Ji and Marolyn Johnson
Norman Mailer and Norris Church
Marvin and Jeanne Mandel
Prince Rainier and Grace Kelly
Princess Caroline Rainier and Philippe Junot
Paul Simon and Shelley Duvall
Arthur and Alexandra Schlesinger
Willie and Cynthia Shoemaker
Jerry Stiller and Anne Meara
John and Lilla Tower
Paul and Katie Williams
Robin and Valerie Williams

Flouting the dissimilar-height taboo takes courage. One man of 5'7" who is married to a taller woman said he ignores the public outcry and puts up with every indignity except two: he won't help his 6'2" wife on with her coat and he won't hold an umbrella over her head. Other such mismatched couples have told me of giving up in despair over the hoots, whistles, jeers, howls, and insinuating remarks that are their constant lot in public. As the old joke reminds them, "Confucius say: Man who date taller woman end up with bust in mouth."

Mismatched couples are always good for a laugh in our culture. Some mismatchees even laugh at themselves. When once asked what he wished for his 4-inches-taller wife, Dustin Hoffman replied, "Growth . . . shrinkage . . ." When a woman is too much taller than the man, words aren't even necessary for humor. Sammy Davis, Jr., used to include a tall

Facing the taboo

woman in his act whose main job was to stand next to him on stage so the audience could laugh at the head's difference in height between them.

In Irwin Shaw's story, his 5′6″ Lothario calls a taller woman named Rebecca for a date. Her roommate Beulah answers and, shielding the mouthpiece with her hand, says,

"That beautiful boy from the bookstore is on the phone. He's invited me to dinner. But —"

"That *dwarf?*" Rebecca said.

"He's not so small, actually," Beulah said. "He's very well proportioned."

"I don't go in for comedy acts," Rebecca said. "He'd have to use his ladder even to get into scoring territory."

This gets to the heart of the aura of humor, fear, and fascination that surrounds couples with a great height disparity. The most common question contemplated if not asked about them is, "I wonder what it's — like?" Or, "I wonder how they, you know — get it together — know what I mean?" Since this book is about answers, as part of my research I've sought some about . . . you know, what it's — *like.*

"When you're making love, body length doesn't matter that much," said a 6-foot woman economist who's had lovers of various heights. "With a smaller man there's no problem whatsoever. Things are equal when you're lying down." She went on to say that her best physical relationships had actually been with smaller men. "To generalize, I don't find large men active enough. They tend to be sort of phlegmatic. Tall men generally are slower-moving — even in pursuits they enjoy."

Several tall women echoed this observation. "I think smaller guys tend to be more energetic lovers," said another 6-footer, a dance teacher, about her smaller mates. This woman said the "best sex" she ever had was with a man 5′9″ whom she called "sexually the strongest, most centered man I've been with." A 5'9" woman reporter recalled an ex-lover of 5'5" as "terrific — the best I ever had. He was a great overachiever."

Beyond such general evaluations, tall women have more specific points to make about the mechanics of mismatched sex. "Physically," said a 5'11" counselor, "having a small man on top of me can be comfortable. I could lie there for hours and be comfortable the whole time. With a tall man on top of me it can get uncomfortable very quickly." Others cite the imaginative possibilities unique to the body of a taller woman involved with that of a smaller man; with strong thighs she can even lift him into the air just by bracing her heels against a bedpost and using her body like a trampoline.

Vertical lovemaking has particular appeal for a taller woman with a smaller man. "Standing-up sex is better with a smaller man," explained the 6-foot dance teacher, "because he doesn't have to bend his legs." She stood to demonstrate, arching slightly and pointing to the vicinity of her hips. "Say with my vagina here and his penis there, it's much more comfortable. I'm not the one who has to go through all the gyrations to get everything even. I prefer to hug a man my own size, though. Our pelvises are together. You get a better rush."

By contrast, a 5-foot farmer's wife complained on a questionnaire, "I have rarely experienced a man's hard-on anywhere but too high! It's taken me years to break the habit of standing on my toes while dancing, kissing, hugging."

A 5'2" woman I talked with was about to marry a man nearly a foot shorter than her first husband, who was 6'4". After leaving her big husband, the woman said, "I got into men more my own size. I feel like small bodies just fit together better." She spread her hands over her abdomen to demonstrate. "Our pelvises just match.

"With my first husband I was aware when we made love that

I had to scoot down'' — she squeezed low into her chair — ''and manipulate my body more than with someone closer to my own size.'' She laughed. ''I did have an experience once with a football player where I thought I'd die — the size *and* the weight. I thought I couldn't *breathe*.''

Because we see them together more frequently, speculation about what it's ''like'' between small women and big men is less feverish than about the reverse pairings. But such couples told me that they too have discovered possibilities unconsidered by bodies more closely matched. Two different men in the 6-foot range, for example, described the pleasures of making love in the shower with their respective tiny, light partners, whom they could lift up and onto them.

A man well into the upper 6-foot range reported experiences at both ends of the line. Once he was accosted in a bar by what he called ''a drunken Amazon'' who grunted: *''You. I want you.''* That turned out to be nice, he said — to be with somebody his own size for a change. But he'd also been with women as small as 4'11", and ''That's nice too. It's very nice to be able to pick somebody up and walk around making love. That's interesting. The extremes are very interesting.'' He grinned. ''So are the in-betweens.''

Actually, the boring truth of the matter is that sex between partners of disparate height is not all that different from any other kind. The reason is simple — and, as I say, boring. As is apparent in any room full of seated bodies, height variation above the hips isn't nearly as great as that below. Most difference in height involves the legs. Thus, with rare exceptions, the only real difference in sex between partners whose height is matched and those whose isn't is that when mismatched partners make love lying down, their toes don't touch. So unless you're a toe fetishist, there's no reason not to look up or down when seeking a partner for sex.

To raise a touchier question — whether relative genital size in mismatched bodies can cause actual problems of fit — I consulted medical psychologist Richard Clopper of Johns Hopkins University. Clopper does sex counseling of short-statured adults, including some who are married to taller spouses. "Stature itself is not correlated with [physical] problems in intercourse," Clopper told me, "because the vagina is so plastic."

The question of whether penis size is related to height is somewhat more ticklish, because the issue of penis size is more ticklish in general. Since time immemorial, legends — often self-serving — have existed about small-men's big ones and big-men's little ones. (Stephen Jay Gould pointed out that the legendary ultrahung little guy could simply stem from the fact that a normal-size penis looks larger relative to a smaller body.) But few people put credence in such legends. In fact, the nervousness surrounding big men with little women could really have most to do with the opposite assumption — that penis length is directly, not inversely, proportional to body length.

The accepted medical wisdom on this question can be found in G. A. Piersol's *Human Anatomy:* "The size of the penis has less constant relation to general physical development than that of any other organ of the body." That was written in 1907, based on data collected earlier. Perhaps because taking measurements in this area is a problem, no confirmation of Piersol's observation was offered until six decades later, when William Masters and Virginia Johnson measured the penises of 312 subjects aged twenty-one to eighty-nine. As the two subsequently reported in *Human Sexual Response,* their findings

supported Piersol's contention that there is no relation between man's skeletal framework and the size of his external genitalia. The largest penis in the study-subject population, measuring approximately 14 cm.

long in the flaccid state, was in a man 5 feet 7 inches tall weighing 152 pounds. The smallest penis, measuring just over 6 cm. in the flaccid state, was in a man 5 feet 11 inches tall weighing 178 pounds.

In other words, there is no way to judge the penis length of a man who's dressed. Height per se has no bearing on size of genitals.

So if height has no relation to genital fit between mismatched bodies and doesn't reflect penis size, what *is* the problem? The problem is strictly psychological. As with most taboos about height, the source rests less with our bodies than our minds.

To the best of my knowledge, only one major psychological study has ever been made about height as it affects American male-female relationships. This study was done in 1954 by psychiatrist Hugo Beigel. Its findings seem up-to-date. Beigel found that among men he studied, a desire to be taller than a woman was related to a need for dominance. The more dominating a man wished to be, the more he wished to look down on his female partner. A 6'1" male subject, for example, said his ideal female would be 5'3" tall because: "I am the domineering type. I like her to be dependent on me at all times. I like to be waited on by women." Nearly three-quarters of the men who said they wanted a greater-than-average difference in height between them and a woman also expressed a greater-than-average need to feel dominant over her. By the same token, women in the study who wished for a less-than-average height difference between their mate and themselves also tended to be frustrated by the traditional woman's role; and in all cases but one, those women who wanted more than an average height difference expressed a desire to be submissive to their husband. In the only other study I know of bearing at all on this subject, Seymour Fisher in 1964 found among a group of college men that those who expressed the strongest belief in male superiority over women also expressed the greatest overall desire for a taller body.

So here, as elsewhere, what's at issue isn't relative size so much as relative power. Not wanting to disturb the balance of power was the principal theme I found in women's explanations for not wanting to go out with smaller men. "Men shorter than I am make me feel too dominant," explained a 5'2" coed. "I am a dominant person, so I feel the men need the height to equalize my personality." Another coed, 5'4" tall, said she feels very uncomfortable seeing the top of a man's head "like a *little boy.*" Similar reasons were given repeatedly by coeds at Cedar Crest for not wanting to violate the shorter-date taboo:

• A man who is shorter than I am seems somehow less superior. [A 5'3" coed]

• I would hate feeling bigger or taller than my mate because I'd feel domineering or something. [5'4½"]

• I would feel the urge to dominate him. [5'4"]

• I don't want to be overpowering. [5'6"]

• I hate having guys look up to me. I feel very uncomfortable and overpowering. [5'8"]

So once again we're caught in a chink in our values. Height attitudes between the sexes may be changing as increasing numbers of women and men try to narrow the power gap that separates them. Tallness per se is already less a source of shame and more a source of open pride than it used to be among women. But the American woman who wants to look down on her man is still as rare as the man who wants to look up to his woman.

Even Sandy Allen of Shelbyville, Indiana, who at 7'7¼" is certified by *Guinness* as the tallest woman in the world, has said that although she might go out with a smaller man, she wouldn't marry one. "I've got this old-fashioned idea that I will never marry anyone smaller than I am," she explained. "I just have the idea that the man should be bigger than the woman. I would feel dominant otherwise, and I wouldn't like to, in a situation like that. I feel the husband is supposed to protect his wife and look out for her.

"Maybe that'll change if Mr. Right comes along, but it hasn't yet. So I really don't expect ever to get married."

8 At the Ends of the Spectrum

God likes to do funny things; here you have the long and the short of it.

> — ABRAHAM LINCOLN, during an audience with Tom Thumb

A notice in the paper announced the First Annual Eastern Conference of Tall Women. It would take place the following Saturday afternoon at a local shopping center. Any woman over 5'10" could take part. And Sandy Allen would be there.

"See how tall!"

"She's the world's tallest woman!"

"Seven feet seven-and-one-quarter inches, I heard!"

"Man, if I was that big, could I ever dunk the ball!"

The kids buzzed and jostled for space among the hundreds of people who jammed the mall. Towering overhead like a thick flagpole was the object of their fascination — Sandy Allen — her broad, impassive face rising up out of a blue T-shirt. One side of the shirt was lettered PEOPLE LOOK UP TO ME; the other side read WORLD'S TALLEST WOMAN.

Only a table protected Allen from the crush of bodies before her. On this table she scrawled her name on slips of paper, then pushed these into waiting hands. Filling the air around her were the snap of camera shutters, the flash of bulbs, and the whir of Polaroid prints emerging.

"Let's go," a short, graying man beside Sandy Allen kept repeating. "Keep it moving. Let's go. Okay, you saw her. Move along. Give somebody else a turn. Let's go!" The man was dressed in brown checks and a tweed hat. His face looked permanently harassed.

After a few minutes, the object of the crowd's attention sank slowly into a chair. Like air rushing from a balloon, the crowd's mood sank with her. What just a moment before could be seen with a simple glance aloft now called for strained tiptoeing. Looks of awe and fascination changed to ones of simple irritation, which soon was voiced.

"When's she gonna stand up again?"

"I can't see her."

"Tell her to stand up!"

"She will in a moment," said the man beside Sandy Allen. "Just be patient." As she continued signing autographs from her seat, Allen seemed oblivious to the discontent crackling around her.

"Stand back and you'll all see," the man beside her finally announced. "Stand back!"

Bracing her arms against the table, slowly, hesitantly Sandy Allen pushed herself out of the seat and gradually up, onto her feet. As she did so, the crowd's muttering ceased. At last the object of their curiosity stood erect. And as their eyes followed hers upward, hundreds of mouths together let out a long, slow "Ooooooohhhhhh . . ."

"Watch the car! Please! Watch the car!"

Followed by a skipping, giggling, pointing pack of children, Sandy Allen's motorized golf cart slowly made its way down the shopping-center mall. Looking back at the bodies dancing about her, Allen's face had the resigned, bemused look of a queen off to the guillotine. The cart came to a halt by a service exit. Standing nearby was a group of women who towered over the man escorting Sandy Allen. "No," he was telling them testily. "No, there's no symposium." His listeners looked rebellious.

Finally the man gave in and asked, "Are there any tall women here?" Though the question seemed superfluous, they answered anyway.

"Yes."

"Right here."

"I'm one."

The man departed for a few minutes, then returned and with a wave of his arm led the group up a stairway and into a room equipped with a conference table and perhaps twenty chairs. After most of them were filled, Sandy Allen engulfed the doorway, stooped her way through, and with a smile eased herself slowly into a seat at the table's head.

"This is Sandy Allen," the man standing beside her announced. "You've read about her — a very lovely young lady.

"I've been around a lot of extraordinary people in my checkered career. I handled the Shrine Circus for twenty years. I did publicity for Ringling Brothers at one time. I did publicity for Clyde Beatty.

"Sandy is, ah, different. She's not like the circus people. The circus people are wonderful people — don't get me wrong. But Sandy is different. She's intelligent. She's a normal person.

"You ladies have never met her, I presume, right? Okay, we'll hold the symposium. Let's make it informal and off-the-cuff, so to speak. I think it's best to start off by asking Sandy questions, don't you think?"

Throughout this speech, Sandy Allen looked halfway between bored and embarrassed. The call for questions was met by silence.

"You want to ask Sandy questions?" the man repeated.

"Any kind of questions, varied questions, that Sandy will attempt to answer to the best of her ability."

More silence.

The man shot Allen a puzzled look. She looked back with a noncommittal sigh.

Finally a participant in the symposium stood. She had curly blond hair and in any other setting would have seemed gigantic. "I came today hoping I was going to be one of the little people," this woman began. "But I'm told I'm the second one down." She then recited in some detail her problems at 6'2" in finding size-13 shoes and clothes anywhere near her size.

Sandy Allen smiled slightly and said, "Well, as far as helping anyone find where to get clothes . . ." The group laughed. "I'm afraid I'm not much help. I haven't bought clothes in a long time. A seamstress has to make all of mine." Despite her deep, husky voice, Sandy Allen's manner of speaking was relaxed. Soon others relaxed too and questions began to flow.

What about shoes?

"Those old clodhoppers I have on now were sixty-five bucks." She raised a golf-type shoe over the table to illustrate.

How many pairs do you own?

"Three. That's all I can afford."

Where do you work?

"As a secretary for the Animal Board of Health in Shelby-ville, Indiana."

What do you drive?

"A van. But I used to drive a Gremlin. From the front seat yet."

Any health problems?

The answer to this question took a bit longer. Allen, who was carrying over four hundred pounds on her frame (down fifty from the year before), had had some knee trouble a few years ago that required surgery. Also, doctors had recently cut a tumor out of her pituitary gland. This tumor had been making her pituitary pump 200 to 1,000 times the normal amount of growth hormone. That's why Sandy Allen at age three was as big as a seven-year-old, had reached 6'3" by age ten, and was over 7 feet tall when she started high school. Adolescence was the hardest time of her life, she said — "putting up with all the b.s. and wisecracks."

In recent years, however, she's come to mind her height less. Without it, Allen told the group, she'd be just another secretary; this way she's a world record. "Sometimes I wish I wasn't so *much* taller," she conceded. "Especially when it comes to looking through catalogs and I see the pretty clothes that other women can wear."

A woman attending the symposium pointed out that, should the occasion arise, there simply is no such thing as tall maternity wear. The woman said that she guessed it meant tall women just weren't supposed to have children. Allen joined in the sympathetic laughter that followed. After it died down, she said that one noteworthy aspect of her notoriety were the periodic proposals of marriage that she receives in the mail. They "are always very interesting," she said. "Most of them are from guys who are interested in taller women. But most of *them* are under six feet. Just my luck." She smiled and looked around the table. "Could I give anybody their addresses?"

We all should make the peace with ourselves that Sandy Allen seemed to have made with herself. There's no question that she'd been hurt by her role in life. In case one missed it in her face, it became clear upon talking to her. But at twenty-four, she was resigned and good-humored about her height.

In a conversation after the "Symposium," the world's tallest woman told me that she thought whatever serenity she had came from emotional support back home. Her grandmother especially, with whom she'd lived since an infant, was very much the "stand up straight, get your shoulders back, be proud of your size" type. Paradoxically, this attitude may have contributed to Allen's height: by trying to downplay their concern about the girl's tallness, the family didn't seriously seek medical treatment for it until too late. When she was ten Allen was taken to a hospital in Indianapolis where doctors offered to try stunting her growth. But, having no idea of the height she ultimately would reach, granddaughter and grandmother jointly agreed not to risk something that sounded so experimental (to say nothing of expensive). Only after she'd hit 7′5″ at age twenty was the tumor on Sandy's pituitary discovered. And only two years and 2 inches later — when blindness threatened — did she allow doctors to cut through her skull and remove the tumor.

"She feels like it was her fault," said the unusually tall woman about her grandmother's feelings. "That she didn't get it discovered sooner." Her voice strained slightly. "I do my best to keep her from feeling that way, because it wasn't her fault."

Away from a crowd, Allen was less casual about her role in life. Of her difficult first year in high school, she remembered: "I hated even to see people for fear that they were going to say something. I would go home sometimes and just cry because I was so mad. What the hell did I ever do to them to deserve all this baloney that they gave me?"

But she certainly seemed unscarred, I suggested, less than I expected I might be in her shoes.

"Oh, gosh," Allen replied. "People are people. If I kept all of that stuff inside me and, you know, kept remembering all that stuff, I don't know what kind of mental state I'd be in today." She laughed her deep, throaty laugh. "It's not too good as it is right now."

Sandy Allen's broad face with its oversized lips was not pretty in any classical sense, but over time her grace gave it a soft appeal not apparent at first glance. She was an attractive woman. Only a bit too much rouge and eye shadow got in the way, I thought. At first this puzzled me. What was the need? But her makeup made more sense after Sandy told me one last story:

I was in Chicago at a manufacturer's convention. They wanted me to attract attention to their exhibits. I was passing out candy and stuff. Then I walked into the rest room. Some lady was there washing her hands. She looked up at me and said, "You're not supposed to be in here." And she went running out the door. I knew exactly what it was; she thought I was a man.

I thought, gee, all she has to do is draw a whole lot of people in here to get me out. So I followed her out. I knew there was a guard, so I went to him. And there she was, telling him about me. When she looked up and saw me coming around the corner, she threw her hands up and took off running like I was coming to get her. Oh, it hurt my feelings.

So I thought, if I'm that grotesque to look at, what am I doing here? I wanted to crawl into a big hole and bury myself. It still hurts even to think about it. I think if I had seen that woman again I would have spat in her face. It just really hurt. It made me ask questions about myself. What do I look like to other people? Am I that grotesque-looking?

Do I look like a man?

*Sandy Allen
and coworker*

Lee Kitchens (right)
and coworker

"When I was in first grade they put us in line by size. The lady in charge took one look at me and said, 'You'll have to go home. You're too small for first grade.' I went home in tears. After that one incident I didn't feel so affected by my size in grade school. But when I hit high school I panicked. It was a big school. Everyone seemed so tall. I felt so inferior. I panicked."

Heads bobbed sympathetically as this story was told by a dark-eyed brunette named Eileen. Although in her early twenties, Eileen looked younger because her body wasn't much over 4 feet tall. Nor were most of the bodies surrounding her at a workshop for young people with restricted-growth problems. A couple of the women Eileen's age were taller than she because they'd received growth-hormone treatment. But these women, too, nodded sympathetically. As they recalled from their pre-treatment days, the episode had a familiar ring.

Two younger boys who were still well below 4 feet looked uneasy. One of them then told the group how life was for him as an undersized twelve-year-old. In school, PE was a particular sore point. At times he was only allowed to keep score. At other times meaningless positions were created just for him — "second goalie" or "fourth fielder." Animated and wide-eyed, with longish black hair, Mike said he was used to being picked last for teams if picked at all. If not picked he'd go lift weights by himself. Mike said that he didn't mind. In an offhand way the boy added that although he and everyone else knew it was his size that kept him off teams, nobody would say so. "They just make up an excuse like you're not good enough," he explained, "or that they hate me or something."

The half-dozen people taking part in this conversation were what's commonly known as midgets — proportionately formed human beings in miniature. They themselves don't care for that term, though they hear it a lot, from kids especially. A 3′6″ social worker named Herman who wore a mustache and carried a walking stick was sitting in on the conversation. Herman said that it was curious: in an attempt to be inconspicuous, some little people dress like kids and try to pass. But kids themselves are never fooled. "They come right up and say, 'Are you a midget?' " The others laughed and nodded. No one could remember ever being mistaken for a kid by a kid, though no one was quite sure why.

Grown-ups are another matter. They not only mistake smaller people for kids, but even try to push them into that role with constant head pats, lap pulls, and offers to pick little people up and carry them about. The very small person's dilemma thus becomes an exaggerated version of all short people's: give in and become a jester or fight back and become an extra-little Napoleon.

A delicate-featured twenty-five-year-old Oriental woman named Susie talked about being the smallest person by far at her parochial school. Every year she was chosen to give the monsignor his birthday present. To do this she was lifted off the ground and held up to him. The task was both an honor and a humiliation. But at least people knew who she was. "To this day," said Susie, "I'll walk down the street and people will say, 'Did you go to St. Francis?' "

Susie went on to say that other than finding work, her biggest problem since leaving school was dating. She said that she particularly resented people trying to fix her up with men on the basis of height alone. With sarcastic mimicry, Susie told the group that whenever a short man was led toward her, the sentiment always seemed to be, "Here's a good one for you."

The other women present murmured in agreement. A blond secretary who'd reached a height of 5 feet with the help of growth hormone said that she personally preferred 6-footers. Being half of a ''cute little couple'' set her teeth on edge. The shortest man she'd recently gone out with was 5'10". Although the little men present kept their counsel during this part of the discussion, none of them looked too pleased.

As always with those at either end of the height spectrum, talk eventually came around to the hated questions and insensitive comments from average-sized people.

''There's no phrase I hate more than 'You're not really *that* short,' '' said a grown woman of 4'8". ''It's like 'You're not really *that* fat,' or 'You're not really *that* awful.' ''

Herman said he was so tired of being asked why he was short that he'd taken to telling people it came from drinking too much milk as a kid. Or because an elephant stepped on him at the circus. Herman, who is in his early thirties, said that he had only recently become less sensitive about his size; for most of his life he hadn't been able to joke about it at all. What broke the ice was a Little People of America convention he attended in his late twenties. On a bus with one group of conventioneers, he spotted another group coming out of a building. ''So,'' he recalled, ''spontaneously we all just lowered the windows and started yelling, '' 'Hey! Look at the freaks. What is this — is the circus in town?' ''

Everyone laughed at the story. Herman grinned broadly.

''We all were so shocked. I certainly was. It was the first time I realized you could joke about it.''

My own feelings while visiting this group were mixed. Partly I felt a sense of ease at being among people for whom shortness is a given and height is matter-of-fact as a topic of conversation. On the other hand, I felt uncomfortable looking down on so many adults all at once. I felt gawky. I found myself sitting as soon as possible, then scrinching as low as I could get in my seat.

My small companions themselves were excellent company — lively, affable, not too touchy about their height. When the rap session ended I hung around to chat a bit further with Susie and two of her friends. Susie was wearing enormous heels — 4 inches at least. Unable to guess, I asked her height.

"Four feet five," she replied.

"Is *that* all?" I gasped. The words just picked themselves up and walked right out of my mouth. What else could I do at that point but bury my head in my arms as Susie and her friends cackled and jeered at this "student" of height and how little he'd learned?

At a later gathering, I attended a discussion of "Sex and Related Topics." Most of the participants were what's commonly known as dwarfs — smaller people with some limb distortion. The group of twenty or so was led by a married couple, with two full-sized psychologists assisting as consultants. Early in the session participants wrote out questions anonymously, then passed them up front to be read aloud. One such question had to do with premature ejaculation. What could be done about it?

"Alcohol works for me," advised a male voice.

"Try abstinence," suggested another.

"Or whistling Dixie."

Other questions were on topics such as women's orgasms, venereal disease, and methods of contraception. For those of short stature, birth control poses particular problems. A diaphragm, for example, cannot be properly inserted by some little women because their limbs and fingers simply are not long enough. IUDs also are problematic, because malformation of the uterus is common among women with growth problems. Nor can the pill normally be used, since its dosage is based on a full-sized system. For these reasons, one of the consultants present recommended that those of short stature rely on "any barrier method followed by foam."

Other than such contraceptive difficulties, the psychologist went on, there are no real physical limitations on sexual activity involving smaller people. A woman raised her hand to say that she'd heard that short-statured people shouldn't have intercourse sitting up.

"Who says?" asked a male voice across the room to a wave of laughter.

Discussion then turned to the advisability of short-statured people becoming involved romantically with those of conventional height. The male group leader led off with his opinion: if such a couple were well-adjusted, why shouldn't they?

"My parents are the proof of the pudding," agreed a young woman of about 3'6". "Daddy's three-foot-five and Mommy's five-eight."

No one who spoke up seriously suggested that smalls should stick to their own kind sexually. But one man pointed out that simple eye contact could be a problem when there was too much vertical distance between a man and woman. Although he didn't say so then, this man was talking from experience; I later learned he'd once been married to a woman considerably taller than himself. Their marriage lasted only two years, he told me. In retrospect he thought that the physical gulf between them was just too great to bridge psychologically.

A small woman listening in on this post-workshop conversation said that she thought the whole question of sex between the sizes had been "resolved" too easily by the group. For her, a basic but rarely discussed question was whether smalls should "stay sexually in a safe community of little people or wander." She smiled up at me. "But we would have needed more trust to go any deeper into that issue."

As this conference drew to a close, I chatted in a motel room with a man named Lee Kitchens. Kitchens, whose 4′1″ stature results from what he called "a syndrome whose name is too long to remember," is one of America's most prominent little people. He's been featured, among other places, on the "Today" show and in *People* magazine. This man is credited with playing a key role in developing transistor radios and hand-held calculators at Texas Instruments, where he's a design engineer.

Kitchens is also a past president of the Little People of America, the 2,500-member group formed in 1957 for those 4′10″ and under. "In the past," he explained, "many little people when they met another one of the opposite sex grabbed on to each other first, thinking that might be their only chance. With this [the LPA] you have a chance to see a wide spectrum of people."

When Kitchens himself graduated from college and began thinking he might like to get married, no such organization existed. Realizing, as he put it, that "the probability of satisfactory arrangement with a normal-sized person was not too good," and being of a practical bent, as his first order of business after college Kitchens sought out smaller companionship until he met the 3′11″ woman to whom he's married. The Little People of America has today simplified the dating process for others in a similar predicament.

"That's not to say a marriage between a normal person and a person of short stature is doomed," Kitchens is quick to add. "That's not true either. We've seen several beautiful examples of how that can work, but we've also seen some where it doesn't."

Barrel-chested, dark-haired, and wearing dark-rimmed glasses — he could pass as a banker — Kitchens told me that he would be a delegate at a White House conference on problems of the handicapped the following week. He expressed concern about some of the "militants" who were certain to be there. On issues involving the handicapped, Kitchens said that he counts himself a moderate and thinks those with physical problems must adjust to the world they live in rather than demand that the world adjust to them.

"But I think I have to change my thinking to the extent that architectural barriers are unnecessary," he added. "It's not absolutely necessary that all federal buildings and courthouses have a flight of one hundred and ten steps in the front. And why have counters in the post office that can't be reached by a little person or a person in a wheelchair? Or how about a child? The guy working behind the counter can't even see the kid. There's no need for high counters there or in banks or anywhere else. It's not necessary. It's habit. And unfortunately we've had to introduce legislation to correct it."

As we left his room to go back downstairs, Kitchens gave me a little tour. From his perspective, the room's bathroom was well designed, with a low sink, tissue holder, and mirror. The closet was another story. Whipping open its accordion doors with a loud *thwap,* Kitchens proclaimed: "Useless!" Even on tiptoes he couldn't reach the crossbar overhead. "I hang my clothes on the doorknob," he explained as we left the room and I flicked off the light switch on the wall. Both it and the adjacent thermostat were beyond Kitchens's reach. So was the elevator button, which I also pushed. "They're at 'eye level' simply from habit," Kitchen explained as we descended.

"So much of what we do is just a matter of custom."

9 Big Bucks in the Boardroom

The most frequent question I'm asked is "How do I get promoted?" My answer: "The easiest way is to be born right and born tall."

— GERARD R. ROCHE, President,
Heidrick and Struggles, Inc.

While personnel director at the University of Pittsburgh, Leland Deck was to meet with a candidate for university vice-president at the city's exclusive Duquesne Club. Since his guest was delayed, Deck amused himself by watching members of Pittsburgh's establishment go by. One thing about them was unmistakable: their height. "They were," recalled Deck, *"uniformly* tall."

This observation intrigued the personnel director. He decided to explore the matter further. What Deck did was to survey a sample of Pittsburgh's graduates and compare reported height with starting salary. His results were striking. Among 91 graduates of one class, Deck found that on the average there was a $1,000-a-year salary penalty for being under 6 feet as compared with the preferred and best-rewarded height of 6'2". Those under 6 feet averaged $701 a month in starting salary, followed by 6-footers at $719, those 6'1" at $723, and those 6'2" at $788 (above this height the figures declined once again). The overall salary bonus for being 6'2" rather than 5'11" was 12.4 percent; the bonus for being cum laude was 4.2 percent. A followup study three years later confirmed the results. "Employers with first choice," Deck concluded, "get to pick the tallest candidates. Those with lower salaries choose from among the shorter.''

His conclusion did not apply just to the science and engineering graduates he had studied. Taller college teachers and librarians as well, he found, were starting at higher salaries. Among librarians, the bonus for being in the upper half of the height pool was more than three times the bonus for being in the upper half of their class academically. ''This is a scream,'' Deck told me after completing that part of his research, ''but nobody seems to want to do anything about it.'' Leland Deck's findings, compiled between 1968 and 1971, were the first real confirmation of something suspected for a long time: that the rewards for being tall in this society include money.

We'd had some inklings of this already. Three decades before Deck's study, the Provident Mutual Life Insurance Company surveyed its policyholders and found nearly a perfect correlation between body height and policy value. The average policy worth $6,180 held by those 6'4" contrasted with an average of $2,979 in life insurance bought by those 5'0" tall. Of course, amount of insurance carried doesn't prove an income differential, but it's one indicator. Here is the policy-by-height table compiled by Provident Mutual:

Height in Inches	Number of Policies	Actual Average Amount in Dollars	
60	152	2,979	
61	303	3,292	
62	828	3,176	
63	1,945	3,713	
64	5,328	3,608	
65	10,861	3,903	
66	21,165	3,976	
67	30,986	4,215	*(cont.)*

Height in Inches	Number of Policies	Actual Average Amount in Dollars
68	40,975	4,336
69	40,700	4,468
70	40,023	4,660
71	34,210	4,825
72	22,652	5,070
73	10,838	5,366
74	5,435	5,261
75	2,173	5,468
76	834	6,180
77	189	5,906

Although Provident Mutual has done no recent study of this issue, someone else has. Adam J. Boxer, an investment banker with Merrill Lynch White Weld Capital Markets Group, produced a study on the relationship between height and income. These findings provide our most thorough and most striking confirmation yet of how height influences income.

In conjunction with labor economist Lee Benham, Boxer correlated income with height in a sample of 17,000 Army Air Corps cadets who were measured in 1943. Of this group, 10,000 reported their salaries after twelve years, and 5,000 after twenty-six years. As rounded off, these figures are as follows:

Height	Mean Initial Salary	1968 Mean Salary
5'3"–5'5"	$3,500	$14,750
5'6"–5'7"	3,750	16,500
5'8"–5'9"	3,900	17,000
5'10"–5'11"	3,900	17,500
6'0"–6'1"	4,100	19,000
6'2"–6'3"	4,000	18,500
6'4"–6'6"	3,700	19,500

Obviously, in such a large and diverse group, factors other than height influence income. But even after allowing for such factors as IQ, educational level and marital status, Boxer and Benham concluded that those 6 feet and over could still count on making around 8 percent more money annually than those below 5′6″ simply as a reward for size. Boxer's terse summary: "We found a very definite income differential we could attribute solely to height."

Subsequent to this study, a telephone poll of 1,067 Canadians found that men who reported their annual income as being in the $5,000–10,000 range also reported their heights as 3.7″ shorter on the average than those who put themselves in the $25,000-plus bracket.

What's going on?

The evidence that tall people make more money than short people could just be an illustration of supply-and-demand laws at work. If taller bodies are in greater demand but in shorter supply than smaller bodies, employers will have to pay more to get one. Salary premiums for tall workers could simply be the marketplace's way of confirming that there's competition for such employees. Is this the case?

In the only study I know of that posed such a question directly, marketing professor David Kurtz of Eastern Michigan University asked 140 sales managers who they would choose between two equally qualified candidates — one who was 6′1″ or one who was 5′5″. Seventy-two percent of the sales managers said they'd take the taller candidate, 27 percent expressed no preference, and one alone said he'd take the smaller guy. After his results appeared in print, Kurtz said that the biggest response he got was from corporate personnel officers — "most acknowledging it was true."

On the other side of the interviewing table, economist John Kenneth Galbraith said that he's experienced his tallness as a competitive asset on the job market. At 6'8", he explained, "my height gave me a range of opportunity that I would never have had otherwise, because people always remember the guy whose head stands high above the others when they are trying to think of somebody for a job."

But such a hiring bias is extremely hard to document. Although discrimination in hiring against racial minorities, ethnic groups, and women has been studied to a fare-thee-well, discrimination based on height is virtually untouched as a subject of serious inquiry. When he was unable to find any research preceding his own on the subject, Leland Deck suggested that perhaps "we don't talk or write on the subject because we don't want to offend tall people or discourage short people. We don't want to imply that the tall man obtained his present level of success with an advantage that is, in fact, meaningless. We don't want to tell the short youngster that it is better to be tall and at the bottom of the class than to be short and at the top of the class."

In a rare attempt to survey job discrimination based on height, *U.S. News and World Report* concluded that although such bias could affect up to half of all Americans, it is virtually impossible to get the subject out in the open. Even those who are targets of such discrimination may not want it brought out. A short midwestern banking executive sent word to the magazine through his secretary that he didn't even want to be *mentioned* in an article on height discrimination. A further problem, the article suggested, is that vocational bias against the short can be quite subtle. A short person turned down for a job due to lack of stature will not normally be told the reason. "It's like fighting a ghost," one employment firm executive said of his difficulty in confronting height discrimination by employers.

A pro-tall bias in hiring can be so subtle that even those employers engaged in it may not realize what they're doing. Harry

Scharlatt, who conducts management development seminars for Union Carbide, told me that during workshops on interviewing he sometimes asks personnel administrators to tick off in a stream of consciousness the qualities that impress them favorably in a job candidate. "Tall" is an adjective that regularly recurs high on such lists. At 5'8½" Scharlatt may find this a little disconcerting, but it doesn't really surprise him. At the outset of his seminars participants break up into buzz groups and pick leaders. Scharlatt said that at times he'll convince such groups he's a wizard by betting he can choose their leader before he's told. All he does is point to the tallest member, and generally that's the person who's been chosen.

Once, however, he was wrong. A shorter buzz-grouper had been chosen leader. Inquiring further Scharlatt discovered the source of his error: the tallest member had indeed been elected leader, but had refused the job and turned it over to someone smaller.

To discover more about height biases among employers, I polled some executive recruiters. Robert Half, president of the country's largest employment agency for accountants and financial officers, said indeed it's been his experience that tall people have an easier time being hired because "they fulfill an image — they look the part." Half has also found that the better paying the job, the more short candidates — like overweight ones — are penalized. "But in my opinion short is worse than overweight," he said, "because overweight something can be done about. Short . . . if you're short, you're short. It's worse because it's cruel."

One executive recruiter on Wall Street who did not want to be quoted by name told me he's found that for high-visibility jobs especially — corporation presidents, executive vice-presidents, stockholder representatives — and especially for consumer-oriented companies with big ad budgets — tallness was nearly a prerequisite for candidates. He and his colleagues find this value so implicitly adhered to in filling jobs that pay $50,000 a year and up that they consider it a joke. "You send over two people who are equally qualified," he explained, "and they'll pick the taller, better-looking guy every time. They always seem to want Gregory Peck."

Tall himself, the recruiter added that on occasion clients have come right out and said that they wanted prospects as big as he. It's a matter of "cosmetics," he explained. "Sometimes, being professional, I'll recommend a guy who doesn't look as good. But they'll keep on pushing. Sometimes they get stiffed and deserve it. A short guy might have been better."

Other recruiters said that they find it uncommon, especially in today's legal climate, for a client to specify a particular size for candidates. But such a desire can still be implicit. Recruiter David Chambers, president of the Manhattan firm bearing his name, said that height is part of a complex of client preferences it's his business to pick up — often by simple intuition. In general, he said, people tend to hire in their own image, including height. Thus talls at the top may perpetuate themselves. But it can also work the other way. Chambers once had a 5′10″ candidate rejected as "too tall" for a sales manager's job. All his salesmen were short, the company president explained, and he was sure they'd be uncomfortable working for a bigger boss.

So in hiring, it's the connotations of height that are at issue. As Chambers discovered, this can cut both ways. But to the degree that an employer values the "look" of extra height — "the tall, dynamic, jut-jawed type," in the words of one — he will seek the extra inch.

Consider a company such as IBM. IBM's former Director of Corporate Information Tom Mechling told me that for visible representatives of that company — salesmen, public relations people, corporate officers — an unwritten rule has historically given preference to talls. This never was spelled out, said Mechling, recalling his years at IBM in the mid-sixties. People just knew what "image" was expected in such slots. "It was a tradition," he explained, "that IBM had a big, robust sales staff. In appearance they wanted salesmen to look domineering, aggressive. Tallness was part of that." Since corporate officers tended to percolate up from the sales staff, Mechling added, this hiring bias imbued the whole company — from the Watsons, father and son, through himself (6'2"), to former Director of Stockholder Information Carter Henderson (6'7") and T. Vincent Learson (6'6"), who ultimately became the company's chairman. Learson has been described in a book on IBM as "among the biggest of the hundreds of big men in a corporation whose leadership over the years looked with favor on outsized specimens."

One corporate consultant told me that the executives with whom she works seem tall overall. A major source of her observation is personal perspective: at 5'3", she spends the most painful parts of her business day looking up. "I do my best work sitting down," she added. "Actually, I do my best work standing up when everybody *else* is sitting down." Unfortunately this isn't always possible. Especially when the day's done and everybody goes out for drinks, the consultant said, she finds she spends a lot of time with her neck crooked. Recently, at a post-consultation cocktail party, this woman was cornered by another woman who asked, "How can you be a consultant to a major corporation? You're *short.*"

Let's look at the record. Is there any evidence that tall people work better than short people? Outside of basketball and lumberjacking, I've yet to find any such evidence. But there is data to the contrary, from two sources in particular: performance records of salesmen (which are easily judged by sales volume) and court cases involving height requirements.

At North Texas State University, Dr. Joseph Murrey devoted his 1976 Ph.D. thesis to evaluating the sales records of life-insurance salesmen (and a few women) relative to their size. A medium-sized former insurance salesman himself, Murrey assumed he would find that talls sell more. It always seemed to him that they did. And sales managers he polled were nearly unanimous in expressing their opinion that this was the case. What Murrey discovered, however, was that the height of an agent did not have much bearing on the amount of insurance that individual sold. The tallest agents among 72 Murrey studied did not sell significantly more insurance than the rest. "The results of this study," he concluded, "do not enhance the fact or fiction of 'height' alone as a factor in sales production." But the companies involved obviously thought otherwise. Their salesmen averaged 5'10.85" — more than 1½ inches above the national men's average.

Murrey's findings have been confirmed repeatedly in other, less ambitious studies of sales performance relative to height. Such studies generally have found that taller applicants are more likely to be hired as salesmen, but not more likely to have a better sales record than shorter colleagues. If anything, salesmen of average height have been found to be the most productive.

Perhaps sales managers are working on a false premise: that fear creates a good sales climate. "What the study showed," said Eastern Michigan University's David Kurtz of his finding that sales managers uniformly prefer tall employees, "is that some people think the blond Teutonic that comes hulking into your office is more intimidating and therefore a better salesman."

It could be the other way around. Clothing consultant John T.

Molloy once kept a video recorder focused on salesmen and purchasing agents during several weeks of transactions. The agents didn't know they were being taped. Reviewing these tapes later, Molloy was impressed with how rude, bordering on abusive, such prospects became when confronted with a sales-man taller than themselves. "After some in-depth questioning," Molloy reported later in his book *Dress for Success,* "I came to the conclusion that when a man who is selling is much larger than the man who is buying, he can and often does frighten the buyer. . . . A frightened man . . . will escape from you, even if it means throwing you out of the office."

Molloy said that when he mentioned this hypothesis to two large salesmen, both agreed readily that scaring clients posed a real problem for them. Yet both were successful salesmen. How did they compensate for their size? Explained the first: "When I walk into a man's office and I catch that glimmer of fear in his eyes . . . I simply fall down. I pretend I've hurt my leg and have him help me. That puts *me* in the defensive position and enables me to make the sale." Said the second: "Whenever I see a man on the defensive, I simply drop my papers all over the floor and start groveling for them. Often the man comes around and helps me, and when he does, I usually have a sure sale."

What's suggestive in both these cases is that sales success was equated not with dominance but submission. Faced with the danger of overpowering a client by their physical size alone, both salesmen did their own version of a kowtow.

One could even speculate that the shorter salesman has an ad-vantage because he's less threatening to prospects of all sizes. In fact, a study of 37 insurance salesmen done before Murrey's found somewhat higher sales figures for shorter salesmen. And the acknowledged national leader in life insurance sales — Ohio's Ben Feldman — is a known short person. But sales managers, like so many employers, will probably continue to give preference to tall applicants for the same reason that Frederick William preferred tall soldiers: somehow they just *look* more up to the job.

David Landsberg said one reason he's a comedian today is because his size made straight work so hard to find. Landsberg tried without success to break into marketing or sales, but got the distinct impression that at 5′2″ he didn't impress employers as the take-charge type. He then applied to be a wildlife officer. What would ducks care? he thought. But ducks don't do the hiring. The people who did, said Landsberg, turned him down on the ground of height. "They said," he recalled, " 'You are too short. You are too tiny. There is a height requirement of five-foot-six.'

"So I said, 'Well, Jeez, the animals will really understand that. I can just see some duck saying, 'Oh, fuck him. He's only five-two.' "

In recent years such height requirements have been challenged repeatedly as discriminatory against women and some minority groups. Most such challenges have been in the public sector — in the field of law enforcement especially. In 1973, 97 percent of the police forces surveyed by the Police Foundation had minimum-height requirements averaging 5′8″. "It has long been the shared belief of the law enforcement community," this report pointed out, "that the height of a police officer has an important effect on the officer's job performance."

But defending this belief with evidence has proved difficult. In one celebrated case, a 5′5″ woman took the police force of East Cleveland to court, demanding that officials justify a height minimum of 5′8″. The subsequent "justification" consisted largely of testimony from members of the police department that height was necessary to their work in terms of strength and credibility. Challenging this contention were expert witnesses

Herman

"Surely you can appreciate we need a height regulation in the police force?"

Herman

"I don't know if they told you outside but I never employ anyone over 5 feet tall."

who testified that modern police methods deemphasize brute strength in favor of "leverage strength," which may in fact be exercised better by smaller bodies than larger ones. (East Cleveland's police were at that very time being taught jujitsu by a 5'2" woman.) These witnesses further testified that there was no evidence tall bodies absorbed blows better or that they deterred violence by their appearance alone. In fact half of the thirty assaults on East Cleveland police officers in the three years preceding had involved assailants smaller than the officer. Such testimony went unrefuted by the police. In striking down East Cleveland's height requirement, the judge ruled that he was "unable to find rational support for the height and weight requirements" and concluded that "the requirements are based solely on the stereotype of the large male officer." The judge added that no decision he could find anywhere else had reached any other conclusion.

A body of such decisions have made height requirements largely a thing of the past not just for policemen but for such other officials as firefighters, lifeguards, and professional baseball umpires, whose 5'10" minimum would have excluded even "the legendary Bill Klem," as one judge pointed out. The crowning blow was a 1977 U.S. Supreme Court decision striking down minimum-size requirements for Alabama prison guards. The state of Alabama, explained Justice Potter Stewart for the majority, "produced no evidence correlating the height and weight requirements with the requisite amount of strength thought essential to good job performance. Indeed, they failed to offer evidence of any kind in specific justification of the statutory standards."

On occasion height standards have been upheld in court as clearly necessary for the work involved. In one such case a minimum-height requirement for Ozark Airline pilots was retained (though lowered two inches, to 5'5") because cockpit controls were designed for that minimum size of user. On the other hand, when an application to be a "trainman" by a 5-foot woman named Carol Wagner was rejected by the Long Island Rail Road ostensibly because 5'7" was the minimum height necessary to reach ceiling buttons for signaling the engineer, her lawyer pointed out that exceptions had already been made for men shorter than 5'7", who didn't seem to be having any problem on the job. The company responded by transferring these men. Eventually the courts struck down the trainman minimum as discriminatory against 95 percent of the nation's women. In her victory statement, Wagner hailed the decision as a victory "for all women and all short people."

This statement in fact was a bit redundant, because in vocational terms, most women *are* short people.

It has often been alleged that vocational height requirements are a subterfuge to keep women and minorities from certain kinds of work. But I wonder if these minimums may not be sincere — sincerely biased against all short people regardless of race, creed, or sex. "One of my prime hypotheses," Leland Deck emphasized, "is that the alleged employment discrimination against women is more a matter of discrimination in favor of tallness." Deck found that in his study men under 6 feet and women in general both made salaries averaging 10 percent lower than men 6 feet and over. Although he found little bonus for being a taller woman (his sample didn't include many), Deck did find that the penalty for being under 5'4" among women teaching college was $440 in annual salary relative to the salaries made by women 5'4" and over doing the same work.

A small woman, being that much shorter than a short man, has double trouble on the job market. One of the primary complaints made by such women in interviews with me and on the questionnaire was their unusual difficulty in finding work. At times employers' rejections were explicit. A 5'1" woman in public relations was originally turned down by a stock exchange for being too short to chalk up figures on their quotation board. A 5-foot secretary was told by a major Boston department store that she was too small to fit in with the rest of its sales force. (At least they weren't lying, the woman added; to this day she has to look up to all the sales help when she shops in that store.)

U.S. Congresswoman Shirley Chisholm, not much over 5 feet tall and weighing just 90 pounds, couldn't find work after college even as a teacher's aide until, with characteristic indignation, she exploded, "Don't judge me by my size!" and was given a successful tryout.

But employment bias against short women seldom comes out in the open. "They just say things like, 'Um, we're not sure you could handle the work,' " explained a 5'1" recent college graduate of her problems finding a job as an administrative assistant. "I've had to resort to my highest heels and most aggressive manner just to get interviewed." Though this tactic finally succeeded and she found work at a major university, even on the job this woman said she still felt the need to be extra tough and hard-bitten to keep from being treated like a china doll.

Marilee, the 5'2" woman I chatted with in La Jolla, had recently given up in despair after a year as the first woman of any height working as a day manager of a local restaurant. Some of the problem was with customers. To illustrate, Marilee pantomimed:

[*Looking down*] Could I speak to the manager?
[*Looking up*] You are.
[*Looking down*] No, the *real* manager.
[*Looking straight ahead*] It used to make me soooo mad!

Deliverymen were a constant aggravation, she added; they refused to believe that this little slip of a thing had the authority to sign for supplies. But the biggest problem was with tall male subordinates. Marilee vividly remembered one guy in particular, a big waiter who hovered over her one day, hands on hips, openly defying her right to tell him what to do. She made her order to him stick, but regular repetitions of such scenes grew exhausting.

Over time the metaphor for Marilee's frustration became her problems with the restaurant's high shelves. "I can't tell you how angry you get when you can't reach something," she explained. "I can't tell you how many times I stood there and just felt like *screeeeam*ing!

"And all those guys would be standing around saying, 'Marilee can't do it. She's the boss and she can't do it!' And I'd get so furious that I would pile chairs on top of chairs before I'd let anyone help me."

Other than Deck's work, I know of no attention paid in this country to vocational bias against short women as such. After noting the demonstrated discrimination based on height found among male job hunters, 5-foot Judith Wax commented, "I've never seen a similar survey about the size/hire ratio for women, but I *do* know that a lot of people tend to treat us as if an undersized brain is the inevitable complement of your cute little body." A survey in Scotland once found that twice as many working women classified as tall (4 inches or more over Aberdeen women's average of 5'2½") had done professional or clerical work than had those classified as short (2½ inches or more below the average). The shorter women, it was found, were three times more likely than the taller ones to be working in unskilled jobs.

The only bit of American data I have along this line besides Deck's is Joseph Murrey's finding that the 22 women among the larger insurance agents he studied were an inch taller than the national average. Also, the 5'3" consultant mentioned earlier said that not only the men but also the women she deals with at the top of the corporate world seem much taller than she.

It would be foolish (and risky legally) for someone with an available job to eliminate short women out of hand. But when I inquired informally of those with job openings whether they'd fill them with a short woman, the clarity of response was striking. No one I asked said he would seriously consider a short woman for an "outside" job. For an "inside" job, such as clerical work, perhaps — but not for a job involving public contact. "I've got enough problems without clients getting my representatives confused with their teenage daughter," explained an advertising executive. The issue in his case was not hypothetical. The man had just reluctantly turned down a "dynamite" woman of 4'11" who had applied to be an account executive — a job for which he'd already hired a woman of 5'11". "A good-looking tall woman can be taken seriously," he said, "a good-looking short woman is dead."

These words were echoed by a corporate officer who said he'd be reluctant to hire a saleswoman under 5'8". "Height is part of attractiveness," this man explained. "Her whole image is just more impressive if she's attractive."

Short women in business have a real credibility problem. Even when they make it big their success is recognized with a titter. "Barely 5 feet tall," said *Newsweek* of the head of Waterman Pen, "blond and attractive Francine Gomez seems more like a pretty china doll than the chairman and chief executive of a well-known French corporation."

Letitia Baldrige once commented to reporter Fred Katz that she didn't think her career in business would have progressed nearly so well had she not been 6 feet tall. After working for firms such as Burlington Industries, Tiffany's, and Chicago's Merchandise Mart, Baldrige set up her own public relations firm. Assessing the vocational value of her height, she told

Katz: "I feel a woman in business who is tall commands a certain amount of authority which if she were five-foot-two with eyes of blue she might not be able to command. Perhaps it's because men are willing to accept that she has the same intellectual capacity that they do."

In responding to my questionnaire, two different teachers, one of 5'8", the other 5'9", both used the phrase "I can hold my own" to describe the advantage they felt their height gave them in dealing with colleagues and superiors at work.

"It gives me the upper hand in some ways" is the way a 6-foot financial analyst for a Wall Street investment firm told me her height influences life on the job. Among men especially, she reported no problem being taken seriously, due in part to the credibility inspired by her size. She didn't doubt that a degree of intimidation might also be involved, especially with smaller male colleagues. But this can also present problems. Her boss, for example, who was more than half a foot shorter, would often bark: "Sit down! I can't talk to you. You're like the Eiffel Tower!"

Actress Nancy Marchand (who plays the publisher of Lou Grant's newspaper) has said that at 5'10" her problems at work have had a lot to do with the sensitivities of short producers. "Certain producers," she explained, "told me that when they first met me they thought, 'You're so tall that I feel like a worm!' I worked for a certain short producer in New York who wouldn't speak to me when I was standing up. He would look like he didn't recognize me, and I didn't understand, because at other times he was warm and cordial. Then I realized he was only warm and cordial when I was sitting down."

Taller working women have special problems keeping everyone comfortable about their height. This often calls for imagination, and strategy. Meeting a smaller client being shown into one's office, for example, may make it necessary to lean over and shuffle papers on a desk before looking — *up* — with a greeting. Colleagues pose a different set of problems for the tall woman. ''It's very important to sit for your boss but stand over a subordinate,'' explained a 5′9″ media executive. In the wintertime, she added, the ''politics of boots'' becomes important and makes it essential to leave a pair of flats in the office for the occasions when her extra inches pose too much of a problem for a smaller person with whom she must do business.

Managing heels is a wonderfully complex issue for taller women at work. Terry Smith, who at 5′7″ thinks she was the tallest woman during two recent years on the Democratic National Committee staff, said the more important the meeting she had to attend, the higher the heels she noticed she'd wear. On days of DNC Executive Committee meetings Smith found herself choosing a particularly uncomfortable pair of bone sandals with 3-inch wooden heels. ''For a long time I never knew why I was even getting those shoes out of the closet,'' she explained. ''Then I realized it was because I was going to be in a crowd and wanted to stand out. I realized I was wearing those torture chambers just to look big.''

Smith, an attractive brunette with a voice full of Alabama, said she feels the greatest need for a lift underfoot when first meeting a man with whom she must do business. After establishing her credentials and her competence, she can then switch to more comfortable, lower shoes. But at times this strategy becomes a gaffe, particularly when the man she's meeting for the first time turns out to be shorter than her 5′10″ in heels. ''Then,'' she said, ''I spend a lot of time sitting down.''

Women at least have the option of putting on or taking off high heels. Men must be more resourceful — smaller ones, that is. Tall men needn't exercise much imagination in their height maneuvers at work. All they have to do is sidle up to a smaller colleague and glare down upon him, or rise *slooowly* from their chair at a meeting and let others observe inch by inch the grandeur rising before them. But smalls must be creative. "Sitting on the desk is a great move," suggested Harry Scharlatt. "Anything that gives you any kind of height above somebody taller than you."

As part of his training seminars at Union Carbide, Scharlatt includes a section on "non-verbals." This always is a popular workshop, he told me — especially the part on equalizing height differentials. "Basically I just tell them to pull some tricks," explained Scharlatt with a grin beneath his blond mustache and devilish blue eyes. "Give that person looking down on you a smaller chair. Stand up while he's sitting down. Wander around the room even, so that he won't get up also. Sit on the desk. Anything that gives you any kind of height above him. If you can't get it, back away from him so you've got more distance. Or put a barrier between you. Put your desk between you and the person coming in. Then height's not as important anymore, because you're not so close." (Scharlatt was quick to add that such tactics are unnecessary around a taller colleague with whom the shorter person feels comfortable. He pointed out with a laugh that he feels so good about his own 6'2" boss that he can even remain seated while the taller man is standing and feel at ease.)

Trained in behavioral sciences, Scharlatt uses a number of means during his workshops to demonstrate the body maneuvering that goes on in business dealings. One such technique is to videotape and play back role-playing exercises. Recently he had one participant play a government affirmative-action officer arguing with a company representative. Both were tall. "The company guy was losing his argument with the government," Scharlatt said, "and the guy in the government stood up and started to point at him without realizing it. So the other guy stood up to equalize his position. When he thought he had won his point, he'd sit down. Then the other guy would. Then one of them would stand again. It was like jack-in-the-box.''

According to Scharlatt, such activities usually strike a responsive chord among participants, who start looking around to see who's taller and who's smaller. Commonly they start talking about height interactions in their personal lives — with wives especially — in addition to those at work. During one session a participant insisted that the head of his division had cut 3 inches off the legs of the chair facing his desk to get an extra edge in eye contact. Scharlatt chuckled at the memory and went on: ''He said, 'Yeah, my boss cuts three inches — I swear.' We were laughing hysterically.''

Whether due to the changing legal climate, the rise of Al Pacino, or the fall of Randy Newman, there are small, hesitant signs that the employment picture for smalls may be improving. Recruiter Robert Half said that, unlike a few years ago, he is no longer asked to send only candidates 6 feet or over for certain jobs. At Manhattan's Life Extension Institute, Dr. Harry Johnson recently tabulated the measured heights of 500 executives who had undergone physical examinations and to his surprise found they averaged 5'9.2" — a mere fraction of an inch over the male norm. And at IBM, Frank Cary, who is reportedly under 6 feet tall, is at this writing chairman of the board.

So perhaps we're not as hung up on height in employment as we once were. But that isn't to say there won't always be certain lines of work more suited to particular sizes of body by aptitude, tradition, or stereotype. In the course of my research I've collected bits of information on types of work that supposedly are suited either to talls or smalls. Perhaps this list will prove useful in determining which jobs to choose or avoid.

A Hardly Definitive List of Jobs for the Tall or Small

TALL JOBS

Airline Customer-Service Agent: Defending in court its decision to hire a 6′4″ man over a 5′4″ woman for this job, Braniff Airways pointed out that height was helpful for reaching cargo-bin doors — in Boeing 727s especially.

Basketball Player: *See* chapter 12.

Chorus Girl: Tall showgirls historically have been paid more and displayed more prominently in the middle of chorus lines than shorter "ponies" on the end. A typical call: "Attractive female dancers (especially tall, large-proportioned girls) needed for chorus line." The Lido in Las Vegas advertises for "Female Dancers — 5′8″ and up."

Criminal: In defending the need for tall cops, the Texas Department of Public Safety made the point that the FBI and other compilers of such statistics have found that criminals are generally above average in height. Anthropometric measurements of criminals in the 1930s found talls especially well represented in the robbery and homicide categories.

Doorman: Commenting on the observation that talls dominate executive rolls, an industrial psychologist once observed, "There is little doubt that a similar survey of doormen would bring like results."

Lumberjack: A study of champion Finnish lumberjacks found them taller than average and concluded that their "work output was positively correlated with general body size."

Miss America: A statistical study of 20 Miss Americas through 1978 found that they ranged from 5′4″ to 5′10″, 5′7″ on the average — the height of 1979's winner, Cheryl Prewitt. An earlier report about this tendency to tallness suggested that "the pageant management does not see a short girl as representing the Miss America mystique."

Model: Female models traditionally are tall. One report said of top model agent Eileen Ford: "[Her] standards *are* high — at least five feet seven." Ford herself has said the ideal woman's model measures between 5′7″ and 5′9″.

Stock-and-Bond Salesman: On top of the general predisposition for height among salesmen, this particular branch is crowded with ex-jocks.

Superintendent of Street Cleaners: A study of forty occupational groups made early this century by New York University Professor Enoch Gowin found that members of this profession were the tallest of all.

Teamster: Champion truck drivers at one rally were measured and found to be taller than participants as a whole.

SMALL JOBS

Astronaut: Smaller bodies (e.g., Charles Conrad, Frank Borman) fit into space capsules better; special indentations must be made for taller bodies. The first Polish astronaut had to sleep on the ceiling "since I am a very tall guy." (His shorter comrades got to sleep on the walls.)

Ball Club Mascot: Ted Giannoulas won his job as the San Diego Padres' fabled "Chicken" because at 5′4″ he was the only applicant who fit inside the costume.

Blacksmith: Pennsylvania blacksmith Jim Hall has said his 5′7″ height is an advantage when shoeing horses: "Being so close to the ground, I don't have to stoop as much as a taller guy would."

Entrepreneur: From Andrew Carnegie to McDonald's Ray Kroc, smalls have found a big advantage in not being subject to personnel departments. "Thank God size doesn't matter when you're self-employed," said the owner of Shorty's Bakery in Taylor, Michigan.

Military Hero: Geneticist Francis Galton once estimated that larger soldiers were at least one-third more likely to get hit in battle. "The enemy's bullets are least dangerous to the smallest men," he wrote, "and therefore small men are more likely to achieve high fame as commanders than their equally gifted contemporaries whose physical frames are larger."

Photographer: Alfred Eisenstaedt, Francesco Scavullo, E. J. Bellocq, Imogen Cunningham, Yousuf Karsh, Mathew Brady, Andy Warhol — all small. One short news photographer has cited an advantage in being able to squeeze up front in crowds. Had victims realized that professional photographers tend not to be tall, they might not have been duped by a 6′3″ impostor who pretended to be the much smaller Richard Avedon.

Psychologist: In the words of two such professionals — "Psychologists are just like everybody else, only shorter."

Radio Reporter: A tall newspaperwoman once observed that "radio reporters are shorter than most people. They tend to burrow up from the ground at crowded press conferences, slinging their mikes like medieval bludgeons."

Rock Star: Recent smaller rock 'n' rollers include Peter Frampton, Mick Jagger, Billy Joel, Elton John, Bette Midler, Van Morrison, Suzi Quatro, Linda Ronstadt, Leo Sayer, Neil Sedaka, and Ringo Starr. Of an earlier rocker, the late Bobby Darin, a profiler once noted: "Like [Paul] Anka and most of his contemporaries, he is short."

Sailor: From John Paul Jones through Horatio Nelson to Hyman Rickover, there have always been good opportunities for small people afloat. After studying naval records through the Revolution, Harvard anthropologist Gordon Bowles speculated that "ship's masters chose the shorter men because they were steadier on their feet, took up less room, and ate less food."

Saint: From tiny Saints Francis of Assisi and Xavier, to the recently canonized "Little Bishop" John Neumann of Philadelphia (and recent Nobel laureate Mother Teresa), there's lots of opportunity for sainthood among smaller people. The ancient Egyptians worshiped gods who were midgets — as was Gregory, Bishop of Tours some centuries later. When geneticist Karl Pearson determined that excavated skeletons of medieval Anglo-Saxon bishops were short, he suggested that "probably the bishops were men unsuited for fighting, and showing a lower degree of physical development." Neither Popes John XXIII nor Paul VI were tall men, and although Popes John Paul I and II were somewhat taller, upon taking office the former referred to himself as "a little man, accustomed to little things."

Theatrical Agent: The William Morris Agency's renowned overall shortness has been called "the rule of Tom Thumb." After doing business there, one 6′6″ screenwriter reported: "Whenever I had to go into the [William Morris] office, I felt like Gulliver. I kept thinking they were going to throw me down and tie my hair to the carpet."

STUMPERS

Comedians: Before discovering the tallness of Jerry Lewis, Sid Caesar, Chevy Chase, David Brenner, et al., I thought "tall" and "comedian" was a contradiction in terms; combine them with smaller comics Mel Brooks, Woody Allen, Don Rickles, the Marx Brothers, David Steinberg, Bob Newhart, George Burns, Jack Benny, Bob Hope, George Carlin, et al. and call this a Divided Zone.

Politicians: Another mixed bag . . .

10 Voting by the Inch

Jimmy Carter, Ted Kennedy and Jerry Brown will stand throughout their 90-minute debate in Des Moines, Iowa, Jan. 7 [1980]. Carter's representative had argued that the participants would be more comfortable sitting down — and, of course, the 5-foot 9½-inch President wouldn't look that much shorter than the 6-foot 2-inch senator if both were seated.

— News item [On Dec. 29, 1979,
President Carter withdrew, and
the debate didn't take place.]

As a child Jimmy Carter always was small. Not only was he shorter than most of his classmates, he also was shorter than his younger sister Gloria for most of the years they were growing up. "He wasn't shy," she has reminisced about her brother at this time. "He was little. . . . He was always wondering if he'd ever grow."

Like most smaller men, Carter doesn't talk much about his height except to deny on occasion that it's affected him. A rare exception was the President's explanation of why he got so much pleasure from seeing women lined up to dance with him at White House social functions. "You don't know what it's like," said Carter, "being a 5′3″ kid in high school."

This was Carter's height when he graduated. Although he recalls growing 3 inches in his first year out of high school, Carter was still able to play under-140-pound football throughout his tenure at the Naval Academy.

Jimmy Carter is remembered as being neither very large nor very imposing during his earliest days in politics. A Georgia newsman who covered his statewide campaigns recalled him as "a shuffling, timid, bird-faced little guy with no presence."

Repeatedly those who have met Carter tell me how stunned

they are by his smallness. "We established chin-to-eye contact" is the way 6-foot Carter delegate Robert Ellis Smith described his first meeting with the Democratic candidate. A subsequent visitor to the White House told me she was startled to note how close in size First Lady Rosalynn Carter was to her husband.

Carter's success at fooling our eye is due to a number of factors. In the first place, we see him most often on television, which reduces size differences of all kinds. In the second place, during his first campaign for the presidency Carter was especially careful to avoid being put in positions that would betray his lack of stature. Though other factors were involved, the fact that Ed Muskie towered over the Democratic nominee by a good 8 inches did not improve the Maine senator's prospects for being chosen as Carter's vice-presidential running mate. Clasping hands and raising arms with Muskie would have forced Jimmy Carter to spend a lot of time on tiptoes, if not dangling in the air. My hunch is that the moment Muskie reached down to shake hands with Carter in Plains, the smaller man began to consider someone closer to the size of Walter Mondale. Carter himself is not known to have commented unfavorably on Muskie's relative size, but members of Carter's campaign staff thought the tall senator physically ludicrous as a potential running mate for their boss.

The climax of Carter's efforts to keep us from realizing his height occurred during his first debate with Gerald Ford. Carter's camp was jittery at the thought of their candidate standing right next to the 6'1" Republican President for all the world to see who was bigger. For this reason they initially demanded that both debaters be seated. Losing on this point, the Democrat's negotiators finally settled for the candidates' lecterns being placed far enough apart that the two men's height difference would not be so apparent. (In return, the Democrats agreed to a background pale enough to camouflage Ford's paucity of hair.)

When the opponents finally faced off on national television, Jimmy Carter made their moment of physical proximity as short-lived as possible — by sticking his arm out stiffly to hold the President at bay as they briefly shook hands, then scurrying back to the safety of his lectern.

The incredible thing was that Ford let him get away with it. It made you wonder if this guy was just too nice to be President. A killer-instinct politician such as Lyndon Johnson would have known just what to do with such a heaven-sent opportunity: grab the smaller man's extended hand and hang on tight, then reel him in slowly like a flounder before draping a big arm low about Carter's shoulder in the friendliest fashion and scooting him under one armpit just long enough for the American people to get a good, long look at who was bigger, who had the most stature, who appeared most — like a President. But to Jimmy Carter's everlasting relief, Gerald Ford just shook hands politely and sauntered back to his lectern.

As a result of the care he took, no one since Mae West did a more effective job of fooling the American eye than Jimmy Carter. Among 305 responses to my various questionnaires filled out early in his presidential career, 52.46 percent thought Carter was as tall or taller than Nixon. Part of Carter's success was due to the gimmicky stuff — the carefully placed lecterns, the appropriate-sized running mate. But the man was also subtle. Jimmy Carter just didn't act like a little guy. He walked slowly, talked softly, held himself straight, but — here's where the genius comes in — not *too* straight. Carter walks with just the hint of a slouch, as if he had an inch to spare.

"He stands erect," said psychiatrist and presidential adviser Peter Bourne of his former boss. "He keeps his body motions to a minimum. There's an economy of movement one associates with greater stature."

Elevator shoes?

"Oh, no."

Sure?

"As a matter of fact," Bourne said in his soft Oxford-Atlanta accent, "I have spent a lot of time with him in his sock feet and found him little shorter than when shod."

Subsequent to our conversation, Dr. Bourne had to vacate his White House office due to a problem with a prescription. Up to that time Bourne was, in Jimmy Carter's words, "about the closest friend I have in the world." They continued to visit regularly even after Bourne resigned. Acquainted with Carter since the chief executive was governor of Georgia in the late sixties, Peter Bourne is credited with writing the first memo suggesting that Carter run for the presidency. Bourne was subsequently part of that campaign until its successful conclusion.

Bourne confirmed that Jimmy Carter's relative lack of stature was of some concern to his political advisers. And this didn't relate just to Gerald Ford. During their initial brainstorming while Nixon was still President, Carter's Georgia mafia had pegged former Texas Governor John Connally as the probable Republican nominee. Since "Big" precedes "John Connally" like "Jimmy" precedes "Carter" in commentators' mouths, the inches and pounds separating these two men were taken seriously indeed. But once Nixon resigned and Ford became the GOP threat, attention in the Carter camp turned to tall rival Democrats.

Oddly enough, 6'5" Congressman Morris Udall was not the opposing candidate whose size most concerned them, said Bourne. Since the Arizonan's height bordered on freakish, they figured it might actually work against him — make Udall seem a Goliath bullying Carter's David. Of greater concern to Carter's people from a height perspective were Democrats such as Indiana Senator Birch Bayh and former Peace Corps Director Sargent Shriver, who with their few extra inches of height each "looked more presidential." But, Bourne said, there wasn't much they could do about those early size match-ups other than be grateful that most group debates among candidates took place while they were sitting down.

Assuming Carter was renominated and ran for reelection in 1980, Bourne thought that from a height standpoint an ideal opponent would be Senator Howard Baker of Tennessee. Since he's as short if not shorter than the President, Baker's nomination would neatly neutralize size as a campaign concern. John Connally, on the other hand, would present as big a problem as always. But by the time you got up to a Big Jim Thompson — Illinois' 6'6" governor — you were back to Goliath country where Carter could once again play an effective David.

"I see this whole thing as being a sort of bell-shaped curve," the psychiatrist concluded, "where there is sort of an acceptable range in the middle — five-foot-nine to six-foot-one or so. Within that range, slight differences matter. So with a five-foot-ten candidate against one six-foot, say, the six-footer might be perceived as of greater stature." Bourne smiled at his choice of word.

Ever since smaller John Adams complained that taller George Washington was "like the Hebrew sovereign chosen because he was taller by the head than the other Jews," relative physical stature has been a regular item on our presidential agenda. At 5'4" — our shortest President — James Madison was subjected to constant ridicule for his lack of stature. Madison tried to compensate with a tall hat and taller wife, but he only succeeded in making himself look smaller in comparison. "A withered little apple-john," Washington Irving called the fourth President. Madison's wife, Dolley, affectionately called him "little Jemmie."

"Being so low of stature," a contemporary observed of Madison, "he was in imminent danger of being confounded with the plebeian crowd, and was pushed and jostled like a common citizen — but not so her ladyship! The towering feathers and excessive throng pointed her station wherever she moved."

From Madison through Stephen Douglas to Jimmy Carter, the issue of height has continued to bedevil presidential hopefuls who felt they didn't have enough of it. During the 1948 primaries, Thomas Dewey stood more than half a foot smaller than his 6-foot-plus principal opponent, Harold Stassen. After being mousetrapped into standing right next to Stassen during one joint appearance, Dewey subsequently showed up wearing elevator shoes.

During the 1968 presidential primaries, a Michigan woman pulled off Robert Kennedy's size-8½ shoe as a souvenir. Inside she discovered an arch support. Whether this was intended for anything more than support of his arch was never made clear. Two years before, when *Newsweek* had asked the surviving Kennedy brothers to pose jointly for a picture, Bob sent word via Ted that he really didn't have time for such foolishness. If they had to have a joint photograph, the magazine was told, then a stock picture of Bob could be pasted next to one of Ted; but it *must* show the older, smaller Kennedy standing slightly above his younger, taller brother.

Concern about height by those who hope to be President is not simply a matter of vanity. For years it's been gospel that the taller candidate normally wins. According to Peter Bourne, this piece of information was one among many that Carter's team considered seriously in their early planning. But is it accurate?

For the past decade a University of Chicago statistics professor named William Kruskal has made a hobby out of bird-dogging the data on which the taller-candidate-wins conclusions is based. So far he's come up empty. Kruskal thinks the "statistic" originated with a 1960 article in *This Week* titled "The Tall

Man Gets Elected.'' When queried, the author of this article was unable to locate for Kruskal the files on which his conclusion was based. Yet many others have reached the same conclusion since — sometimes offering evidence, more often not. Kruskal contacts them all.

''When I tried to find documentation,'' he wrote, ''I met with consistent frustration. Authors of the articles were evasive or just quoted one another, and I ended up unsure of the facts. Height, after all, is not that well defined; it varies with age and time of day, and it depends on whether shoes — Adlerian or not — are counted in. The height differences between candidates have often been small, and ex post facto distortion — or choice of one of several height values — may have happened.''

History lost a great opportunity to get impeccable information on the height of at least one President when Theodore Roosevelt died before anthropologist Ales Hrdlicka could put measuring instruments on his body. Earlier this century Hrdlicka was conducting research on the physical measurements of ''old Americans.'' Hearing of his project, Roosevelt wrote volunteering his own body as one to be measured. But before the anthropologist could do so, the ex-President died. ''The loss of this record is to be deeply regretted,'' Hrdlicka later commented. ''The data would have been of much historic value. . . . Accurate records of this nature — as well as faithful life busts — should be preserved of every President.''

Which only goes to show that Hrdlicka was a better anthropologist than he was a politician. Presidents do not necessarily *want* their size to be known — at least not accurately. Even big Lyndon Johnson, the tallest President since Lincoln, when having his picture taken with 6'6" reporter Frank Cormier made sure Cormier stood on a step below.

Johnson was a politician who understood the value of height. He was famous for getting his way by scooting up close to

. . . or Other Steps
Can Be Taken

lesser men and glowering down upon them with the same promise of protection and threat of power they may have felt at one time for their father. Reference constantly was made to Lyndon Johnson as "larger than life," "Texas-sized," and exercising a "6′3″ style of leadership." Even liberal journalist Robert Sherrill observed of the thirty-sixth President, "Whatever his failings, Johnson is at least no pipsqueak."

Is tallness in fact a political plus? Unfortunately, there are grounds other than dubious statistics to suggest that it is. In the first place, if a politician such as Johnson is *seen* as having the advantage of size, this perception can become self-fulfilling. As I am writing this, Illinois Governor James R. "Big Jim" Thompson is being discussed seriously as a presidential prospect. Considered high among the governor's assets is his height. "Because he is new," wrote one commentator only semifacetiously, "young, 6 feet 6, and not a right-wing loony, the nation's leading political writers have all but proclaimed Thompson the GOP nominee." Thompson's tallness itself may not lead to the White House. But our assumption that it could is grease on his skids.

The Illinois governor himself doesn't deny that there are political overtones to his size. Why else, he asked in response to my inquiry, did his last political opponent — who was a full head smaller — refuse to have their picture taken together? "A taller candidate seems to be more visible in a crowd," Thompson added. "Also, if television is present, it sometimes gives the taller candidate more visibility."

Covering the victory celebration of 6′5″ former basketball player Bill Bradley after his nomination for the U.S. Senate, a New Jersey television commentator noted how much easier his job was when a candidate's head stood so high above the mob. "It's always easier with tall guys," an advance man once explained as he funneled voters over to his candidate — New

York's 6'5" U.S. senator-to-be Daniel Patrick Moynihan. Prior to working for Moynihan the same aide had worked for 6'3" New York Mayor John Lindsay.

As if such natural advantages weren't enough, clever aides can magnify their big candidate's edge with a little imagination. During the 1976 presidential primaries an assistant to Morris Udall went early to an auditorium stage where the candidates would later be debating and slipped a few reams of paper beneath the lectern. This raised the podium enough to put the microphone right at Udall's mouth. The other candidates then had to strain just to be heard, let alone seen.

Such demoralizing of smaller rivals by clever larger candidates can be subtle. It's not all that difficult. A gesture so small as making sure a milk crate is provided behind the lectern at which your opponent is about to speak can do wondrously bad things to his morale. With a chuckle one Republican campaign consultant told me of the time Texas Senator John Tower kicked such a planted crate clear across the stage.

But there are limits to this approach. The consultant recalled one 6'5" congressional candidate with whom he worked going overboard to remind voters at every opportunity who was the taller of the two candidates. "The guy probably hurt himself this way," this adviser said of his unsuccessful client. "It seemed like he was picking on his smaller opponent."

Looking like a bully is a particular danger for a tall candidate whose opponent is significantly shorter. Restraint is necessary. When 6-foot Herman Badillo ran unsuccessfully against Abe Beame for the New York City Democratic mayoral nomination, he at first used his height effectively by maneuvering his 5'2" opponent right next to him for pictures. But Badillo then began to charge Beame with being "a malicious little man." Especially in a city filled with Beame-sized residents, this came across as Big Bully stuff. The taller man tried to backtrack, to explain that he really was referring to his opponent's "pettiness of mind." But everyone knew what he was referring to. What Badillo really was getting at was the fact that Abe Beame was nearly a foot shorter than he was.

When the height difference between two candidates is so pronounced, the taller of the two really has no need to even mention this fact himself. Reporters can be a particular help to taller politicians simply by using cliché-words to describe the relative size of candidates. Since most such words for tall have a much better ring than those for small, this kind of reporting grates on the psyche of shorter candidates. When she ran against 6′6″ Lowell Weicker for the U.S. Senate in 1976, then Connecticut Secretary of State Gloria Schaffer grew so sick of reading about herself as a "petite, cute blond," that she got a soapbox, painted it red, and lettered it boldly on one side: I AM NOT PETITE. Schaffer then stood on this soapbox for all her joint appearances with Weicker. Although she'd known her Republican opponent for years, Schaffer said she never realized how much taller he was than she (well over a foot) because she'd never had to stand next to him for so long.

Feeling rather "cowed" by his size, the candidate made herself do things like march right next to Weicker in parades in hopes of overcoming her fear. One parade in particular stands out in her mind, she said. It was a day so hot that the street was getting soft. This made her feel smaller than ever. "As we marched along sinking into the macadam," Schaffer recalled, "I remember thinking, 'I don't feel very tall — he's much more obvious than I am.' "

On reflection, Schaffer doubted that Weicker's size per se won him the election. But she had no doubt that it put her at a disadvantage — in her own mind if not in others. "There was just something in my head," she concluded, "that made me feel like he was really bigger than I was."

When I reached up to shake hands with Lowell Weicker, I could see what Gloria Schaffer meant. The man's enormous. "During the Watergate hearings," said Senator Weicker, settling mercifully into a leather easy chair in his Washington office, "when people would meet me in person they'd often comment on how tall I was compared with television." He chuckled. "They don't realize that most of my six feet six inches is in the legs."

Senator Weicker recalled Schaffer's uneasiness during their joint appearances. During one debate he even remembered her openly referring to his size advantage. But from his perspective, the effect of their physical contrast wasn't so one-sided. Weicker tends to a roundness of face and torso perched atop those incongruously long legs. So on overall "looks," Weicker said, he felt more than edged out by his Democratic opponent.

For years — at least until Wyoming's Alan Simpson, reputedly 6'7", joined him in 1978 — Connecticut's junior senator figured he was the Senate's tallest member. Weicker knew he had a couple of inches on Ed Muskie and was pretty sure of having at least an inch on Pat Moynihan, though they'd never checked it out back-to-back. Years ago, Weicker recalled with a chuckle, he and the late Rogers Morton of Maryland did just that: went back-to-back on the floor of the House to see who was bigger. Each had just been elected to Congress and they figured they'd better get this issue settled right at the outset. Weicker won, by an inch.

Like Moynihan's advance man, Weicker doesn't doubt that for standing out in a crowd, being remembered, and giving the appearance of being in charge, tallness is a political blessing. But he's aware too that some voters can be overawed by his size. Although Weicker didn't say so, this could also be a problem with colleagues. At one point during the Watergate hearings, the Connecticut senator heatedly charged Howard Baker with trying to shut him up. Because both were seated at a hearing table several seats apart, Baker's response seemed to come from nowhere. ''I can't overlook the presumptuousness,'' grinned the senator from Tennessee, ''of a man who's five-foot-seven telling a man six-foot-six to shut up.''

Perhaps because Howard Baker had since become minority leader of the Senate and a serious presidential possibility, Weicker didn't seem eager to discuss that exchange when I interviewed him. He did not think their height differential ruled out a hypothetical Baker-Weicker or Weicker-Baker ticket. In fact, Weicker said, in 1970 he first ran for senator from Connecticut on a ticket with gubernatorial candidate Thomas Meskill. ''Meskill's much shorter than I am,'' he pointed out, reaching his palm quite a bit below his hairline. ''I remember one time when we were together on a platform and I reached down to take his hand and raise it up with mine'' — Weicker demonstrated, then laughed — ''and I ended up yanking him right off the floor.'' But the incident couldn't have been too disastrous. Both candidates won.

Reflecting on being a tall politician, weighing all the pluses and minuses, Senator Weicker knows how he feels on balance. ''On balance,'' he concluded, ''I would have to say it's an advantage to be tall.''

Over a century ago, in 1866, a survey of members of the U.S. Senate found their reported height to average 5'10½'' — well above the male norm at the time (even when adjusted for heels and hyperbole). Professor Enoch Gowin included two groups of politicians in his 1916 survey of heights, and found that the average reported stature of those state governors responding was 5'11.2'', that of U.S. senators 5'10.6''.

Hoping to get fresher information, I conducted my own poll

of such officeholders (see Appendix B), seeking to determine their stature and their thoughts overall about the role of height in government.

At 5′7″, the shortest of 27 senators responding to my poll was Hawaii's Spark Matsunaga; the tallest were Patrick Leahy of Vermont and Edmund Muskie of Maine, both of whom reported themselves as 6′4″. In an accompanying letter, Muskie's aide Robert Rose made the point that on television "everyone looks 'tall' " and wondered if this medium may have reduced any influence height has on politics. Barry Goldwater, himself 6 feet tall, questioned whether shorter candidates actually were at a disadvantage. "Wallace did okay," Goldwater pointed out. Most of his colleagues echoed Goldwater in denying that tallness had any political advantage. Yet the average of their stated heights was 6′0.33″ — 3⅓″ over the national male norm.

The average of 31 governors who reported their height was 6′0.46″. The tallest among them was 6′6½″ Governor Jay Rockefeller of West Virginia, the shortest 5′7″ Otis Bowen of Indiana. Bowen said that he'd defeated rivals up to 6 inches taller but didn't feel the height difference was a factor.

Bruce Babbitt, on the other hand, the 6′2″ governor of Arizona, said of his half-foot advantage over one rival: "I did not see eye to eye with my Republican opponent. Being the tallest candidate, I feel height is of value in predicting success in office. It helps get honesty into government; i.e., 'I can't stoop that low.' "

Most of the governors who commented on this question, like most of the senators, took the approach that relative height shouldn't and doesn't influence politics. Governor William Milliken of Michigan, 5′11″, said, "After 30 years in public service, I have never found an instance where height was the measure of the individual." Added 5′9″ Governor John Dalton of Virginia, "My own view is that the philosophy, the personality and the approach of the candidates are far more important than their relative height."

On the other hand, an assistant to 6'4" Governor Rudy Perpich of Minnesota noted hopefully: "It has often been said that the taller candidate has the advantage. . . . The Republican opponent in this fall's election is shorter than the Governor, and we hope it's a good omen." (It wasn't; in 1978 Perpich lost his bid for reelection.)

Whatever role it may or may not play in the political process, height is never far from political minds. It just comes out in funny ways — quips, asides, jokes. A senator the size of Howard Baker is subject to constant "just kidding" references to his size. During the Watergate hearings, a reporter slipped Baker a note suggesting a question to ask of witnesses. The two-part question was: "Is there anything in the White House staff system or in the institution of the Presidency itself, that would prevent a man 5 foot 5 from becoming President? If so, what can we do to prevent this in the future?" Baker laughed aloud as he read the note. What else could he do?

In public at least, Howard Baker is more mascot than Napoleon in managing his size. After he made his crack to Weicker about a man his size not presuming to tell a man Weicker's size to shut up, I dropped the senator from Tennessee a note telling him that this wasn't presumptuous, it was his duty, and that the smaller people of America were solidly beneath him. Baker wrote back saying he was gratified to learn of this support and was ordering the Watergate Committee's 6'5" Minority Counsel Fred Thompson to investigate any influence of a Heightist Conspiracy in the last election. "I shall ask him to slouch while doing so," Baker hastened to add.

Forced as he is in public to grin and shuffle when light is made of his height, a Howard Baker is considered no less powerful in the Senate by virtue of his size (or lack thereof). "After a while you don't think of him as being short," said the senior staff member of a key Senate committee. "Here you think more in terms of power and influence than height. There's a difference between getting here and being here."

This point was made during an informal discussion with members of this committee's staff on the role of height in governance. Once elected, the senior man pointed out, senators get to sit down a lot during committee meetings and hearings compared with all the standing involved in a campaign. In public hearings they not only sit but sit on a raised platform. This staffer also thought a case could be made for a stronger type of smaller man making it into the Senate. "A big man," he explained, "may never develop the voice, the commanding presence, because he never has to."

"Like Pastore [former Senator John Pastore of Rhode Island]," chimed in a younger member of the staff. "He was very short but even in a large room he had this incredible, booming, loud voice with rolling phrases. He was very small but he'd overpower you with his voice. Some people liked him; others found him way too much. I found him amusing, which I guess isn't too respectful."

"He had a lot of power," interjected the senior man. "An awful lot of power."

As we discussed current smaller senators, John Tower was mentioned — the Republican from Texas who until joined by California's S. I. Hayakawa and Kansas's Nancy Kassebaum stood alone at the bottom of the Senate's height ladder. "Tower's traded on it," said the senior man. "What do they call him, the little, little . . ."

"Jerk," said a young man's voice from across the room. All but the senior man laughed.

"Little giant or something," he finished.

Discussing a range of senators these staff members found their actual and perceived heights could vary. Birch Bayh, for example, the boyish Democrat from Indiana, is a 6-footer, but all agreed that he comes across smaller. So does slim Joe Biden of Delaware, who tops 6 feet. And although ex–Harvard football player John Culver of Iowa is physically big, "his presence," I was told, "doesn't fill up the room."

By contrast, senators such as Ernest Hollings of South Carolina and Lawton Chiles of Florida are tall and look it. With his white hair, erect posture, and courtly manner, Hollings, one man said, in appearance is "the quintessential senator." The laconic Chiles is in the Gary Cooper tradition. Then there's Ed Muskie, who's regularly called "Lincolnesque," partly due to his size and cragginess, partly due to his solid legislative record.

As interested as this group was in the whole idea of real or perceived size, no one felt that the relative height of senators had much to do with their influence. "By the time they get here," said one staffer of a taller senator's height advantage, "that's not likely to intimidate people."

But even if no one thought physical size influenced governance much, no one doubted that it could be pivotal in a campaign. The group chortled at the thought of Howard Baker running with Big Jim Thompson on a Republican ticket. "The cartoonists would have a field day," said one staffer.

"A little Mutt-and-Jeff action," added another.

And thirty years later, poor Thomas Dewey remains vivid in political memory. "When Dewey was called 'like the *little* man on a wedding cake,' " chuckled the senior staff member, "it was devastating."

So what can we conclude about the role of height in electoral politics? Probably that for an office*holder* height matters relatively little; but for an office *seeker* it matters a lot. As illustrated by my poll, even those politicians who deny any advantage to tallness may themselves be its beneficiaries. If only for practical reasons — simply by standing out in a crowd — the taller candidate has an edge.

But, depending on what office is being sought, the political assets of height are not entirely one-sided. During a race for mayor of New York between big John Lindsay and little Mario Proccacino, psychologist William Berkowitz sent students into the streets of Manhattan to ask voters their mayoral preference and their own height. Taller voters showed a clear preference for their size-mate, Lindsay. Shorter voters split down the middle between the two candidates. Berkowitz suggested that the marked difference in size between Lindsay and Proccacino put smaller voters in a bind. On the one hand, he thought, we prefer candidates most like ourselves — height included. On the other hand, we value tallness and associate this trait with qualities of leadership. Taller voters, therefore, had no problem being for Lindsay: he was both their own size and impressively tall. But smaller voters in such a contest, as Berkowitz concluded, ''are faced with conflicting cues: the tall candidate is absolutely tall, but also quite different in height from themselves. If both factors are about equal in importance, their vote should be roughly split between the two candidates.'' This, in fact, apparently was the case. And Lindsay won.

But John Lindsay may have been an anomaly all along, both in size and style. Pointing out that New York mayors have traditionally been short, Jimmy Breslin once wrote a funny and perceptive tract asking if John Lindsay weren't ''too tall'' to be mayor. ''Too tall,'' Breslin explained, meant not just 5 to 12 inches taller than his predecessors but ''too Manhattanish, too removed from the problems of the street corners. . . . His head high, his arms folded, the word 'shall' coming out of him.''

Though no such statistics exist, I wonder if a direct correlation might be found between stature of body and of office — if the closer a politician is to the people being served, the less advantage there is in standing above them. This possibility was suggested by Governor J. James Exon of Nebraska in response to my poll. Himself 6'1", Exon thought that a shorter candidate might have a political disadvantage overall, but that on the local level such a candidate "would be better known and as a result physical features would be less important."

From Fiorello La Guardia through Richard Daley to Cleveland's Dennis Kucinich, there certainly has been a long line of small mayors in this country. (Louie Welch, who served five terms as Houston's mayor, said he turned to local politics after being rejected as "too short" for a department-store job.) Even an exception such as New York City's tall Mayor Ed Koch tries to identify in style and fact with his feisty smaller predecessor La Guardia. When he moved into Gracie Mansion, Koch dramatically had the Little Flower's desk moved into the mayor's office — only to find his legs wouldn't fit underneath.

Like La Guardia, smaller politicians seem to do best when they capitalize on their size rather than disguise it. Abe Beame never really got the hang of it, but George Wallace was most effective as the Fighting Little Judge, just as S. I. Hayakawa did a good job of peddling himself as a "feisty little Samurai."

Some of the most successful practitioners of smallness in politics have been women. From the first U.S. congresswoman, Jeannette Rankin, through Clare Boothe Luce, to Shirley Chisholm, there is a distinguished tradition of little women in public life. Two contemporary governors, Dixy Lee Ray of Washington and Ella Grasso of Connecticut, are part of that tradition, as are Chicago Mayor Jane ("The Little Spitfire") Byrne, U.S. Senator Nancy Kassebaum, and such recent congresswomen as Barbara Mikulski, Margaret Heckler, and Chisholm.

In Brooklyn and in Congress, Shirley Chisholm has capitalized on her size-suited vigor. On a national tableau that style hasn't played as well. Of her stab at the presidency in 1972, Chisholm said: "They'll have to remember that a little 100-pound woman, Shirley Chisholm, shook things up." Later she added:

Who knows? It took a little black woman, Harriet Tubman, to lead three hundred of her people out of slavery; it required another little black woman, Rosa Parks, to say she was tired of going to the back of the bus for a seat. . . . It may take another little black woman to "bring us together" in these troubled times of war and worry.

But Chisholm wasn't taken too seriously in that race, perhaps because her size and style didn't seem quite "presidential."

If height matters anywhere in politics, it's in a race for President. Studies of voter preference during presidential races have found voters not only expressing their preference for a taller candidate, but sometimes misperceiving their choice as taller. With a Chisholm such self-deception is difficult. With a Carter it's barely possible. Combining psychiatric perspective with experience gained at various levels of government, Peter Bourne suggested that unlike congressional or gubernatorial races, a campaign for the presidency has to contend with a higher level of symbolism. Height is prominent as a presidential symbol. "That role gets caught up in so many perceptions," explained Bourne, "paternal ones, the kinglike role of the President, the hope that he'll be a Superman embodying everything you want the country to be."

It was revealing to follow the physical terminology commentators used to evaluate Jimmy Carter's standing after he entered the White House. When his popularity fell early on, Carter "declined in the public eye," we were told, and "shrank in our estimation" — he seemed "no longer larger than life." But

The Ups and Downs of Jimmy Carter

"WELL, GLORY BE! I'VE ACTUALLY GROWN A LITTLE BIT!"

ANOTHER DAY . . . ANOTHER POLL

"YOU'RE STILL A BIG MAN IN MY EYES, JIMMY."

Popularity

1977

1978

1979

after picking himself up at his midterm Middle East summit, the President "stood taller" and "gained in stature." Falling once again, he became "a little tyrant," a "frantically spinning little man," and — in the words of columnist William Safire — "smaller than life."

"They say Carter is the first businessman ever to sit in the White House," deadpanned George Meany. "But why did they have to send a small businessman?"

During Carter's roller-coaster ride in the polls, not only commentators but cartoonists took their lead from Gallup in determining what size to portray the thirty-ninth President. Past midterm even the President's own press office had reduced Carter's official height half an inch to 5'9½".

Well into his presidency, Carter experienced the rare luxury of having a White House visitor comment that he was taller than she had expected. Said Carter: "I was taller before I got to be President."

11 Casting to Size

Audrey [Hepburn] is a tall girl. She's 5 feet 7, I think. She'll need tall leading men. Maybe she'll have to wear flat heels in *Sabrina* and Bogart will have to wear high heels. But if we can do it with Alan Ladd, we can do it with anybody.

— BILLY WILDER

The subject of height was fresh in Scott Rudin's mind when we visited in his New York office. An independent casting director, Rudin had just been working on a movie starring Al Pacino. "Pacino is not gargantuan by a long shot," said Rudin. "One woman auditioned who we were very interested in for the love interest. She was a wonderful actress. But when they stood up she absolutely *towered* over him." Rudin raised a hand high in the air to demonstrate, then shook his head. "So we just had to find somebody else."

A 5′1″ actress — Maureen Silliman — then read for the part. But she was too short. "She's so talented," Rudin sighed about this actress. "But she's very small and there is a common feeling within the industry that the American public expects leading women to be two or three inches shorter than the male star. Maureen was simply five or six inches shorter."

So instead of Al Pacino's love interest, Maureen Silliman was cast as his sister. Did her size help her get that part?

Rudin grinned. "It didn't hurt."

Himself average-sized — perhaps 5′10″ — Scott Rudin is husky and bearded. He wore a short-sleeve plaid shirt the summer morning we chatted. Covering the walls all around him were glossy photographs of actors and actresses, sometimes with resumes attached. High on such resumes was the performer's height.

Rudin had a range of stories to tell me about the role height plays in his business. Like the time he almost couldn't cast 5'10½" Sally Kellerman as a World War II USO entertainer because of concern that 1940s styles wouldn't suit her frame. But styles change in casting as well as clothing, and lots of actors — including smaller men — are working today who might have had trouble being cast in another era. Paul Newman, for example, Rudin said, is not tall at all. This was exciting news. Rising to my feet I asked if Paul Newman was taller than I.

Rudin looked me carefully up and down. "No," he said finally. His voice had a definite ring. "I think he's shorter."

Shorter than *I* am?

"I would think so."

Another star Rudin mentioned as being in my height range was Roy Scheider, late of *Jaws, Jaws II,* and possibly *III*. The casting director recently had the rare experience of having to turn down an actress as too short to play opposite Scheider. This actress, Marybeth Hurt (*Interiors*), seemed perfect when she auditioned alone. But standing next to Scheider, she obviously wasn't going to work. The combination of being young and barely over 5 feet tall cinched it. "She did look like a kid," Rudin recalled with a sigh. "If she had been five inches taller I think she would have worked. It was really a shame, because that was a perfect instance of somebody's height keeping them from getting a part."

Rudin's more common problem with an actor such as Scheider or Pacino is making sure an actress doesn't tower over him so far as to make special effects necessary. "If you're doing a film with Roy Scheider," he explained, "you're not going to get somebody who is going to make you put Roy

Scheider on crates. And with someone like Pacino, it would be silly *not* to cast to them. That's the reason the picture exists. They're the focal point of what you're going to see on the screen, so you've got to match that actor.''

Matching actors and actresses looms very large in moviemakers' minds. Height is central to such matchmaking, but in a special sense. Nowhere is height more relative than in a casting director's mind. To those casting a movie, there's no such thing as "to tall" or "too small" — except relative to the rest of the cast. A lot of great movie teams have in fact been on the small side, but audiences never knew it because they matched. Bob Hope and Bing Crosby. Mickey Rooney and Judy Garland. Robert Redford and Paul Newman. Alan Ladd and Veronica Lake. Fred Astaire and Ginger Rogers. Gene Kelly, Donald O'Connor, and Debbie Reynolds.

Before becoming a star himself, 6'7" James Arness spent his fledgling years repeatedly losing roles because shorter actors couldn't be cast next to him. Arness's casting problem was so serious that by one report his agent made it a practice to visit producers' offices in advance, find out where the chairs were, then coach his client on how to make a beeline for the nearest one, slouching along the way. After years of indignities such as playing a human vegetable in *The Thing,* Arness finally began to win some better parts with the help of John Wayne. Wayne said that the only thing that bothered him about the taller actor was the fact that Arness was one of the few men alive who could see his bald spot.

Once James Arness became Matt Dillon and producers had to cast around *him,* the good fortune rippled outward to other tall actors — costars such as Chuck Connors and George Kennedy. Kennedy has credited his first TV jobs to the fact that "Jim Arness needed big guys to hit.''

According to casting director Jane Feinberg of Twentieth Century–Fox, height is second only to overall "looks" among the factors that must be considered in balancing casts for movies and television shows. As soon as an actor or actress walks through her door, said Feinberg, she'll quickly assess the person's general appearance and make a mental estimate of his or her height. She takes her own estimates more seriously than the height listed on resumes. Based on her experience in casting thousands of productions over the years, said Feinberg, "actors lose jobs because of their height all the time." At times this is due to specific requests. Some producers will euphemistically ask for big women by specifying "Swedish" or "German" girls, sometimes adding for emphasis: "No petites." In one case, the director of a television program didn't want anyone under 5'7" because the leading lady was tall and he figured she'd be more comfortable that way.

"We also find that short leading men don't like their coactors to be taller," added Feinberg, who is particularly careful to cast around the star that way. Not long ago she was working on a Richard Dreyfuss movie and had to turn a number of actresses away as too tall for him. A Melinda Dillon could get away with being a tad taller than Dreyfuss in *Close Encounters of the Third Kind,* Feinberg explained, but "we saw ladies who were over five feet ten inches tall and thought we'd better not go that big."

Paying attention to actors' feelings about height is a common problem for casting directors, producers, and fellow actors. "Good Morning America" host David Hartman has said he once actually lost a movie part when the movie's well-known 6'4" lead vetoed Hartman as too tall. Bonnie Franklin nearly turned down Mackenzie Phillips as her daughter in TV's "One Day at a Time" because she'd heard the younger actress was

The last part of this love scene between Sophia Loren and Alan Ladd never hit the scree

"at least as tall as the World Trade Center." (In fact Phillips is 5′7″ or so, 4 inches taller than Bonnie Franklin; once introduced, they got along fine.)

Even in opera, big Beverly Sills at one point grew so weary of singing opposite smaller tenors that she wrote a poem to director Julius ("Chulyuss") Rudel pleading for a 6′4″ tenor named Richard Casilly. It read:

> *I'd like a tenor taller than my ass-illy.*
> *Please, Chulyuss Darlink, can I have Dick Cas-illy?*

She got him.

Of his problems casting around Alan Ladd in *The Blue Dahlia,* producer John Houseman once commented: "Since he himself was extremely short, he had only one standard by which he judged his fellow actors: their height. Meeting another actor for the first time, if his glance hit him or her anywhere below the collarbone he was sure to explain as soon as we were alone that he didn't think he or she was exactly right for the part, and would we please find someone else."

Ladd's sensitivity was understandable. Born twenty years too soon, Alan Ladd was the size of Dustin Hoffman in the age of Gary Cooper. Though "officially" 5′10″, he was in fact closer to 5′4″, a "handicap" that until his late twenties limited the

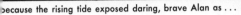

because the rising tide exposed daring, brave Alan as ...   ... no man to look up to!

well-built blond actor to small movie roles and lots of work on the radio.

Ladd's breakthrough came when he was cast opposite Veronica Lake in *This Gun for Hire* (1942). Herself barely 5 feet tall, Lake matched Ladd perfectly. Both were stunning physically in every respect except size. Together on screen the pair sizzled. Alan Ladd and Veronica Lake soon became the country's favorite love team — bigger at the box office than Tracy and Hepburn even, or Bogart and Bacall.

The beginning of Ladd's end came when he was mismatched with 5'8" Sophia Loren in *Boy on a Dolphin* (1957). Once the casting gaffe was realized, every gimmick known to moviemakers was employed to fool our eye. Crates were placed under Ladd's feet, and trenches dug beneath Loren's. Neither star was happy with this situation. From where he stood Alan Ladd compared working with Loren to ''being bombarded with watermelons.'' She pouted about having to spend so much time sunk in the ground. Jokes about the mismatch consumed *Dolphin*'s set and eventually spread to the public at large. Ladd, it was said, was twice Loren's age but only half her size. (Later they would say the same thing about her husband Carlo Ponti.) Even *Mad* magazine got into the act with a panel showing the actor standing on a ship's rail to kiss Loren. Alan Ladd, *Mad* concluded, ''quite obviously is no man to look up to.''

All odd-sized actors at one time or another are subject to help underfoot. Even Jimmy Cagney, whose identity was based on feisty smallness, was forced up on a 2-inch apple box for close-ups with Claire Dodd in *Footlight Parade*. And Humphrey Bogart, who made no bones about wishing he were a foot taller, used to joke regularly about the "wedgies" he so often had to wear on camera. After first donning elevators for some early westerns, Bogart remarked, "I walked around as though I was on stilts and felt like a dummy."

When Sylvester Stallone was filming *Rocky II* in Philadelphia, I followed him around for an afternoon and was impressed both by his 2-inch heels and by the way his pant cuffs were cut low in back to drape over them. Although not much taller than I am, Stallone has so convincingly presented himself as a gigantic heavyweight that he's even been used by one writer as a metaphor for size — "as big as Sylvester Stallone." How did the actor pull it off? With a diverse and imaginative set of strategies. First comes the help underfoot. Then there are eye-lifters, such as running up the art-museum steps in *Rocky* and its sequel. But most important in Stallone's case has been the use of his own height as the focal point when casting. Heavyweight boxer Ken Norton was originally expected to play Rocky's opponent Apollo Creed. But next to Norton's hefty 6'3" frame, Stallone looked like a middleweight. So the part went to Stallone's size-mate Carl Weathers. Other supporting roles were filled with even smaller actors, such as Burgess Meredith, Burt Young, and Talia Shire. By contrast Rocky looked huge, and the illusion brushed back on the man playing him. "Stallone is a big man," one reviewer subsequently wrote, "impressive in wrath and sheepish in love. . . ."

Undoubtedly there's more than a little ego involved in such a strategy of self-enhancement. But for an actor, apparent size can be a simple matter of food on the table. One reason Stallone ended up producing *Rocky* himself was that the studios he first solicited thought him too small to play a heavyweight. But for a resourceful filmmaker, "too small" (or "too tall") simply means that extra care must be taken to cast within a limited range of heights.

Not taking such care creates problems for tall and small alike. Nick Nolte, for example, is an ex–football player making a strong bid to become a male lead of classic stature — a tall Robert Redford. His height has caused costar problems. For *North Dallas Forty,* singer Mac Davis, who is considerably shorter than Nolte, was cast as the quarterback of a professional football team — Nolte's teammate and pal. Luckily their team was set in Texas so that out of uniform Davis could wear high-heeled cowboy boots. In uniform, during huddle scenes, he reportedly stood on a box. By watching this movie closely, one can notice that full-body views of Davis normally were shot from a distance with him standing alone; when he stands next to Nolte, their feet disappear from view.

A boost underfoot is still so common for actors that a standard joke around Hollywood goes:
"One of these days,   (fill in the wearer)   is going to fall off his heels and hurt himself." A custom shoemaker in Los Angeles once listed among his contemporary lift customers Cliff Robertson, Kirk Douglas, Rod Steiger, Andy Williams, and Burt Reynolds.

Reynolds also wears some very impressive heels at times. "You know," he once told a woman admiring his physique, "when I take these boots off, I'm five feet four inches."

"You look closer to five eleven to me," his admirer responded.

"Lady," said Reynolds, "no actor is five eleven. There's not an actor in the world who isn't over six feet."

Painfully aware that the closer they are to the norm, the

greater their chances of getting work, odd-sized actors at both ends of the measuring stick do whatever they can to claim or deny inches. Alexis Smith, for example, whose "real" height (according to her) is 5'9", once confessed that her "official" height has varied over the years depending on the size of man she was being considered to play opposite. When cast next to a shorter man the tall actress was forced to play scenes barefoot (with Charles Boyer, for example, in *The Constant Nymph*).

For any tall actress, wearing no shoes at all is the counterpart of wearing elevated shoes for a short actor. This is what 5'8" Melanie Griffith said was required of her for love scenes she played with Paul Newman in *The Drowning Pool*. Bare feet were also required of Ingrid Bergman when she played opposite smaller actors such as Bogart, Boyer, and Yul Brynner.

When introduced to David Selznick shortly after she came to this country from Sweden, Bergman said, the producer's first words to her were: "Would you take your shoes off?"

"It won't help, Mr. Selznick," the actress replied. "I am this tall."

Moaned Selznick: "Oh, my God."

The producer then cabled an assistant: "I NOTE BERGMAN IS 69½ INCHES TALL. IS IT POSSIBLE SHE IS ACTUALLY THIS HIGH, AND DO YOU THINK WE WILL HAVE TO USE STEPLADDERS WITH LESLIE HOWARD?"

In Howard's case stepladders turned out to be unnecessary. But throughout her career Bergman has been plagued with the need to create the illusion that she was shorter than men over whom she towered. In *Casablanca,* for example, Humphrey Bogart was somewhat shorter than she was, and Claude Rains considerably so. As a result dual catwalks were built for Bergman's two costars to walk on beside her when filming indoors. For outdoor shooting it became her turn: to walk in a specially dug trench between the two men.

Bacall, Bogart, and Hepburn

It all gets back to match. Maureen Silliman, the 5'1" actress Scott Rudin cast as Al Pacino's sister, said that during two years she spent on ''The Guiding Light,'' New York–based soap operas were known among actors as ''tall soaps'' or ''short soaps.'' ''Search for Tomorrow'' was tall. ''Ryan's Hope'' was short. ''Guiding Light'' was small when she joined, but gradually grew tall as some men over 6 feet were cast — and eventually women to match.

One symptom of ''Guiding Light'' going tall was the casting of a 6'6" actor as Silliman's love interest. Walking to the middle of her Manhattan apartment, the actress stretched her legs outward like a dancer contemplating a split. ''He used to have to stand like this all the time when we played together,'' she said. ''It was so hard for the cameraman to get us both in.'' The tall actor played a doctor who goes through a harrowing cesarean delivery of the Silliman character's illegitimate baby. Later the script called for her to reward him with a kiss. Such proximity posed a particular problem. Without help, both wouldn't fit in the range of the camera. Silliman smiled at the memory, saying ''so I stood on a box and kissed him.''

On ''Days of Our Lives,'' 5-foot actress Patty Weaver had a similar problem with an unusually tall actor. ''I came up to his crotch,'' she explained, running her hand across the top of her head. ''The cameramen are dying. They're in stitches on the floor. They kept having to collect themselves to shoot the scene.''

So out came the crate. Weaver chuckled mirthlessly at the memory. Then she described a similar episode involving her and Ronnie Howard of ''Happy Days,'' when they worked together in a television movie. Since Howard is relatively short, Weaver figured that there would be no problem when they had to kiss. ''So there I am and I'm reaching and I'm reaching to kiss him. And he can't reach down because I'm supposed to kiss him. So they say to bring on an apple box. Half-a-one. Even on that I'm still too low.

" 'Bring in a full one,' they said.

" 'This better work. Because I'm not bringing in a second one.'

"That's appalling, embarrassing. Humiliating. How much can you move around on an apple box?"

Cheerleader-pretty in her mid-twenties, Patty Weaver is blond, blue-eyed, vivacious, and curvacious — in short, a classic knockout. But short. When she auditions for parts, Weaver said, the first thing she's asked is her height. "I just say, 'About five foot, hm, hm . . . Would you believe five-foot-ten?' "

The day we met for lunch at the NBC commissary in Burbank between "Days of Our Lives" tapings, Weaver had recently been the dinner partner of an influential television executive who was casting a new show. They were looking, he had told her, for a "very elegant woman." What constitutes "elegant" she had asked. Well, for starters: tall. That ended the conversation.

"If you're short," she complained, "you're not considered elegant. When you're short, you're cute and perky. A short woman can even be thought of as lovely, but never elegant."

Size is so symbolic of a given look that actors tend to be less concerned with their height per se than with the "type" implied by their height. To get a sense of how height and type interplay, one simply has to read the casting calls in theatrical trade papers. Here are some examples:

• *Danny:* leader of the Burger Palace boys, well-built, athletic & nice-looking, with an air of cool. Must be at least 6' and have sex appeal & charisma.

• *Leon Zucker:* 60's, Bessie's husband who sells TV sets, a short pedantic man who has all the zeal of the newborn middle-aged student, plaid jacket and blazing two-tone shoes.

• *Vadinho:* handsome, well-built, sexual male, preferably tall . . .

• *Miss Lacy Seward:* 25, Anglo-Saxon beauty; tall, blond, assured in manner & speech. Very thin, lovely.

• *Mouse:* 18 years old, small in stature with large forlorn-looking eyes. She is one of Sarah's sorority sisters.

• *Gino:* late 20s, tall and lean tough guy. Could be black.

• Seeking Italian kid who is really big — at least over 6 feet tall and with a thick build; a guy who is really a hulk — preferably tall and heavy and menacing. Also . . . Irish-looking kids (the Irish must be under 5'4" tall).

• . . . black male performer, 18 years and older, 4'10" and under to play an animal in a new major Columbia film.

Height is integral to type. It's basic. Actors talk matter-of-factly about getting "typed out" of certain roles by the appearance their height suggests. "Sissy Spacek types" do not usually audition for roles specifying a "Sophia Loren type." Nor do Al Pacino types normally compete for work with Gary Cooper types.

Richard Dreyfuss for years was consigned to a Dustin Hoffman–type slot. "Anyone," he explained, "who wasn't six feet tall with a face like Robert Redford was called a 'Dustin Hoffman type.'

"My agent says, 'Listen, if you'd gotten the part in *The Graduate,* Dustin would have become known as a 'Richard Dreyfuss type.' And it's true."

Meyer Mishkin, who's been Richard Dreyfuss's agent since the actor was in high school, said that until recent years directors regularly would brush Dreyfuss off with the comment, "He's too short." "When one television executive asked me how tall Rich was," added Mishkin, "I said, 'One-and-a-half inches taller than Dustin Hoffman.' If they are going to buy him inch by inch, that's the only way I can answer.''

Neither Mishkin nor his client will reveal just how tall the small actor is. Published estimates range from a generous 5'8" to a credible 5'6". Although Dreyfuss himself doesn't like to discuss his shortness (except obliquely, by expressing an interest in playing Napoleon) others have done so for him throughout the actor's career. Commentators regularly note and comment on Dreyfuss's lack of stature. The Oscar winner has been compared to dogs in reviews — small dogs — terriers, pugs. "Maybe that's the price one has to pay for being only 5'6½" tall," suggested reviewer Rex Reed, who himself called Dreyfuss "Mickey Rooney–sized."

But — as Mishkin predicted — since his client's first break in the matched cast of *American Graffiti,* followed by his hit performances in *Jaws, Close Encounters,* and *The Goodbye Girl,* producers who can't afford to say, "Get me Richard Dreyfuss!" are today saying, "Get me a Richard Dreyfuss type!"

It is possible, of course, to be cast against type. This is how Dustin Hoffman got his start. According to Scott Rudin, a "young Jimmy Stewart type" was originally sought to play Benjamin Braddock in *The Graduate.* But Hoffman was so suited to the role that director Mike Nichols cast him anyway. Even when leading lady Katharine Ross (who had already been cast) complained that her costar-to-be looked "about 3 feet tall," Nichols stuck with his miscast star and made history. In Hoffman's case the effect of being cast against type was revolutionary. By challenging the leading-man type, Hoffman turned that type around.

"Since Dustin and Pacino and Dreyfuss all those shapes are changing," Joel Grey pointed out. Barely ten years ago, he explained, it was inconceivable that actors his size could play leading men. Even Grey's own Oscar-winning 1972 performance as the master of ceremonies in *Cabaret* is one he might have had difficulty being cast for just a few years earlier.

During the early part of his career Joel Grey was limited to the roles casting directors assumed suited his size. As he recalled, such parts consisted largely of "the wisecracking kid next door; the buddy of the good-looking, tall leading man; the sidekick. Billy the Kid on 'Maverick,' Littlechap in *Stop the World — I Want to Get Off.*"

But Grey thinks such stereotypes have given way to talent and reality. "America," he said hopefully, "is getting closer to the European ideal of people on the screen being the people one meets during the day, not this idealized thing of bigger-than-life." He grinned. "I think it's healthy."

Healthy or not, this trend poses problems for movie producers. If smaller leading men were growing popular in conjunction with smaller leading women there would be no problem. But in a casting director's nightmare, even as the size of leading men has shrunk, that of leading ladies has lengthened. Diane Keaton. Candice Bergen. Jill Clayburgh. Meryl Streep. Even Jane Fonda and Faye Dunaway, who aren't especially tall, give the impression that they are. "I think everybody expects leading women now to be on the tall side," confirmed Scott Rudin. "I can't really think of any women you might know who are short who have become real movie stars. There are comic ladies who are. I think Streisand's not that tall, and people like Judy Holliday."

But, paradoxically, the recent casting scene is such that Lee Majors's manager has peddled him about Hollywood as the "only" young leading man over 6 feet; and the suggestion has been made that Sally Field won a movie part opposite Henry Winkler because there were no other leading ladies his size.

Perhaps for such reasons Scott Rudin and his colleagues are less sanguine about the trend to smaller leading men than are its beneficiaries. "I think, frankly," said Rudin about the origin of this trend, "that it's just by accident. I think what happens is that every so often an actor comes along who is so good that he defies his type. You talk about a Pacino or a Hoffman — you can't ignore that talent. I mean you can't *not* use Dustin Hoffman in *The Graduate* because he's not as tall as Jimmy Stewart. You would hurt your own picture. And then an actor like that becomes a star, then you've got a Pacino, and they become the prototype. At this point, when people think of a man for romantic leads, frequently they think of Pacino."

As a consequence, Rudin was having trouble casting talented actors who are too tall for today's tastes. One such actor he described as "terrific-looking, blond, all-American, Gary Cooper and all that. Too much of a hero."

Another promising young actor is Randy Quaid, who Peter Isacksen sees as his major competition for "tall parts." Quaid has given several wonderful performances, including roles as a goofy suitor of Cybill Shepherd in *The Last Picture Show* and as a sailor off to the brig in *The Last Detail*. Recently, Rudin said, he wanted to cast Quaid as best friend to James Caan for an upcoming movie. The part called for a bumbling but lovable character who was a real friend — not a sidekick. Therefore the conclusion (probably valid) was that such a person had to be more or less Caan's size — not too small, not too tall. Since he was taller than Caan, Quaid typed out.

The day we talked, Rudin had just been through a major disappointment with a tall actor named Jeff Goldblum. Goldblum, who's received good notices for his performances in such movies as *Between the Lines, Invasion of the Body Snatchers,* and *Next Stop, Greenwich Village* is quite tall and unusually slim. When Rudin tried to cast him for an upcoming comedy, studio executives turned thumbs down on the basis of Goldblum's looks alone.

"They thought he was too tall," said Rudin of producers' reactions to Goldblum. "They were all so afraid to take a chance. . . . Jeff is so tall, and no one looks like him — he doesn't look like Woody Allen, he doesn't look like Richard Dreyfuss, he doesn't look like George Segal — everybody who you think of as a comic actor, he doesn't look like."

Rudin scowled.

"It's a terrible shame. The shame is not for Jeff. Because eventually someone in a position of power will make a movie with Jeff playing the lead and he'll be a big star."

Rudin smiled.

"Then every movie star who plays 'Jeff Goldblum roles' is going to be tall."

12 Choosing Up Sizes

What difference does it make? Harry is a hell of a lot bigger than the baseball.

— PERRY CHAPPAS on the 5'4" height of his son Harry, shortstop for the Chicago White Sox

Mario Andretti is among the calmest, most gracious of men. It helps to be tops in your field. Winner at least once of every major auto race in the world, Andretti is generally considered the best overall driver racing today. Some consider him the best ever. Such status is conducive to graciousness.

But about one particular episode in his life, Mario Andretti is not gracious at all. This episode took place at age twenty-one when he had just started trying to catch on as a sprint-car driver. Lacking the money for his own car, Andretti stuck a helmet beneath one skinny arm and made the rounds of tracks near his Nazareth, Pennsylvania, home. One of his first stops was at a track in upstate New York. There the young Italian immigrant was told flatly that he was too small to handle race cars — that he should go home and find something less strenuous to do.

Recalling the incident seventeen years later and the particular guy who tried to shoo him away, Mario Andretti's voice took on an uncharacteristic edge. "I never forgot the son of a bitch," he explained. "He could have said, 'I got somebody else lined up.' He could have said a lot of things. But he had to pick on my size. It was unfair. It was a malicious put-down."

Having said this, Andretti's voice smoothed once again and he chuckled. ''I come across the guy now and then and he's all peaches and cream. You know, I never held a grudge against any individual in my whole life, except him. And I'll never forget it.''

During an hour's conversation Andretti returned repeatedly, insistently, to this early slight and the injustice — the stupidity — of someone saying he was too small to race cars. ''In our sport,'' explained Andretti, ''whether you are as big as a mountain or just average size, it's still up to you to set up the car in such a way that you can drive it properly. You don't have to wrestle it every inch of the way.

''In the early days they thought a successful racing driver had to be a big guy with big barrel muscles on his arms and big wide shoulders who looked like he could wrestle that thing forever, and twist it and turn it every way he wanted to — which was wrong anyway.

''I often said as long as I don't have to carry the car on my shoulders I'll be able to set it up so I can drive it.''

If any sport should be blind to size of participants, it's auto racing. What difference can the height of a driver make? If anything, as with jockeys, the virtues of light weight in conjunction with shortness may bestow an advantage.

In recent years not just Andretti but other small men, such as Jackie Stewart and Gordon ''Wee Gordy'' Johncock, have excelled at auto racing, as have bigger men, such as Dan Gurney and A. J. Foyt. And even more recently, Janet Guthrie — tall for a woman, short for a man, and echoing Andretti's line that she drives the car, doesn't carry it — has taken her place at the Indianapolis 500 starting line.

Arguments still rage in this sport, as in others, about the relative advantages of being big or small. Particularly with today's lighter, sleeker, custom-designed Formula 1 cars, a case can be made for the virtues of lighter, smaller drivers, who save the designer cockpit space.

Andretti feels that the big-versus-small argument is simply irrelevant when it comes to auto racing. "You've seen big guys and small guys win championships," he explained. "Even in the olden days — past Indy winners, prominent drivers like Pete De Paolo, who's exactly my size.

"That's why it hurt when a guy could dish it out to me because I wasn't established. I was nobody. I was just twenty-one. It hurt me so much that this guy could say, 'You aren't big enough to handle these things.'

"I'll never forget it. He's been so kind to me in many ways — complimentary and even makes jokes about certain things that he remembers. But that was such a flat put-down. No one will ever tell me it wasn't done maliciously and because of that, I'll never forget it."

All smaller athletes, it seems, have such a story in their backgrounds. Reviewing even the records of champions among them, one is struck by such stories' similarity. Nate "Tiny" Archibald, who later went on to win a National Basketball Association scoring title, wasn't even allowed to try out for that sport until his senior year of high school. The Philadelphia Phillies' short All-Star shortstop Larry Bowa was cut three times by his high school baseball coach. And Hank Aaron, before going on to break Babe Ruth's career home run record, was turned away from a Brooklyn Dodgers tryout camp as not big enough to play baseball. Even Joe Morgan, the National League's Most Valuable Player in 1975 and 1976, a decade earlier went directly to college out of high school because every major-league team considered him too small, at 5'7", to be drafted.

Eight years before he won the 1976 Cy Young Award as the

National League's best pitcher, Randy Jones was told by scouts that he was too small to pitch in the major leagues. "I remember when I was coming out of high school — a scout for the Los Angeles Dodgers talking to me after a ball game," Jones told me as he suited up for practice in the San Diego Padres' locker room. "He said, 'I like the way you pitch, but you're a little small.'"

Did this bother you?

"Oh yeah," replied the pitcher, concentrating on his laces. "Everybody else was getting drafted out of high school and that bothered me." He looked up with a slight smile. "But winning twenty ball games makes you grow. [His 1976 record was 22–14 on a losing team.] You grow with every win."

Soft-spoken, curly-haired, all taut, wiry muscle, Randy Jones isn't really that short. Listed officially as 6 feet, he's actually 5′10″. But today's pitchers are increasingly basketball player–sized, so he's relatively short for his position. Jones also is slight, and he relies on a low sinker pitch that overpowers no one but makes most batters hit lazy little ground balls to the infield. As a result Randy Jones is constantly being called "the little left-hander" and takes a lot of ribbing about his size. "Pete Rose is always calling me a little guy," he said. "He called me 'the little dabbler.' A dab here. A dab there."

How do you respond to that sort of thing?

Jones smiled as if to himself and toyed with his glove. "I just smile a lot," he finally said. "I don't want to wake anybody up. Pete didn't get many hits off me last year."

As Jones, Bowa, and others have proved in baseball, as Archibald and 5′9″ Calvin Murphy have shown in basketball, as Andretti in auto racing and smaller colleagues too numerous to list in all other sports (including football) have demonstrated, the prejudice against smaller athletes can be just that — a bias defying evidence to the contrary. Like casting directors, most coaches have "types" in mind and will not be shaken free from such stereotypes, often to their subsequent horror. (How would you like to be the Dodgers scout who sent Henry Aaron home to grow? The coach who cut Bowa? The one who told Archibald not even to try out?)

But coaches simply reflect their society's values. In America, it's been said, our teams are modern hunting bands. One foreign observer called American sports a "substitute frontier." In such a setting tallness isn't necessarily a virtue, but it tends to make everybody feel better all around. "Americans have made it very clear that they find big men much more entertaining than small men," noted English sportswriter Paul Gardner. "There is a long-standing American idea that bigger means better. . . . one of the reasons why football is cherished is because it is one of the few areas of life where the idea actually works."

Of a recent crop of National Football League draftees, *The Sporting News* told us: "The trend to size is more marked than ever in football. After San Diego drafted a 300-pounder this spring, Philadelphia opted for a defensive tackle weighing 275. He is 6′8″ . . . ." Of the New York Jets' draftees, the *New York Times* reported: "They look big, they act big, and, in fact, they are big. . . .

" 'Big, durable, physically sound. Hitters,' explains Coach Walt Michaels. 'I didn't want to go for the flash in the pan.' "

For centuries the question "Can a good little man beat a good big man?" has been grist for barroom debate. In America's favorite sports the answer clearly is no. Because traditionally we've defined our sports in such a way that size is rewarded and its lack penalized. From log-splitting to football, sheer size and strength are unquestioned assets in those pastimes Americans cherish. And this is not just a male phenomenon. A group of women participating in intercollegiate athletics was recently found to average 5'6" in height — nearly 2½" above the women's national average, and an inch taller than college women as a whole.

The self-fulfilling prophecy of American sports is that tall players are better suited to them because our sports are better suited to tall players. At UCLA a coach once ran a series of physical tests that he later reported "proved" big men were better athletes than small men. What tests constituted his proof? Baseball throw, football punt, quarter-mile run — all events known to favor bigger bodies. No diverse series of tests, including those such as chin-ups or distance runs (which favor smaller bodies), has ever found any correlation between size and athletic ability overall. The physical virtues of size depend entirely on the sport.

One way in which women have been discriminated against by major American sports has been the simple fact that such sports reward the male size advantage. Sports in which smaller athletes (including women) can excel — soccer, gymnastics, cycling — have until quite recently been considered sissified in America. Even when a game we do like has no inherent reward for bigness, Americans are ingenious at devising such rewards. Golf, for example, is a sport suited to many sizes of people. Yet at least one smaller professional golfer, Larry Hinson, has complained that the trend in American golf courses has oriented this sport to talls. "There's no need for a 7200 yard course with fairways close to 700 yards long," he explained. "Every player shouldn't have to be 6'4" and over 200 pounds."

Volleyball is another sport in which the virtues of size depend entirely on the way the game is played. Elsewhere, in the Orient especially, a defensive, scooping style of volleyball favors bodies that can retrieve balls about to hit the ground. In the United States, a booming, power-ball style rewards tall bodies better able to spike and defend against spikes. The leading American women's volleyball player, Mary Jo Peppler, is 6 feet tall. When he gave up basketball, Wilt Chamberlain went right into volleyball and became one of that sport's standouts. An all-star volleyball match was subsequently hyped in this fashion: ''7-foot-1 basketball legend Wilt Chamberlain and 6-foot-3 Garth Pischke — with a 46″ vertical jump — face each other across the net!''

Even soccer has been given a characteristic American twist as that sport grows in popularity here. In theory, soccer is the most size-neutral of major sports. The game was invented by the English Football Association in 1863 specifically to reward skill over size. As played in most parts of the world, smaller bodies even have something of an advantage owing to their greater dexterity and speed. A group of champion Yugoslav soccer players were actually found to be shorter on the average than all the players in their area and than the male population as a whole. Kin-Itsu Hirata, who in 1964 measured and compared a range of Olympic athletes, concluded that ''the physique of soccer players is rather small and a little stout. As soccer needs strength of feet and endurance, such a physique will be the most suitable.''

Perhaps because size and strength matter so little in soccer, the United States has literally been the world's last major country to succumb to its charms. But inevitably, as soccer has caught on here, an ''American'' style has evolved — one emphasizing body contact and power shots up the middle by big players in contrast to the deft footwork displayed by smaller bodies playing this sport. Compared to the finesse of the game played abroad, ours, in the words of an American college soccer coach, is one based on ''strength, size and kicking people around.''

The best example of our genius at adapting a game to favor size is the only major American-invented sport: basketball. Hard as it is to conceive of today, basketball was not intended to favor talls at the outset. When Dr. James Naismith in 1891 tacked peach baskets to facing balconies of the YMCA gym in Springfield, Massachusetts, then gave his charges a soccer ball to aim at these baskets, his intention was not to invent a game favoring larger people. Naismith mostly was trying to create something more interesting than calisthenics for his boys to do in the winter. His peach baskets were set ten feet off the floor (where today's hoops remain) because that was the height of the balconies to which they were attached. By having to place the ball so high in the air with such accuracy, Naismith figured, basketball players would be rewarded for grace over strength. How little he understood our values.

It did take Americans a while to figure out how suited basketball was to talls. Until World War II the game was played by many sizes of people. In those early days greater emphasis was placed on outside shooting, which smaller players could do at least as competently as larger ones. In the 1930s the original Boston Celtics had a center no taller than some guards today: 6'4".

But during the war average- to small-sized men were drafted by Uncle Sam rather than by the pros, while those over 6'6" were considered too tall for military service and were left home to play basketball (among other things). Since then, the average size of basketball players has shot up far more quickly than that of men in general. A comparison of the 1948 University of Kentucky basketball team with that of 1968, for example, found both groups taller than men generally, but those in 1968 by a far greater margin. During that twenty-year period, the height of Kentucky players rose an average of 2 inches (2½ inches for the starting team) while the average height of American men overall rose less than an inch. Ten years later, in 1978, a study of basketball players at 253 colleges found they averaged 6'4.66", an increase of more than one-tenth of an inch over the year before, and of more than one-third of an inch over the 1972 average. During the same period, the height of American men in general had stabilized.

A comparable trend has been found in other sports. Members of Harvard's 1942 crew team, for example, were found to average 5¼ inches taller than those of 1867, a rise more than double that of Harvard students in general. More recently, a comparative study of football players at the University of Texas between 1899 and 1970 found the average increase in their height to be 2.6 inches and the average gain in weight 35.3 pounds. Anthropologist Robert Malina, who conducted this study, estimated this seven-decade rise in the size of Longhorn football players to be double that of their male classmates overall. Dr. Malina attributed the disproportionate rise in size to recruitment and styles of play favoring bigger players, and to training methods that increased bulk. Although it has not been proved, the high-protein meals provided at training tables for football players as young as junior high age may increase not only heftiness but height.

While such studies of American athletes have found them growing taller over the years than Americans in general, comparable studies of foreign athletes competing in sports less popular here have found that the foreigners' internal organs grow larger over time but their height rises no faster than that of the population at large. This is true of athletes in sports such as distance running, swimming, skiing, and cycling.

Cycling provides an illuminating case study of size in American sports. The racing of bicycles actually began in the United States late last century. Until World War II bike races at Madison Square Garden and hundreds of other "velodromes" around the country regularly attracted fanatic sell-out crowds of thirty thousand or more. But after the war Americans' pent-up hunger for cars and growing passion for sports such as football and basketball (exacerbated by conflicts among cycling promotors themselves) reduced interest in cycling to practically nothing. By 1955 only two American velodromes were still operating.

In many other parts of the world cycling is rivaled only by soccer in popularity. When both were active, a bike-racing star such as Belgium's Eddie Merckx was nearly as widely known as the fabled soccer star Pelé. Because there is opportunity for all sizes of people in cycling, this sport, like soccer, is one in which no country need feel at a disadvantage.

Recently cycling has begun to come back in the United States, but in a characteristically American fashion. For a time I lived near one of the country's leading velodromes in Trexlertown, Pennsylvania, and the local newspaper covered the bicycle races in season. As one might imagine, most ink was devoted to big, beefy, sprint champions such as Jerry "The Gentle Giant" Ash. Women's events got less attention. And barely mentioned in tag lines at the end of cycling coverage were winners of the longer races in which the need for endurance favored smaller, less glamorous racers.

The beauty of sports is the accuracy with which they reflect their host culture. As five minutes in any locker room will confirm, sports are just society without manners. They let us know where we stand without equivocation. One drawback about American sports in particular is that they're set up in such a way that smaller bodies are generally left standing outside the locker room.

I say "generally" because when one tries to make a case that little people are discriminated against by our athletic system, some coach or other will always come along with a noisily defensive rebuttal. Names such as Calvin Murphy or Joe Morgan are trotted out and paraded around. Then a series of clichés is set loose — most prominent among them: "It's not the size of the dog in the fight, it's the size of the fight in the dog."

Such points have merit. Newspapers and magazines are constantly studded with inspiring stories of smaller athletes who bucked the odds to not only master but excel at sports favoring bigger bodies. Like the Morgans and the Murphys, a 5'7" Charlie Criss, who at twenty-eight made the National Basketball Association as a rookie, encourages us all, as does the Cleveland Browns' superb 5'7" running back Greg Pruitt and the California Angels' 5'4" All-Star shortstop Freddie Patek.

But such smaller stars must pay a tax beyond the physical toll. This tax is their first name. In the mouths of sportscasters, especially, the given name of a smaller athlete invariably becomes his middle name as "Little" takes over the first spot. Little Calvin Murphy. Little Randy Jones. Little Charlie Criss. In the case of Freddie Patek, for most of his career the smallest player in major-league baseball, announcers sometimes skip his first name entirely and just call him Little Patek. (Floyd Little, the small former running back of the Denver Broncos, generally was able to hold on to his first name by virtue of his last.)

Don't think such linguistic indignity doesn't bother the smaller athlete. Joe Morgan said that he originally signed with the Houston Astros because their scout was the only one to call him a "good player," not a "good little player." Portland Trailblazer guard Dave Twardzik said his goal as a professional basketball player is to erase the "little" always stuck in front of his name.

But such an aim is fanciful. Even when bigger people try to "understand," they don't. "There is many a place in pro football for the little man," said one news report, "a term all of these tykes detest."

A "short-but" syndrome confronts all smaller people, though no one more than the smaller athlete. ("He's short, but he's strong"; "He may be small, but he's got the heart of a lion"; "The guy's little, but he's got exceptional speed.")

Kids reading the sports page, listening to the radio, or watching television can't fail to miss the message of such commentary. Nowhere better than in sports commentary do we get more precise or more frequent information about where smaller people stand on the American scale of things. Just for the hell of it, I sometimes jot down what they're saying over the air about professional athletes of smaller stature. Here are some examples:

• Surprising power from this little fella. [Howard Cosell about Los Angeles Dodger Ron Cey]

• For a little guy he can hit the ball. [Jim Palmer about Texas Ranger Mickey Rivers]

• I don't know how any NFL quarterback would be able to spot the little tyke once he planted himself over the middle. [Los Angeles sportscaster Jim Healy about former San Diego Charger Johnny Rodgers]

So, yes, it's not the size of the dog in the fight, and it is the size of the fight in the dog. All it costs successful smaller athletes is their dignity.

And even if the Calvin Murphys of this world are an inspiration to some, they exemplify nothing to many people with less talent and determination. So long as American games are geared to talls, the average-sized athlete of average talent is set up for failure. A football or basketball player in the mid-six-foot range doesn't have to be terribly talented — that's just a bonus; but players in the mid-five-foot range must be brilliant to succeed. Inspiring as such cases may be, they pave no path for the less gifted who might like to compete in popular sports but haven't a prayer because these sports are geared to talls. What options are there for such players?

One suggestion often made is that the rules of sports be revised to give everybody an equal chance — that categories of competition be created in all sports based on size: short, average, and tall leagues, say. But this approach creates more problems than it solves. In the first place, a spirited athlete wants to take on all comers, even if lack of size puts him or her at a disadvantage. In the second place, were we to categorize athletes by height, our biases being what they are, the tall league would immediately become the major league, all the rest the minors.

More fruitful than ghettoizing athletes by size would be to broaden the pool of major sports to include more activities in which all sizes of athlete can compete equally. Odd as it may seem to the American imagination, size isn't necessarily an asset in general athletic performance. In terms of fitness overall, there is no known advantage to being any particular size. As a single example, a test battery administered to Navy recruits that included squat-thrusts, sit-ups, push-ups, squat-jumps, and chin-ups showed "no noticeable change in physical fitness mean scores with an increase in height."

However, bodies of different height do perform certain tasks better than others. Owing to their higher center of gravity, tall athletes are favored in all jumping events — high jumping in particular, because they start off much closer to the bar. Throwing events — discus, shotput, hammer throw — have always been more suited to those who can project a missile with stronger muscles, using greater extension. In general, tall bodies also seem suited to quick bursts of strength, and therefore excel in shorter events.

Smaller bodies, on the other hand, have the advantage when

endurance is rewarded. The average height of Boston Marathon winners from 1897 to 1965 is 5′7.1″. Smalls also do better than talls when lifting the body is called for, as it is in gymnastics. And the lower center of gravity common in a smaller body helps the gymnast's balance, as it does that of the skier.

Of course, generalizations such as these must step aside periodically to make way for the dedicated exception. "The outstanding high jumper," advised a 1970 text on physical performance, "is without exception a tall individual." Eight years after this was written, 5′8″ Franklin Jacobs leaped to a new world indoor record of 7′7¼″.

For those without Jacobs's extraordinary talent and drive, it could be useful to know how body size affects one's prospects in particular sports. For that purpose I've put together the following brief summary of information correlating height with performance for a variety of physical activities.

A Sport-by-Sport Review of Prospects by Body Size

Archery: Since equipment is size-adjusted and strength per se is not central, this is a good sport for all sizes and both sexes.

Auto Racing: There's room for all sizes in the driver's seat — but some penalty for being too tall and having to squeeze into the cockpit.

Baseball: Despite a trend to tallness, baseball has always had room in its heart and on the field for smaller players — particularly at shortstop and second base. Pitchers are getting gigantic.

Basketball: Unless unusually talented and dedicated — with a high tolerance for humiliation — a small player should find another sport.

Bicycle Racing: Cyclists come in all sizes. Talls have an edge in sprints, smalls in marathons.

Bowling: A sport favoring precision over strength, bowling offers no reward for size; tallness increases the distance necessary to set the ball down. According to former Professional Bowlers Association official Jerry Levine, despite exceptions in their ranks, "Ninety-five out of a hundred bowlers on the tour will tell you, 'The smaller the bowler, the better the bowler.' " Physiologically, a bowler is best helped by sturdy legs and a lean frame that permits free arm swing.

Boxing: Owing to weight divisions, boxing is good for all sizes. There's a reach advantage in being tall for one's weight.

Chess: This game is size-neutral (although Woody Allen once claimed to have failed the height requirement for his high school chess team; and the shorter Anatoly Karpov demanded an elevated seat for the world-championship matches in which he defeated Victor Korchnoi).

Dance: Average height is classically considered most aesthetically suited to ballet; modern dance is hospitable to a wider range of sizes.

Fencing: Since equipment is size-adjusted and finesse counts more than strength in fencing, there's no penalty for smallness; the reach advantage of talls is offset by their presenting a larger target. Fencing has been suggested as ideal for man-woman competition.

Golf: Suited to all sizes, within extremes. Since club length varies to fit height, there's some penalty for size extremes, which make custom-made clubs necessary.

Gymnastics: Among the few sports with a clear advantage for smallness.

Hockey: Prospects here are like those in baseball. Though the trend is changing, historically there's always been room on the ice for smaller men, more so at some positions than others (on offense in particular). Professional defensive players, especially, are mushrooming in height. The increasing popularity of brawling in this sport gives talls a sideshow advantage.

Horse Racing: The only sport in which one simply *can't* be very tall (because of weight limits). A Shoemaker or a Cauthen excepted, horses are generally better known than the men who ride them.

Lacrosse: Indian-invented, with an emphasis on speed, this game is good for all sizes. It's growing in popularity, which soon could make it necessary for smalls to defend their turf.

Racquetball: Good for all sizes. Smalls are among current champs in this sport, which is rapidly becoming more popular. Though power shots, predictably, are also getting more popular, the compact, enclosed playing area doesn't limit such shots to talls. Whole families can play mixed doubles.

Rodeo: Plenty of room for smalls, in riding events especially (where balance helps). Longtime (former) champ Larry Mahan is not tall.

Rowing: The ideal rower has a long torso, long arms, and short legs; since such a combination is rare, long everything is second best, so talls dominate this sport.

Rugby: Not quite as much advantage for size as in football, but almost.

Skiing: A low center of gravity helps in most events. One study of champion skiers found them below the average height of contestants overall.

"If you're 5'6" tall and you stand with your toes touching the baseline, this is what you see when looking through (and above) the net."

"A solid net helps convince the 5'6" player that he or she had better have respect for that high barrier which stops so many shots."

"This is the baseline view for a six-foot player. Did you six-footers ever realize that from your own baseline you have to look under *the net tape to see a shot land in your opponent's court?"*

Soccer: A game for all sizes, depending on the style of play and the position (talls have greater opportunity on defense). Most styles of play in the world today give an edge to the agility and speed of smalls.

Surfing: A low center of gravity makes surfing easier.

Swimming: Tall bodies and longer limbs are favored in all events save diving (Alan Ladd was a champion diver in high school) and very long distance races.

Tennis: There's a real reach and stride advantage for talls, but smalls can compensate with hustle. In most settings other than at Wimbledon, etc., tennis is relatively size-neutral.

Track and Field: More events favor talls than smalls — throwing and jumping events in particular, as well as hurdles and middle-distance races. Smalls have advantage chiefly in long-distance running; sprints are a divided zone.

Volleyball: Small Americans ought to look elsewhere; smalls elsewhere should stay with it (one study found no correlation between size and volleying ability).

Weight Lifting: Even within individual weight categories, smallness is an advantage since arms closer to the ground have better leverage.

Wrestling: There's an advantage for wrestlers in being short for their weight, but not as much as for weight lifters.

SUMMARY

Good for Smalls: Diving; gymnastics; horse racing; long-distance bicycling, running, and swimming; rodeo riding; skiing; surfing; weight lifting; wrestling.

Size-Neutral: Archery; auto racing; baseball, hockey, and soccer (depending on style and position); bowling; chess; fencing; golf; lacrosse; racquetball; amateur tennis; volleyball (depending on style of play).

Tall Advantage: Basketball, boxing, football, jumping events, rowing, rugby, sprint cycling and swimming, tournament tennis, throwing events, middle-distance running.

As you can see, among the full variety of sports, there is room for every size. Our choice in America to emphasize those sports favoring talls penalizes small and tall alike. A surprise for me has been discovering that real frustrations are felt among those supposedly favored by our society's athletic values. A 6-foot friend, for example, who was tall as a child, told me that he always envied the "Phil Rizzutos" and "Peewee Reeses" among his playmates, who seemed to get extra recognition if they did well on the ball field because less was expected of them. But if he dove successfully for a fly or snared a hot grounder or hit the ball for distance — well, that's what big kids are supposed to do. At least that's the way it seemed to him.

Even in professional sports, larger athletes can feel unappreciated by virtue of their size. "Nobody roots for Goliath," Wilt Chamberlain once said. "Everybody wants to see Goliath lose," echoed Kareem Abdul-Jabbar.

"I remember as a kid," Jabbar later added, "seeing a picture in the New York *Daily News* of Wilt Chamberlain with four teeth knocked out. I felt very sorry for him. And I bet I was the only person in New York City who did."

To some degree everyone's a loser in the American approach to sports. By our compulsion to reward size we teach kids a cruel but accurate lesson: in American sports, as in American life, height produces champions. This lesson is unfortunate for all sizes of people. It leads to little people feeling left out, big people feeling unappreciated. In sports, particularly, such feelings are generated early and indelibly.

On the questionnaires I distributed, men and women alike repeatedly mentioned school sports as the activity that best taught them where their height placed them on the American scale of values. A 5'7" graduate student, age thirty-six, who was always small recalled that in grade school PE a team captain counted off for volleyball as follows: "1, 2, 3, 4, 5, 6, 6½ (when he got to me)."

A 5'2" mother and writer in her early thirties said she still can remember from girlhood volleyball courts "the utter joy on the faces of the opponents when I was next to the net! The tall, athletic types would 'spike' the ball over the net and down on me so hard that it frequently hit me in the face. Yuk!" Her husband, a 5'8" television newscaster, stopped growing in the eighth grade. As a result he progressed from being one of the tallest to one of the smallest members on his high school basketball team. Or, as he puts it, "from first string to the bench in just four years!"

Happily, sports are one aspect of American life in which prospects for people of all sizes seem to be getting better. The growing popularity of auto racing, gymnastics, skiing, long-distance running, racquetball, soccer, and cycling are all encouraging signs. Unlike football or basketball, such sports will always have room for smaller participants, no matter how hard traditional American athletes may try to alter this reality. The total of two U.S. cycling velodromes in 1955 has increased to some fifteen today, with more on the way. Growing numbers of facilities across the country are becoming hosts on weekends to little girls competing gymnastically. Kurt Thomas, who is 5'5", recently brought the United States its first gold medal in international gymnastics competition since the 1932 Olympics. An American soccer player of the same height, Billy Gazonas, not long ago was named College Player of the Year and subsequently turned pro. Kids' soccer teams across the country today rival or even exceed in popularity those of football. During a three-year period in Charlotte, North Carolina, one park's football program declined from 200 to 75 participants; during the same period, the number of kids playing organized soccer in that city as a whole went from 0 to 500.

If such trends continue — if our historic preference for sports that favor talls is balanced by the rise of sports that favor smalls, or, better yet, favor no size in particular — people of all heights will come out winners.

13 Putting Height in Perspective

Host: Why do you think kids are shorter than adults?
Kid 1: Because they're born after 'em.
Kid 2: I think it's because kids need someone to look up to.

— Children's talk show on ''America 2-Night''

So what does it all mean?

Why should something so silly as a few inches between bodies create such psychological chasms?

And how did it come to pass that tall got such a better reputation than small?

To put in perspective why relative height is so basic to our feelings about ourselves and each other, probing the adult mind is less useful than examining the child's mind that clings to it.

"Every adult," psychiatrist Erik Erikson has written, "was once a child. He was once small. A sense of smallness forms a substratum in his mind, ineradicably. His triumphs will be measured against this smallness, his defeats will substantiate it. The questions as to who is bigger and who can do or not do this or that, and to whom — these questions fill the adult's inner life far beyond the necessities."

To understand why this happens we must go back to the time when we looked up at everybody — back as far as the crib. It's difficult to re-create how the world must have looked from that perspective. But we can imagine. Flat on our back. Barely able to move. Helpless. Huge objects looming overhead. Enormous bodies moving about. Giants. And these giants control us utterly. Our life is literally in their hands. Whenever they want they can pick us up, put us down, roll us over, roll us back again. Their wish is our command.

As babies in a grown-up world — as midgets among giants — we make an accurate association between size and power. Bodies bigger than ours control us. The bodies we look up to are very strong. Every one of them. This equation probably is one of the earliest in a baby's consciousness, and one of the most lasting.

Psychologist Layne Longfellow has suggested that the primitive size consciousness of the child is imbued with a sense of magic. "Big people can perform magic," explained Longfellow, describing the infant's early perception of the world. "They can make it light or dark, they can create sound or turn it off by pushing a button. We can't even push the button yet. They can put clothes on or off us. They can move around. They can walk. They can do anything. They can perform magic. And they're big."

Presumably some spark of this infant's perspective smolders throughout our lives. So perhaps we can forgive ourselves when we continue to associate size with power long after the association is invalid. The grip of the infant's eye is very strong.

The principal size-power equation we make as babies involves our parents. They're the big people who most control our lives. At times they nurture and protect us; at other times they cause us pain. Always, they control. And always their control is from on high.

Parents know about power from above. At times they yield it: to stop a child's crying, they may lift him to eye level. To make him delirious with excitement, they can lift him high into the air. But when they want to show who's boss, they set him down far, far beneath them.

"My son is 2½," explained a twenty-nine-year-old mother,

"and about a yard high. When I'm in a reasoning mood, I stoop down to his level so he sees us as equals. But when I'm *really* mad (do you know about 2½ year olds?), I feel more effective glaring down at him."

Those who counsel parents to help them bridge a gap with their kids will commonly begin with the size disparity. An author working on a fatherhood manual told me his first exhortation for men trying to do better by their young sons is "Down on your knees!" Too many fathers, he pointed out, won't even reach down to hold their boy's hand; the child has to reach up. Thus does the father become in his son's eye a huge, looming, ominous figure. Asked to describe their fathers, preschool boys interviewed by this counselor would refer first to that parent's gigantic size. "Tall as the ceiling!" they'd say. "Big as a tree!"

No world is more height-obsessed than the child's world. There, everything is sorted basically by size: little kids, big kids, grown-ups. When learning to speak, words for size are among the first a child acquires. "In addition," as psychologists Allan Katcher and Max Levin have pointed out, "much of the child's early verbal training provides repetitive references to size distinctions. The child also receives numerous reinforcing examples of the role of size in determining status and value judgments in our culture. One has only to examine children's storybooks, records and movies to be impressed with the obvious force of this kind of cultural emphasis."

Around the globe, perhaps for all of time, children's stories have portrayed worlds of big and small, giants and dwarfs, elves and monsters, fairies and witches. From Jack the Giant Killer to David and Goliath, the powerful but clumsy big figure eventually is felled by a crafty smaller person — a person closer in size to a child. This is the outcome we pray for as children.

Yet the giants who threaten little people in such tales often turn out to be gentle within. Something like our parents.

Unlike their fairy tales, in which giants are cut down to size, children's jokes often mock big people by exaggerating their size and making them grotesque. In a study made of children's humor, psychoanalyst Martha Wolfenstein found such mockery the most common form. By making fun of the size to which they aspire, Dr. Wolfenstein concluded, children work to alleviate the "growing up" anxieties all of them feel.

Sensing how anxious their children are about this subject, parents everywhere manipulate growing-up worries to achieve desired ends. As a reward for what the parents want, growth is promised. All it takes is eating your spinach, drinking your milk, and getting to bed on time. An eighteen-year-old college student, 5'2", wrote me: "I can still recall my mom saying, 'Eat your vegetables, because if you don't you will be like your grandmother' (who's 4'8"). Since I hated vegetables I only ate a few and snuck the rest under the table to the dog. Maybe mom was right because I'm on the short side of the family, but the dog turned out to be a huge German shepherd."

Stunted growth, by contrast, is threatened as a punishment for doing what the parent doesn't think is a good idea — smoking, drinking, masturbating — or whatever else children oughtn't to be doing these days. The specific activity for which shortness is the punishment varies depending on the culture. Smoking seems to be America's favorite source of stunted growth. The Hopi Indians are very stern with children about having sex too young and warn them that it will result in their becoming dwarfs. To the best of my knowledge, none of the common taboo activities for which stunted growth is the threatened punishment has been shown to actually hinder growth. When someone once wrote advice columnist Dr. Hip Pocrates (Eugene Schoenfeld) to ask if sex stunted growth, he replied, ''I have noticed no decrease in average stature among Berkeley youths.''

One would think parents might do more to soothe rather than aggravate their kids' size anxieties. But that would involve giving up a measure of control. ''Even the kindest of parents,'' Seymour Fisher has noted, ''is impressed with the power contrast that is obvious in the size differential between the child and himself.''

Some parents do go out of their way to lessen certain aspects of this differential — at times with outside help. One technique of ''family therapy'' involves equalizing size and eye level by having kids stand on crates to achieve eye-to-eye contact with their parents, or having parents stoop to their knees for the same purpose. After attending a workshop where such techniques were demonstrated, a thirty-five-year-old mother began experimenting with her three-year-old girl by getting down on the floor so their eyes could meet directly. The mother told me that the positive effect on her child's mood was so startling that three years later she was still making a habit of lying, stooping, or sitting with her daughter whenever possible.

In another case, a young mother reorganized the whole family living quarters after realizing how it must look to her kids. This mother's realization came from visiting a house specially outfitted for an ultratall couple. ''I, at 5'4'', felt miserable and infantile,'' she wrote. ''My feet dangled on the toilet, I had to stand on tip-toes to put a towel or coat away. I had to reach across a high sink to wash. This brought back vivid feelings of childhood frustration and anger at having to live in a place which didn't suit my body. Immediately upon returning home I adjusted *our* home to better suit our toddler. Low hooks, better stools, little low toy shelves, etc. He was thrilled and started hanging things up and putting toys away.''

So parents can and do sometimes soothe their kids' height

ZiGGY

BY Tom Wilson

WHEN i WAS A LiTTLe KiD, AND i'D GeT DepreSseD, MY MoTHeR WOULD ALWAYS SAY TO ME.. "ZiGGY," SHe'D SAY, "THiNGS ARe NeVeR AS BAD AS THeY SeeM" ...SHe ALWAYS SAID THAT

©1973 Universal Press Syndicate

...AND WHeNeVeR i'D GeT DiSCOURAGED, AND FeeL AS THOUGH i'D MADe A MeSS OF eVeRYTHiNG, SHe'D SAY, "DON'T WORRY ZiGGY, TOMORROW'S ANOTHER DAY"...SHe ALWAYS SAID THAT TOO..

...AND ONCe WHeN iT SeeMeD LiKe i'D NeVeR GeT TO Be GROWN UP, MY MUM SAID TO Me ...."DON'T Be iMPATieNT ZiGGY, JUST eAT YOUR GReeNS AND DRiNK YOUR MiLK, AND YOU'LL GROW UP TO Be BiG, AND TALL AND STRONG"

....FiRST TiMe SHe eVeR LieD TO Me !!

Tom Wilson

anxieties by taking a little thought. The problem is that it's so easy to be thoughtless and keep reminding a child of who's bigger. This isn't hard for grown-ups to do. All it takes is continual use of affectionate terms and phrases such as "squirt," "tyke," "little man," "kid," and "Oh, you're such a cute little thing." Not resorting to such diminutives when talking with a kid is next to impossible. I've tried. Generally I last about five minutes.

A practice that even more effectively reinforces children's height anxieties involves standing them against a door jamb for regular measurement. Not seeing enough distance between the marks on such a doorway can horrify a smaller child, just as seeing too much distance can trigger a bigger child's fear about growing into a giant. But with their special love of statistics Americans in particular seem to need some such data with which to report their child's progress to the world.

"I am puzzled by the curious habit of American parents when

asked about their children,'' a recent immigrant once wrote Ann Landers. ''Why, so often, do they respond by telling the boy's height and weight? . . . These statistics are announced with great pride, as if it were a great achievement. Why?''

Landers wasn't sure. Perhaps, she thought, in the absence of anything better to brag about, ''parents can always fall back on height and weight.'' Later she published a letter from a South Dakota mother complaining about ''insensitive and crass people who compare the size of children.

''My son is small for his age,'' the mother explained. ''I'm tired of biting my tongue when acquaintances (I'd hardly call them friends) make remarks such as, 'Is he the shortest child in his class?' Or, 'I can't believe he's seven. Look at how much taller my son is!' ''

For a child anxious about his size, grown-ups of all kinds can be a source of stunning insensitivity. It doesn't usually involve out-and-out cruelty — just a little ''overlooking'' of how acute a child's sensitivities can be about where he or she stands in the height sweepstakes.

Take lining up by height. Being at the front or back of such lines was the painful childhood memory most often mentioned to me by adults who once stood there. One middle-aged man remembered this feeling as one of being ''out on the edge,'' rather than safely in the middle. A woman in her twenties who was shortest in her class said that since the ''punishment'' for being late was getting sent to the back of the line, she was late on purpose constantly. ''Thank God for Marvin Ackerman,'' said Stephen Jay Gould, ''who stood in front of me in line (I was always second).''

When the young Ruth Gordon boasted to her father that she was to lead the entire eighth-grade graduating procession, at first he was pleased. As the actress recalled in her autobiography:

" 'Why, Snuggy!' he said proudly. 'You got the highest marks?'

" 'No, I'm shortest.'

" 'Chosen on account of a deformity,' he said."

Standing at the other end of her school's lines was big Alexis Smith. Recalling her deep feelings of inadequacy while growing up, the tall actress once explained: "I was always at the end of the line in gym. Everybody stopped, and I just kept growing.

"I was the dud the pretty girls would have around for contrast."

Who's last or first or second or third among kids neatly organized by size may seem like a trivial matter to those concerned with bureaucratic aesthetics. But to those arranged in such lines, where one stands is an issue of the first magnitude. I've heard people more than half a century removed from the experience describe in painful detail the humiliation of being a piddling little "daisy," say, on the end of a flower line, rather than a proud sunflower in the middle.

One woman of sixty-five still remembered vividly the times her elementary school PE class was lined up inversely by height to march outside for exercise. Always the shortest in class, she was always last on this line. "We then paired up for various dances or games," she recalled. "If there were an even number of pupils, all was well. I had a partner. If not, I usually had to go through whatever motions — of clapping or whatever, turning where someone was supposed to hold my hand, etc. — quite alone. This humiliated me since I tended to be clumsy anyway, but doing alone what everyone else was doing with a partner made me feel excruciatingly isolated.

"Every nice day that we went outside, I frantically started counting the number of students lining up, praying that there would be an even number."

Teachers have many means at their disposal with which to

confirm students' suspicion that people of contrasting size get treated differently. Other means, besides lining up students by height, are more subtle but every bit as reinforcing of size-value equations. Bigger kids are given tasks that seem suited to their size — pulling the shades, erasing the high boards, keeping order while teacher's gone. Smaller kids get smaller chores — picking papers up off the floor, erasing the low boards, taking attendance.

Unfortunately, it's nearly impossible *not* to treat children as being the age we perceive them to be based on size rather than the age they are. John Money has attributed this to our "tyranny of the eyes," explaining: "All human beings have an automatic, unthinking capacity to orient themselves toward other people on the basis of stature and physique as indexes of age and mental maturity."

As a result, those who were small or tall as children have very different memories, compared to those who were average-sized, about what school was like. "I always had to sit in the back of the room," recalled a 5'9" teacher who was big as a girl. "I was always chosen first for teams. People expected more of me in achievement as related to my 'advanced' growth." Another woman, who eventually reached 6'1", remembered being so big at age five that they put her in first grade instead of kindergarten for fear she would "scare" the other children.

Looking so much older than one's peers leads to constant problems. In grade school Kareem Abdul-Jabbar had to carry around his birth certificate to get kids' discount rates, as did Lynnie Greene. But the worst problem overall is being told constantly to "act your age," when the age referred to is the one a tall child appears to be, not the one he or she actually is. The ambivalence can be strong here. On the one hand, it's nice to be treated as older. On the other hand, it's confusing. If you look eight at five, you're not given as much leeway as your same-age playmates to run and jump and shout and cry and carry on as five-year-olds do but eight-year-olds can't.

Living up to the expectations of an older body puts a heavy burden on the tall kid. Such a kid may not like pulling down shades in class, may not want to be chosen first for teams, may prefer *not* to be team captain or class president or whatever the leadership spot is that seems to need a tall body to fill it. A booklet of tips for King-Size Clothes customers cites "leadership pressure" as a lifelong burden that must be shouldered by those of above-average height.

"What people 'expected' from me I never quite 'discovered,' " author Albert Payson Terhune once recalled of his tall boyhood. "All I knew was that, whatever they expected, they weren't getting it."

At the other end of the spectrum, a contrasting set of expectations entirely faces those growing up small. What's "expected" of them is childlike behavior. Looking younger than they are because of their size, such children get treated as younger — even by bigger kids their own age. To provide something fresher than her own memory of growing up small, a 4'11" teacher gave her questionnaire to her eight-year-old daughter so the child could tell me what it's like to be littlest in class. Here are some of the girl's responses:

• *Nicknames:* Shrimp, shortcake, midget.

• *Opposite-sex responses:* Taller boys like me more, but shorter boys tease me and are too rough.

• *School incidents:* I was the shortest one in class so I had to play Tinkerbell in Peter Pan.

• *Everyday problems:* Reaching for things in cabinets when everybody else can reach it, and reaching tables in lunch.

• *Comments made about your height:* Gosh you're small! Hey little ant. Oops — I think I just stepped on you! Hi Super Shrimp, little one and make motions at me.

• *Height you'd rather be:* Five inches taller.

• *Anything to add:* Telling somebody that won't laugh or tease me and will understand me. I like getting it off my chest and explaining it.

The mother of a thalidomide baby born with short, deformed legs once said that far from being afraid, the girl looked forward to having her legs amputated so she could be fitted with artificial limbs. "If she has two artificial limbs," the mother explained, "then her height can be adjusted upwards as she grows older. It's very important to Joanne to be taller. She is sensitive about being so much shorter than the other children.

"Recently, when she took her first Communion, they lined the children up according to height and Joanne had to go first because she was shorter even than the second-graders [Joanne was ten at the time].

"Sometimes when I buy her clothes I ink in a bigger size to make her feel better. She keeps saying, 'I *am* a big girl.' "

It is difficult to exaggerate how important size is to any child, but to a smaller one especially. This is *the* issue of their day, every day. I remember. Every fiber of one's being is focused on "growing up" — that is, getting bigger.

A basic height problem for kids and grown-ups alike is one of language. The words we use for age and size are so hopelessly intertwined; when we refer to a "little kid," we're describing both. When we say "grow up," we mean a process both chronological and physical. Ideally, the two go together. But they don't always. If a child's body isn't growing fast enough to "keep up with its age," where will he or she find the sophistication to realize this doesn't mean remaining a child forever?

As the end of the growth years draws near, panic is common among those not measuring up. This is when anxious smaller boys, especially, and their even more anxious parents show up in doctors' offices desperate for a remedy, an operation, a shot — anything — to keep from being doomed to shortness. Though there is seldom anything that can be "done" (shortness, after all, isn't a disease), the experience of being taken to the doctor is itself very often a lasting childhood memory. Joel Grey was taken to the doctor by parents worried about his height and remembers the experience with mixed feelings. On the one hand, he felt that his folks were looking out for his health, and for that he was appreciative. Also, he himself wouldn't have minded being taller. But the episode sticks in his mind as "degrading" because "it kind of confirmed there was something wrong with you."

There was nothing wrong, physically, except short parents — if that's "wrong." Psychologically it can feel that way. The whole issue of height-related feelings between parents and children is one that's rarely confronted. Yet such attitudes can influence how we feel about our parents, how they feel about us, and, ultimately, how we feel about ourselves. Genetic guilt may color the feelings of short parents with short offspring. "My children would have been taller," explained a 4'11" mother about why she'd rather be 5'3". Similarly, endocrinologists have told me that tall mothers who feel responsible for a daughter's tallness frequently seek growth-stunting treatment for the girl.

In other cases, tall parents of small children can sometimes barely conceal their frustration over the runt they've helped create. A thirty-two-year-old, 5-foot-tall psychologist said that her shortness had been a constant source of friction between her and her mother. "My mother blamed me for my height," the psychologist wrote, "declaring frequently that I had refused to eat when I was a baby (she never thought about her two packs of cigarettes a day while she was pregnant with me). She urged me constantly to do stretching exercises! She made it clear that I was a disappointment to her. She'd wanted me to (a) be a Rockette and (b) be able to wear large-brimmed floppy hats.''

Parent-child height feelings crisscross in elaborate patterns. Those who surpass a parent in height can establish an entirely different relationship from those who don't. The day one grows taller than a parent is a thrilling day for the surpasser, a traumatic one for the surpassed. ''It was quite exciting,'' recalled Michael Crichton of shooting up past his dad in his early teens, ''but I'm afraid my father, who's six-five, was a little upset. He started walking around the house on tiptoes so he would be taller than I was.''

It's such a commonplace by now for kids to grow taller than their parents that we forget this isn't the way it's always been. J. M. Tanner has estimated that the current trend to taller bodies in Europe and America is something over a century old (elsewhere it's even more recent). Thus for most of man's existence, a father presumably could count on making no worse than eye-to-eye contact with his son; and likewise a mother with her daughter. The fact that this hasn't been counted on for the past several generations probably has had a greater impact than we realize on relations between parents and children. ''I can't seem to 'yell' at her,'' wrote a 5'9" teacher whose fifteen-year-old daughter was about to surpass her in height. ''She and I have talked about this. She psyches me out real well. When she knows I'm really disgusted with her, she'll pull out a chair and tell me to stand on it and yell at her. Do you suppose if she grows a few more inches and becomes taller than her mother she will control her mother?''

We all try to be lighthearted about such transfers of power, but the process can be heavy. A man confronting a son about to look down upon him is caught in a psychological bind. On the one hand, he wants to take pride in having produced such a large specimen. On the other hand, how *do* you grow accustomed to looking up at your baby boy?

One man of 6'2" told me about wearing his father's old Navy uniform to go trick-or-treating at the age of eleven. It fit perfectly. By thirteen his feet had outgrown his father's shoes. Today there's nearly a foot of difference between them. The father tries to be casual about the matter. He calls his thirty-year-old son "a boy you can look up to." But the son thought he always picked up an edge in the comment. Certainly *he* wasn't altogether comfortable about their gap. The man pulled a snapshot from his wallet to show me. He and his father are standing arm in arm on the beach. The son's body is curved nearly into a *C* as he leans over in a desperate but futile attempt to keep things more even.

Grown-ups working out an adult relationship with their parents can draw very basically on relative size. Several people who grew taller than their parents told me that this made it easier to break away psychologically. On the other hand, a woman who outgrew her father found him rejecting her as (in his words) "an overgrown heifer." Perhaps the ideal is that reported by Steve Gould, who stopped growing upon reaching his father's height of 5'8". Characterizing their adult relationship today, on his questionnaire Gould wrote simply, "Better friends at eye level."

I've dwelt here on the height issues affecting parents and children, because such issues have so much to do with our feelings about height in general. Parent-child metaphors are at the heart of our grown-up feelings about tallness and smallness. Isn't the main reason tall people are chosen so regularly for leadership positions that we raise our eyes to theirs as we once did to our parents' — with a similar feeling that this is a person who can take care of us? And don't we assume that bigger people are stronger people less because of their extra muscle mass than because our latent infant's eye concludes that whatever it looks up to is powerful — as our parents once were, looking down on our crib?

The parental role we often impute to bigger people isn't always a positive one. Around tall men, especially, the fear we might once have felt while looking up to a father can make us keep our distance from someone who revives such feelings. More than one tall woman has told me of preferring shorter men for at least part of her adult life because taller men were too easy to confuse with daddy. Unlike the rest of us, taller women do not encounter men taller than they are so regularly as to get used to the sensation — the childish sensation — of looking up to a big father figure. Whether used to it or not, we all have some version of that parent-confusion problem around taller people. Or should I say they have some version of that problem with us?

It's important to keep in mind that the discomfort we may feel around someone too much taller or smaller than we are has less to do with the other person than with our own feelings that are triggered by that person's height. Television hostess Jeanne Parr, a 6-footer, told me that she realized this very young. Nearly as tall in the sixth grade as she is now, Parr was constantly called "Daddy Long Legs" and worse by the other kids. "They teased me all the time and made me cry," she recalled. "I felt like a freak."

Parr remembered in particular the time a smaller boy wouldn't stand next to her in line because she was such a "freak." When she came home in tears and told her father what had happened, he told her to stop crying. The problem wasn't hers, he pointed out, it was her smaller classmates'. With unusual insight, the father made the point that the other kids didn't mind her being taller so much as they themselves minded being smaller. ''And that one comment saved my life,'' Parr said. ''My size never bothered me so much after that.''

It really isn't another person's height that bugs us when it's very different from ours. Who cares? It's the way that person's height makes us feel about our *own* — that's the real issue. Around talls, it's easy to slip into feeling like a kid without realizing what's going on. Looking up so far can release that mixture of awe, fear, and envy left over from the time when everyone we looked up to controlled us. This is why level of eye contact is so basic to the size we judge others to be. At some subconscious level, we estimate another person's size by how we feel when our eyes meet theirs; and how we feel usually is tied to how far up or down we must look to make eye contact.

In the rare instances when a smaller person (a psychiatrist, say) reflects the power of a parent, we judge him or her tall. But when someone taller seems to be as feisty as a kid brother or sister, we judge such a person small. Confronted by someone whose behavior contradicts our stereotype for their size, our mind finds it easier to misperceive that person's size than alter its own stereotype.

Take the case of former New York Yankees manager Billy Martin. Martin's behavior fits the classic stereotype of a little guy: noisy, contentious, defensive. Except Martin isn't little; he's nearly 6 feet tall. But because he ''acts little,'' that's how Billy Martin is widely perceived — a ''fiery little man,'' in the words of one observer; ''the feisty little manager,'' in the characterization of another.

But some heights are hard to misperceive. When confronted with a clear conflict between our height behavior stereotype and reality, we quickly grow confused. Such a conflict lies at the heart of the social difficulties faced by unusually short people who act mature but look young. Those who work with growth-deficient adults say that no matter how long one's done this work, the urge to pat a smaller head or to pull a little body onto one's lap never dies. John Money, much of whose career has been devoted to working with those of unusually short stature, has suggested that such an urge could be innate — that it could be based on the parenting instincts smaller people trigger in taller people. Money explained that ''a dwarf spends a long time being baby-sized and evoking from people responses geared toward the nurturance and succorance of helpless living things. It is well known to animal ethologists that the perceptual appearance of the young of many species triggers various innate releasing mechanisms of parental behavior in adults of the species. In humans, there seems to be an analogous mechanism with respect to the size of another member of the species.''

If this is true not just of dwarfs but smaller people in general, such a response could help explain the dilemma short people face. If smaller people are going around triggering parent-feelings in taller people, this puts everyone in a bind. Looking down at a man with a mustache could be unconsciously arousing an instinct to treat that person as a child, even as the conscious mind says, ''Ridiculous!'' When a smaller person behaves in a childlike manner, this eases the conflict of signals. But if such a person acts grown-up, the paradox is enhanced and liable to get us frustrated. Should we respond to instinct or reason?

The confusion of signals may be a particular problem for a woman confronting a man shorter than herself. I've long been puzzled not by the condescension so much as the actual hostility, the real anger women can exhibit toward men shorter than themselves. But, again, it may not be the man who's at issue in such a case so much as the woman's own feelings in response to him. In *The Bell Jar,* Sylvia Plath (herself tall) wrote of her heroine's reaction to a smaller man she'd just met at a party:

"The thought of dancing with that little runt . . . made me laugh. . . . He was the type of fellow I can't stand. I'm five feet ten in my stocking feet, and when I am with little men I stoop over a bit and slouch my hips, one up and one down, so I'll look shorter, and I feel gawky and morbid as somebody in a sideshow."

If what is really going on in such cases is a confusion of parenting and mating signals, angry frustration is an understandable response. A tall man meeting a short woman may not mind this mixture of signals. A child-woman puts him in a fatherly role that has a lot of history behind it. But a woman meeting a man shorter than herself has more of a problem. Where is the cultural role allowing her to treat a lover as a son?

For such reasons a person of radically different height from ourselves can make us uneasy, confused, frustrated, even angry. But we're rarely conscious of the source of such feelings, and we seldom know how to deal with them, or even what to say. So what we usually end up saying is something like "How's the weather up there?" or "Are you standing in a hole?"

We all develop in a context of reactions to our body size. Students of "body image" say that from earliest childhood we're aware of how others perceive our physical being. Seymour Fisher and a colleague have suggested that this awareness could begin as early as the first six months of life. Throughout our entire life we are shaped by the potential and the limits we perceive our body as having.

"The concept of his body," explained psychologist Boyd McCandless, "is central to one's concept of himself. One lives with his body twenty-four hours a day from birth until death. Its characteristics such as strength, proportion, and attractiveness are intimately related to how society responds to a person. Since social feedback shapes the self concept, it is easily seen that the interaction of body and self concept is inevitable and important.'' The end result, said McCandless, is not a self-fulfilling prophecy so much as a "social fulfilling prophecy," in which our behavior conforms to that expected from someone with the type of body we inhabit.

In a 1975 study made of 69 junior high school boys, two of McCandless's colleagues found that *others'* perceptions of these boys' height had more to do with their evaluation of themselves than the subjects' own sense of their height. "For example," reported Aleonso Prieto and Michael Robbins, "in the present sample teachers' evaluations of height had a higher correlation with self-esteem than did an individual's self-evaluation of his own height. This suggests that others may somehow be communicating their perceptions of a person's physical characteristics to him and this in turn is related to his feelings of self-esteem.''

Ultimately, a continuous loop of such behavior-feedback-behavior throughout a person's life results in what I've called a "size-suited style." In broadest terms this style is born of the expectation that taller bodies are older, more independent, more mature, more powerful, and therefore in need of greater restraint. One mother told me that as her 6'6" husband is approached in height by their teenage boy, he's begun to give the boy "lessons" on how to restrict his body so as not to frighten other people, who are frightened enough of tall bodies already.

Smaller people, by contrast, throughout their life are reminded that they'd better be careful or they might get hurt. Implicit in such reminders is the lesson that physical well-being in the presence of larger bodies can depend on the ability to be agreeable. "If you made somebody laugh," explained 5-foot songwriter Paul Williams of the comic style he learned young, "they weren't going to punch you, you know."

Since they're learned early and indelibly, such size-suited styles can persist into adulthood long after they've lost meaning, validity, or even accuracy. "Peanuts" creator Charles Schulz, for example, is not generally thought of as having a tall point of view. Yet Schulz in fact is nearly 6 feet tall. His height came to him late. As a child Schulz was smallest in his class. When picked at all for teams, he was picked last. His nickname was Sparky. The perspective of Schulz's small childhood obviously is more basic to "Peanuts" (which he originally planned to call "Little Folks") than that of his taller adulthood.

Pete Rose is another example of an adult displaying a style suited to a size he outgrew. The Phillies' star is a scrappy, noisy, all-out player whose lack of inhibition is usually associated with smaller players. "Rose is a big man who plays like a small man," wrote *Sports Illustrated*'s Ron Fimrite (who gave Rose's height as 5'10½"). "Those who have never seen Rose up close tend to think of him as a small man. In fact his smallness is a matter of style, not physique."

But at one time Rose's style *was* also a matter of physique. Rose was only 5'7" when he graduated from high school. He said the late spurt that took him to his adult height didn't come until nineteen. The style of play (and the style of being) he still depends on is one he learned when relatively short. "He developed the habit of playing hard when he was small because it was his only means of attracting notice," concluded Fimrite. "As a result he knows no other way to play." (Rose to this day may perceive himself as smaller than he actually is. To play the lead, if his life story is ever filmed, the baseball player has suggested the shorter but equally feisty Robert Blake.)

In an example of the opposite process, Carol Burnett is a woman who can appear taller than her adult 5'6" or so because this is the height she reached at age eleven, when she was taller than anyone else in her class. By the time everybody else caught

up with her, Carol Burnett was established in the gawky, gan-
gling, clumsy style that is her trademark today, and which we
associate with bodies taller than hers. "In real life," wrote a
surprised recent visitor to the comedienne's home, "Carol Burnett is little and delicate and vulnerable — not quite the gan-
gling, sprawling trouper her television show suggests."

It could be that our height relative to others' at certain early,
impressionable times of life influences our adult style more than
the height we ultimately achieve. If both are the same — if
we're relatively small or relatively tall at all stages of life —
then our style will be congruent with our size. But if our position on the ladder shifts, our style may be incongruent, as with a
Rose or a Burnett. I've long felt that my own size-suited style is
that of an even smaller person, which I once was — compared
to the other kids in school. By contrast, I know average-sized
adults who at one time towered over their classmates and con-
sequently still feel gigantic, just as I know 6-footers who once
were shortest in their class and to this day can't get used to
looking down on anyone.

Breaking the grip of a size-suited style we find obsolete or in-
appropriate is a difficult task. It can be done. There are tall,
feisty, and defensive people in the world. Look at Daniel
Patrick Moynihan. Or Howard Cosell. Or Richard Nixon, for
that matter. It is also possible to be small and restrained, as
Jimmy Carter has demonstrated. But breaking the chains of a
style suited to our body size and developing one suited to another is not easy.

Consider the experience of Helen Hayes. To her early mor-
tification, Hayes never grew much over 5 feet tall. She hated
being so small, thinking a great actress must be a woman of
stature.

At first the critics agreed with her. For an early stage portrayal of Cleopatra, Hayes was lambasted — less for her lack of

talent than her lack of size. The young actress was advised to limit herself to parts more in keeping with her frame.

She did just the opposite. Rather than resign herself to inge-nue roles, Helen Hayes simply learned her craft so well that she could credibly portray *any* character of *any* size. The culmination of this effort was her successful portrayal on Broadway of Mary, the 6-foot Queen of the Scots. "The strangest phenomenon . . . takes place on the stage of the Alvin nightly," wrote a reporter at the time. "Miss Hayes, five feet tall, somehow manages to achieve a physical stature far above her actual height. She actually creates an illusion of tallness, and is not dwarfed by playing between two of the tallest men in the theatre — Phillip Merivale (Earl of Bothwell), and Moroni Olsen (John Knox)."

But Helen Hayes paid a price. "Each night I'm worn out trying to convince the audience that I have classic features and majestic height," said the actress at the time. "During the day I train like a prize fighter. If I haven't enough energy to put into my work the audience will suddenly realize that it isn't Mary, Queen of the Scots on the stage, but just that little soubrette, Helen Hayes, dressed up like a big girl."

The question is whether it's worth it (at least for those of us who don't have to portray Mary, Queen of Scots). Breaking the grips of a size-suited style is a task calling for enormous will, concentration, and self-discipline. It won't necessarily make one happier. Because a size-suited style can be like a pair of shoes that one doesn't especially care for but keeps wearing anyway because they fit so well. In recent years a means has been discovered for treating very small people who are deficient in growth hormone to bring them up to normal or near-normal height. A tragic but revealing psychological reaction often results. Growing so much taller in a short period of time can throw entirely off stride those who have spent years adapting to being so much smaller. Serious depressions have sometimes resulted. The patient may not have liked being so small, but he or she was used to it, and there were certain rewards. A new size calls for a whole new way of being in the world. Learning such a way is "a slow, tedious process," according to John Money, "whereby a child gets used to his new status as a person who will no longer be unique because of his short stature, much as he may have detested that uniqueness."

For those of us stuck with the height we are, our only alternatives are to learn by practice a style suited to somebody else's height or make the best of a style suited to our own. The virtues of the latter path are realized all too seldom. At either end of the spectrum I've found people far more conscious of the drawbacks of their size and its style than the rewards. This includes talls. Just as the rest of us don't like the fact that those with extra inches get added rewards, neither do many of those tall recipients. How could they, if they have any pride? "People frequently comment favorably on my height," explained a 6'2" psychology professor on his questionnaire. "While I like people to like me, I would rather have them tell me I am slim, or intelligent, or hard working — anything else."

Layne Longfellow, 5'8½", who is the only son of a 6-footer, said he's always felt that deep in his heart his father expected him to grow taller, "though this was never really expressed." A few years back the psychologist finally asked his father if this were true. "His response was that he had always been pleased at how small I was compared to him," recalled Longfellow, "that I was kind of neat and compact, tidy and trim and all that. He said he thought that was quite an enviable way to be and he was glad that I didn't turn out to be big and unwieldy."

Discovering how much talls envy about smalls has been a revelation to me. In his wonderfully abrasive, paranoid essay "Troubles of a Big Guy," Albert Payson Terhune said he envied smaller people, especially "the clothes they can wear becomingly and that I cannot wear without looking like a section of a circus parade. . . . I don't believe there is a Big Guy on earth who in the depths of his soul does not crave to wear loud ties and louder clothes and 'extreme' hats. His heart yearns for them. But his common sense, if he has any, tells him his only sartorial hope is to look as inconspicuous as possible."

Terhune then went on to make a long list of other things he envied in smaller people. Some entries on his list included:

• I envy them the fact that they do not loom up above their kind, like monumental sore thumbs.

• I envy them because the people in seats behind them, at the theater or at ball games or prize fights or the opera or elsewhere, don't make audible remarks about the view being totally cut off.

• I envy them because nobody hates them or has a yearning to punch them, unless they have done something to merit it.

This is the aspect of being tall most regretted: the fear talls know smaller people feel in their presence. The worst part is that such fear is not totally unwelcome. "My height," wrote a 6'3½" television producer on his questionnaire, "cuts me off from people, puts me above them, helps me maintain that side of me that wants to be aloof and apart."

The problem seems to be that at any height, we're more conscious of the drawbacks than the rewards, which are easy to take for granted. And every height has rewards.

Asked what they like about their height, smalls most often mention being unthreatening. Kids seem more at ease with them than with taller grown-ups. Officials of foreign countries who are small can deal more comfortably with visiting Americans who look them in the eye (a source of Kissinger's effectiveness?). As both Joel Grey and Wilt Chamberlain have pointed out, small is the only universal size. Everyone once was small, and we all know what it's like. Only a few of us know how it is to be tall. Finally, as Harry Scharlatt observed, shortness can be "like a surprise weapon. Nobody expects that much from you, so when you deliver, they're impressed."

Average-sized people most often mention inconspicuousness as that height's major virtue. Not having to think very much about height is what seems most appealing to those of average size. "It's not an issue," they explain. "I can worry about other problems." One man of 5'11" told me he likes perceiving himself as short or tall depending on the circumstances. Many mentioned being able to buy clothes off the rack with lots of selection as a bonus for being average. And as a man of 5'10" added: "I can sleep on any bed."

Then, of course, there are the many virtues of being tall, which have already been covered fairly thoroughly (and enviously) in this book. In one of the few other listings of height virtues I've seen, Dr. John Eichenlaub groups the benefits of tallness primarily around the inherent look of authority. "We take a big man's word for many things we would otherwise question," wrote Eichenlaub. A more average-sized person, he added, may lack such advantages "in the first-glance department," but makes up for this lack in a greater ability to develop relationships. "After you've settled into a chair beside a medium-sized man," suggested Eichenlaub, "you feel more at ease and more comfortable with him than with someone at either end of the scale."

Smaller people, by contrast, may not be so easygoing but do have most license to act in energetic, attention-getting ways without giving offense — so long as this style is balanced with even a modicum of restraint. "This mixture of uninhibited showmanship, sharpness and modesty is a difficult one to handle," concluded Eichenlaub, "but together these things can easily beat the benefits of large or medium size. After all, midgets have always been more popular than giants.''

Smaller people's potential for authentic popularity is a plus too easily overlooked. In a study mentioned earlier, on ''Height and Attraction,'' the authors found that contrary to their prediction, smaller men were best liked by other men of all heights. For strength and leadership, most men agreed, the taller the better. But for friendship: ''Short men were liked more and rated more positively than tall men.''

Smalls in many fields find their standing especially high with kids. When Abe Beame was mayor of New York, his popularity among children was noted. He himself suggested it was ''because I'm their size.'' In show business, Paul Williams and Henry Winkler have particularly strong followings among the young, based partly on their shortness. Calvin Murphy has said that kids especially seem to enjoy talking with him. ''They don't feel out of it standing next to me,'' he explained, adding, ''Of course, *I* feel out of it, standing next to an eleven year old boy my height.''

Unlikely as it may seem at the time, some later benefit has even been attributed to the trauma of growing up small. Actor-director John Cassavetes once said unequivocally that being 5 feet tall at fourteen forced him to become ''funnier, more outgoing.

''Being short,'' according to Cassavetes, ''is a great character builder, even though it sure as hell doesn't seem that way when you first start out.''

Mel Brooks has said repeatedly that his becoming a professional comedian stems directly from his need as a short kid to get laughs, and his anger at being put in that position. He once characterized the profession that's made him rich, successful, and famous as ''getting even in an oblique way through comedy.'' When *Playboy* advised the comic that he was the only subject to be interviewed twice by the magazine, Brooks whistled aloud at the honor. The interviewer then asked to what he attributed this distinction. ''To my height,'' Brooks replied. ''And the lack of it.

''But being short never bothered me for three seconds,'' he continued.

''The rest of the time I wanted to commit suicide.''

Let's face it. No one *wants* to be small. Not in this society. I know I don't. When all is said and done, I still know what height I want to be: 6'1''. Not only would I play better basketball at that size, but people would pay more attention as I walked into a room, and I could be quieter without feeling overlooked. Also the thinning of my hair would be less noticeable.

Since topping out 5.38 inches short of my goal, I've devoted a lot of energy to wishing I were taller or could at least act that way. Sometimes I'll go to Clint Eastwood movies and study his style for future application to myself: the squint, the presence, the strength held in reserve. Then I'll try out my Clint Eastwood style among friends. It suits me about like a size 42 long. All being Clint Eastwood's ever gotten me is comments such as ''You got something in your eye?'' or ''How come you're so quiet all of a sudden?''

Recently I've been feeling less need to be Clint Eastwood. This has something to do with one of the more important pieces of information I've acquired in the course of writing this book. That information concerns how little the wish to be a different height has to do with the hope of actually gaining or losing inches, and how much it has to do with the wish to have qualities associated with those inches. My own wish to be taller, I've found, is tied directly to my interest in being more intimidating.

At one time this interest was very strong. The fact that I looked down on so few people was not reassuring at all.

But as my wish to intimidate others has declined, so has my interest in being taller. (Neither are gone; both have declined.) In fact, *not* being intimidating is something I've just begun to enjoy. I think not looking like a physical threat, not triggering child-to-parent responses, and not looming over very many people has often made human contact possible when it would have been difficult were I just a few inches taller.

Realizing how symbolic height can be as an ''issue'' gives us the opportunity to confront our assumptions about size — which can be changed — rather than our physical dimensions, which can't. If society moves away from a leader-as-parent approach, for example, we can dispense with our need for tall leaders. Should executives learn better tactics than intimidation for getting their work done, tallness will wane as an administrative virtue. As sex roles broaden, so will our sense of what height a man or woman ''ought'' to be.

None of this will happen soon. Most of us will continue to be frustrated to some degree by how tall we are or aren't. Every height has drawbacks. But it's helpful to know how little our height-related feelings have to do with relative size, and how much to do with the attitudes engendered by size. Understanding how little our ''height problems'' with friends, kids, parents, spouses, and colleagues have to do with size itself allows us to face the real problems of power, control, and parent-child feelings that underlie such ''problems.'' Then we can start exploring alternatives to envy of someone else's height or sullen resignation to our own. Along the way, we may even find rewards for being the size we are — whatever size we are — in forms we've long taken for granted.

The best reward for confronting a height issue directly can be discovering that height itself was never really the issue.

Appendixes

A Twenty Questions about Height

In mid-1977 I sent the following questionnaire to a nonrandom sample of perhaps four hundred friends, relatives, correspondents — anyone I thought might fill out and return the form. About half did.

Twenty Questions about Height

Name (optional) _____ Birthdate _____

Sex _____ Occupation _____ Height ___'___"

1. While growing up did you feel _____ short _____ tall _____ average compared to the other kids?

2. Can you recall any incidents from school in which your height played a role? _____ If so, describe one or more.

3. Did you ever have a nickname based on your height? _____ If so, what was it? _____

4. Was there ever a growth spurt which significantly altered your height relative to that of your peers? _____ If so, did this change of size alter the way you felt about yourself? _____ How?

5. When you began to take an interest in the opposite sex, did you feel your height restricted in any way those with whom you might interact?_____ If so, can you recall any illustrative incidents?

6. Did your parents ever worry about your height?_____ If they did, how did their concern express itself?

7. To what height did you grow (taller, shorter or the same) compared to your father?_____ mother?_____ Has this influenced your relationship with them in any way?

8. Today do you feel _____ short _____ tall _____ average?

9. Do you ever add or subtract inches when reporting your height?_____ If so, how many_____ and why?

10. Is there a height other than your own you've always wanted to be?_____ If so, what is that height ___'___" and why do you think you'd prefer it?

11. What do you especially like about being the height you are?

12. Here are some situations in which height comparisons may be made. Check those in which you've ever found yourself comparing the height of your body to those around you. Elaborate where possible on the back or on a separate sheet of paper.

_____ on a crowded elevator   _____ with kids (yours or others')
_____ standing in line   _____ during games or sports
_____ among co-workers   _____ at a party
_____ with a mate or lover   _____ at a bar

13. Do you ever find that the height of a person of the opposite sex influences your reaction to him/her?_____ If so, how?

14. Are there everyday implements such as chairs, cabinet shelves or cars which are difficult for you to use because of your size?_____ If so, what are they, and what's the problem?

15. Do people ever make comments to you about your size?_____ If so, what are some?

16. Have you ever felt your height was a help or hindrance socially?_____ If so, how?

17. Have you ever suspected your being hired for a job, or given a promotion or a raise or positive job evaluation, was influenced in any way by your height?_____ If so, elaborate.

18. Who would you say is taller, Jimmy Carter or Richard Nixon?

19. How tall would you estimate each of the following people are, or were?

Napoleon __'__"   Jonas Salk __'__"
Shirley MacLaine __'__"   Bella Abzug __'__"
Paul Newman __'__"   Bea Arthur (Maude)__'__"
Warren Beatty __'__"   Charles Manson __'__"
Mae West __'__"   Henry Winkler (Fonzie)__'__"
Joel Grey __'__"   Harry Truman __'__"

20. Is there anything you'd like to say about human height that I've not asked about?

B Height in Government

In mid-1978 I sent the following letter and questionnaire to all United States senators and state governors. About a third of the former and half of the latter responded to my inquiry.

Dear Senator/Governor:

I need your help.

While gathering information for a book on human height (to be published next year by Little, Brown) I've been unable to find up-to-date information on the height of officeholders. The last such survey was made in 1916 by a New York University professor who found Governors averaged 5'11.2", Senators 5'10.6". Could you take a few seconds to jot down your height on the enclosed form and return it to me so I can give my readers fresh information on this topic?

Three further questions on the form concern relative height in the political process. Your thoughts on this subject would be a bonus. At first glance height might not seem a serious political concern. Yet from Lincoln's debates with Douglas through Carter's debates with Ford, it's seriously concerned some candidates. A good reason for such concern is the widely-reported statistic that taller Presidential candidates normally win. But that "statistic" has never been verified. Nor has most of what we assume about height in politics. I hope you'll be able to help me collect reliable data and perhaps add an insight or two which could shed some light on this dimension of our political process.

Height in Government

Name _____ Height___'___"

1. In your estimate what has been the greatest difference in height between you and a rival candidate for office? _____ inches. Were you _____ taller _____ shorter? Did this difference affect that campaign in any way? _____ yes _____ no. If so, how?

2. Would you say a candidate taller than his opponent has an advantage in a race for _____ City Councilman _____ Mayor _____ State Legislator _____ Congressman _____ Senator _____ Governor _____ President? Elaborate:

3. In office, have you observed any instances in which the relative height of people affected their ability to work with each other? _____ yes _____ no. If so, could you describe such an instance?

C Notes

Despite the best efforts of my copy editor, these notes don't strictly adhere to the University of Chicago (or any other) style manual. Rather they are an attempt at no-frills citation — to give credit where due, reveal my basic sources, and suggest paths for further reading. I've tried to give references that are full enough for locating the sources, but seldom fuller. Article titles, for example, are only mentioned when themselves informative (in academic journals, especially, many such titles are so long and jargony that you get dizzy just trying to read them). From long lists of coauthors I've commonly listed only the principal author plus "et al." Only intermittently do I list specific page numbers for citations (when citing a paperback book, for example, whose pagination may be different from a hardbound edition of the same book). I hope this economical approach offers adequate documentation without weighing down the book unduly.

An Introductory Note

p. 3 Both *Current Biography,* 1943, and *Winchester's Screen Encyclopedia* (Maud M. Miller, ed.; London: Winchester Publications, 1948), listed Alan Ladd at 5'10"; *Photoplay,* June 1956, went to 5'10½".

4 According to the November 19, 1976, National Center for Health Statistics report titled *Height and Weight of Adults 18–74 Years of Age in the United States* (hereafter cited as National Center, *Height*), p. 2, the adult American male averages 5'9", the female 5'3.6".

On height variation in relation to time of day, see Albert Damon, Howard Stoudt, and Ross McFarland, *The Human Body in Equipment Design* (Cambridge: Harvard University Press, 1966), p. 50, which indicates that adults gain 0.95" while asleep overnight. See also I. Newton Kugelmass, *Adolescent Immaturity* (Springfield, Ill.: Charles C. Thomas, 1973), p. 70; and J. M. Tanner et al. in *Annals of Human Biology* 1 (1974): 103–106.

5 Mildred Trotter and Goldine Gleser in "The Effect of Aging on Stature," *American Journal of Physical Anthropology* 9 (1951): 311–324 estimate adult loss of stature averages 1.2 centimeters every twenty years; W. E. Miall et al., in a study of adult height loss in two Welsh towns, *Human Biology* 39 (1967): 445–454, found such shrinkage to begin at age twenty-five, accelerate at thirty-five; K. J. Ellis et al. in the *Journal of Laboratory and Clinical Medicine* 83 (1974): 716–727 say such loss of height is a continual process once full stature is achieved, and between the ages of twenty and seventy-five can result in up to a 5 percent decrease in height; in "Stature-Shrinkage and Bone Loss from the Fourth through the Ninth Decades," *Proceedings of the First Workshop on Bone Morphometry* (Z. F. G. Jaworski, ed.; Ottawa: University of Ottawa Press, 1973), Stanley Garn and Kay Larson summarized their finding that such stature reduction is due to actual loss of bone with age.

The discovery about taped-speakers' heights, by Norman Lass, Professor of Speech Pathology and Audiology at West Virginia University, was mentioned in *Time,* December 6, 1976, and was reported by him in *Journal of the Acoustical Society of America* 60 (1976): 700–703.

1   Who's Bigger?

p. 7   Abraham Maslow wrote about the sizing-up process in "Dominance-Feeling, Behavior, and Status," *The Psychological Review* 44 (1937): 404–429 (p. 410 quoted).

8   The President's assistant was Dr. Peter Bourne; on November 3, 1977, we met in his White House office, where I took down the comments used here and subsequently.

9   Robert Ellis Smith, who edits *The Privacy Journal,* also appeared on "A.M. America" and later described this episode to me.

Andrew Tobias discussed Robert Redford's height in *New York,* January 27, 1975, following up his earlier remark about the actor's shortness in the issue dated September 23, 1974.

10   The *Philadelphia Bulletin*'s Rose DeWolf commented on sensitivity about height in a column reprinted by the *San Diego Union,* April 13, 1975.

11   On choosing friends by height, see the discussion of research by William Berkowitz and Sidney Portnoy in chapter 3; on height in marriage, see J. N. Spuhler, "Assortative Mating with Respect to Physical Characteristics," *Eugenics Quarterly* 15 (1968): 128–140, and James F. Crow and Joseph Felsenstein, "The Effect of Assortative Mating on the Genetic Composition of a Population," ibid., pp. 85–97; on height and physical problems, see chapter 2; on height and sports, chapter 12; on height and voting, chapter 10; on height and jobs, chapter 9.

The 5'3" secretary told me about feeling average while we were seatmates on a train from Boston to New York. For the most part such semi-anonymous comments throughout the book grow out of similar conversations and hereafter will not be cited.

16   Elvis Presley's lifts were mentioned by actor Kurt Russell (who portrayed the singer in a TV movie) in *TV Week* (*Philadelphia Inquirer*), August 22, 1979.

The study of ten job applicants by Leland Deck of the University of Pittsburgh was reported by him during a telephone conversation with me in June 1972, and in a two-page photocopied summation dated 1971 (see also chapter 9). Air Force women were reported overestimating their height in *Pediatrics* 52 (1973): 555–560, cited by Robert Malina, William Mueller, and John Holmes in *Human Biology* 48 (1976): 487–500. The third study mentioned, by J. E. Singer and Patricia Lamb, is described in the *Journal of Social Psychology* 68 (1966): 143–151.

17   Philip Caputo's column in the *Chicago Tribune,* October 19, 1974, reported that Italy's 5'3" premier aspirant Amintore Fanfani cited Caesar, among others, as a small predecessor. Correlating tallness and achievement, Havelock Ellis, in *A Study of British*

Genius (Boston: Houghton Mifflin, 1926), p. 278, listed Caesar among history's tall leaders.

17–18   For a summary of historic debate on Jesus's height up to the time of its publication, see J. Rendel Harris, "On the Stature of Our Lord," *The Bulletin of the John Rylands Library* 10 (1926): 112–126; see also Marcello Craveri, *The Life of Jesus* (New York: Grove Press, 1967), pp. 161–165. Teddy Pendergrass's comments are from Maralyn Lois Polak's interview with the singer in *Today (Philadelphia Inquirer)*, September 17, 1978, p. 8.

18–20   The visit to Madame Tussaud's took place on December 15, 1977.

20–21   The TV program mentioned, "Bill Moyers' Journal," was broadcast by the Public Broadcasting Service on February 12, 1979.

2   Is Bigger Better?

p. 23   The Minnesota woman was quoted in *The Arizona Republic,* December 26, 1975.

24   Michael Medved told me about being mistaken for David Wallechinsky in a February 1977 conversation I had with Medved in Los Angeles; Wallechinsky confirmed the experience in a subsequent telephone conversation.

24–25   *The National Enquirer* carried its account of the disparate-sized reporters' experiences in the September 14, 1976, issue.

25   John Kenneth Galbraith was quoted on height bias in *The Christian Science Monitor,* May 18, 1977.

The nursing students' height estimates were reported by W. D. Dannenmaier and F. J. Thunin in *Journal of Social Psychology* 63 (1964): 361–363. The college students' height estimates were reported by Paul R. Wilson, ibid. 74 (1968): 97–102.

San Francisco Examiner on Sargent Shriver, August 6, 1972; *Newsweek* on James McIntyre, January 8, 1979.

26   *Parade* (Lloyd Shearer) on Cornelia Wallace, July 23, 1978; *Esquire* (Nora Ephron) on Bernice Gera, January 1973; *Newsweek* on Floyd Bevens, October 23, 1972; *Time* on Bill Jenkins, October 22, 1973; David Broder in *The Atlantic,* March 1975; *New York Times* on Paul Gann and Howard Jarvis, June 8, 1978; *Newsweek* on Aleksandr Godunov, September 3, 1979; *Parade* (Lloyd Shearer) on Dustin Hoffman, May 25, 1979.

27   *Current Biography,* 1976, on Malcolm Fraser; *People* on Deng Xiaoping, December 25, 1978; *New York Times* on Mike Torrez, August 8, 1978; *Philadelphia Inquirer* on Theodore White, September 17, 1978.

The Maoists' opinion of Deng was quoted in *Time,* February 5, 1979, p. 31.

29   On King Saul, see 1 Sam. 9:2.

On skeleton size in tombs, see: William Haviland in *American Antiquity* 32 (1967): 316–325, p. 320; J. Lawrence Angel, *The People of Lerna,* Lerna Series vol. 2 (Washington, D.C.: Smithsonian Institution Press, 1971), p. 110; and Angel's contribution to Steven Polgar, ed., *Population, Ecology and Social Evolution* (The Hague: Mouton Publishers, 1975), p. 181.

Egyptian wall paintings are discussed by E. E. Rump and P. S. Delin in *Journal of Personality and Social Psychology* 28 (1973): 343–347, p. 343.

Pitirim Sorokin's comment (with emphasis deleted) is from *Social and Cultural Mobility* (1927; reprint ed., Glencoe, Ill.: The Free Press, 1959), pp. 222–223.

29–32 Frederick's Prussian soldiers are discussed in Robert Ergang, *The Potsdam Führer* (New York: Columbia University Press, 1941), pp. 84–102.

32 Nancy Mitford is quoted by Anthony Smith in *The Human Pedigree* (Philadelphia: J. B. Lippincott, 1975), p. 83.

S. L. Washburn and C. S. Lancaster estimated early man's height range in Noel Korn and Fred Thompson, eds., *Human Evolution* (New York: Harper & Row, 1967), p. 70.

The greater vulnerability of tall bodies under stress is discussed by J. Z. R. Young in *An Introduction to the Study of Man* (Oxford: The Clarendon Press, 1971), pp. 397, 563; and Paul R. Nickens in *Journal of Archaeological Science* 3 (1976): 37 (hereafter cited as Nickens, *Archaeological Science*).

32–33 Ashley Montagu writes about size and health in Ashley Montagu and C. L. Brace, *Human Evolution,* 2d ed. (New York: Macmillan Co., 1977), p. 470 (hereafter cited as Montagu and Brace, *Evolution*).

33 On the relationship between diet, size, and health, see: Nickens, *Archaeological Science;* Lawrence Galton, *How Long Will I Live?* (New York: Macmillan Co., 1976), pp. 52–53; Donald B. Cheek, *Human Growth* (Philadelphia: Lee & Febiger, 1968), pp. 638–639; and Gilbert B. Forbes in *Nutrition Reviews* 15 (1957): 193–196.

Thomas K. Landauer and John W. M. Whiting have discussed their findings in *American Anthropologist* 66 (1964): 1007–1028; ibid. 67 (1965): 1000–1003; and (with Thomas Jones) in *Child Development* 39 (1968): 59–67. Whiting and S. Gunders's paper "Mother-Infant Separation and Physical Growth" appeared in *Ethnology* 7 (1968): 196–206. Landauer and Whiting's findings are summarized in their 1978 paper "Correlates and Consequences of Stress in Infancy," photocopy, 41 pp. (p. 24 quoted), to be published in Ruth Munroe, Robert Munroe, and Beatrice Whiting, eds., *Handbook of Cross-Cultural Human Development* (New York: Garland STPAR Press).

34–36 J. M. Tanner's comments were made to me during our meeting on December 14, 1977; quoted remarks by Tanner appearing elsewhere in this book, unless otherwise attributed, are also from that interview. His principal works on height and growth are: *Human Growth* (ed. by Tanner; London: Pergamon Press, 1960); *Education and Physical Growth* (New York: International Universities Press, 1961); *Growth at Adolescence,* 2d ed. (Oxford: Blackwell Scientific Publications, 1962); and *The Physique of the Olympic Athlete* (London: George Allen and Unwin, Ltd., 1964; hereafter cited as Tanner, *Athlete*). Of the scores of articles Tanner has written, the most accessible ones are in *Daedalus,* Fall 1971 (hereafter cited as Tanner, *Daedalus*), and *Scientific American,* September 1973.

35 A preliminary analysis of slaves' heights by James Trussell and Richard Steckel was published in *Journal of Interdisciplinary History* 8 (1978): 477–505; I discussed the findings with Trussell by telephone on June 7, 1978.

37 In *The Futurist,* August 1978, engineer Thomas Samaras makes the point that weight rises disproportionately to height, thereby exaggerating the taller person's greater consumption of resources.

On heat retention relative to body size, see Harry Shapiro, *Peking Man* (New York: Simon & Schuster, 1974), p. 60, and Montagu and Brace, *Evolution,* p. 434.

Gilbert Forbes discusses the relatively greater absolute strength of taller bodies in Melvin Grumbach, Gilman Grave, and Florence Mayer, eds., *The Control and Onset of Puberty* (New York: John Wiley & Sons, 1974), pp. 433–434.

On the relative strength of tall and small bodies in general, see: Jana Pařízkova and Jarmila Merhautová in *Human Biology* 42 (1970): 391–400, p. 397; Per-olof Astrand and Kaare Rodahl, *The Textbook of Work Physiology* (New York: McGraw-Hill, 1970), p. 323 (hereafter cited as Astrand and Rodahl, *Physiology*); and Donald E. Lamphiear and Henry J. Montoye, "Muscular Strength and Body Size," *Human Biology* 48 (1976): 147–160.

37–38 On the relative mechanical virtues of body size in general, see: F. W. Went, "The Size of Man," in *The American Scientist* 56 (1968): 400–413, p. 407; Stephen Jay Gould, "Size and Shape," in *Harvard Magazine*, October 1975, especially p. 49; and David Sinclair, *Human Growth after Birth* (London: Oxford University Press, 1969), p. 36. Dr. Frank Jobe is quoted in the *Los Angeles Times*, January 1, 1976, about finding smaller athletes less prone to injury.

Tanner, *Athlete*, explores in detail the relative advantages of height in various Olympic events.

38 On lungs and height, see: J. E. Cotes, *Lung Function* (Philadelphia: F. A. Davis Co., 1968), p. 354; T. J. Cole, "The Influence of Height on the Decline in Ventilatory Function," *International Journal of Epidemiology* 3 (1974): 145–152, p. 147; and John B. West in *The Lancet*, April 24, 1971, pp. 839–841.

Demonstrated disease vulnerabilities corresponding to body structure are summarized by Albert Damon, "Constitutional Medicine," in Otto von Mering and Leonard Kasdan, eds., *Anthropology and the Behavioral and Health Sciences* (Pittsburgh: University of Pittsburgh Press, 1970), pp. 189–190 (hereafter cited as von Mering and Kasdan, *Anthropology*). On height and headaches in particular, see *Time*, November 7, 1977. David Owen surveys data on XYY chromosomes in *Psychological Bulletin* 78 (1972): 209–233. Juan F. Sotos surveys "Giantism and Acromegaly" in Lytt I. Gardner, ed., *Endocrine and Genetic Diseases of Childhood* (Philadelphia: W. B. Saunders Co., 1969), pp. 142–169.

Dr. Harold Schwarz has specialized in documenting the probability that Lincoln suffered from Marfan's syndrome; see *Time*, May 22, 1978, as well as the letter of Dr. A. M. Gordon, ibid., June 26, 1978, claiming he made the same diagnosis sixteen years earlier. Another letter to *Time*, June 12, 1978, challenged the grounds for claiming that Lincoln might have suffered from this disease. Reed Pyeritz and Victor McKusick wrote about "The Marfan Syndrome" in *The New England Journal of Medicine*, April 15, 1979, pp. 772–777.

David Smith in *Pediatrics* 70 (1967): 463–519, surveyed the fifty-two maladies with which the symptom stunted growth is associated.

On the relative pulmonary efficiency of a small lean body over a tall lean body, see Albert Behnke and Jack Wilmore, *Evaluation and Regulation of Body Build and Composition* (Englewood Cliffs, N.J.: Prentice-Hall, 1974), p. 14 (hereafter cited as Behnke and Wilmore, *Body*).

38–39 On reproductive ability in relation to body size, see: A. M. Thomson in J. J. Van der Werff, T. Bosch, and A. Haak, eds., *Somatic Growth of the Child* (Springfield, Ill.: Charles C. Thomas, 1966), p. 211 (hereafter cited as Thomson, *Growth*); Toshiyuki Furusho in *Japanese Journal of Human Genetics* 9 (1964): 100–109; A. Damon and R. L. Nuttall in *Human Biology* 37 (1965): 23–28 (which has a report on the fecundity of tall Harvard men as cited by Damon in von Mering and Kasdan, *Anthropology*, p. 188); and A. Roberto Frisancho, Jorge Sanchez, Danilo Pallardel, and Lizandro Yanez in *American Journal of Physical Anthropology* 39 (1973): 255–262, p. 258 (on the greater reproductive record of smaller bodies in the Andes).

39 In *Science Digest*, July 1978, and *The Futurist*, August 1978, Thomas Samaras describes his finding that in a nonrandom sample of several hundred deaths (many of celebrities), those of taller people came sooner on the average than those of smaller ones. He also refers to a Michigan nursing-home study of 200 residents that found short people were living longer.

The Metropolitan Life Insurance Company found taller policyholders lived somewhat longer than smaller ones in a study published in *Transactions of the Actuarial Society of America* 50 (1949): 48–58, pp. 57–58. An earlier Metropolitan study, "The Weight Standards and Mortality of Very Tall Men," read at the Forty-seventh Annual Meeting of the Association of Life Insurance Medical Directors of America, October 22–23, 1936, found little mortality difference by height. I suspect that attempting to correlate height and longevity independent of other variables is futile.

Gore Vidal commented on Aaron Burr in *Time,* April 21, 1975, p. 45.

Harry Johnson correlated self-reports of height and of intercourse frequency in his *Executive Life-Styles* (New York: Thomas Y. Crowell, 1974), pp. 87, 201–202.

39–40 In a press release dated November 9, 1972, Betty Roney noted that of 2,000 hair-loss patients, 20 percent, or double the national average, were 6 feet tall or more. She discussed this finding with me (as well as my thinning hair) at her clinic on December 15, 1977.

40 Harry Shapiro discussed size and efficiency in *The New York Times Magazine,* December 15, 1963.

3 In the Mind's Eye

p. 41 Howard Teichmann, *George S. Kaufman* (New York: Atheneum, 1972); p. 269 of the Dell ed. (New York, 1973) is quoted.

Ralph Stephenson and Jean R. Debrix, *The Cinema as Art* (Baltimore: Penguin, 1965), p. 45 (hereafter cited as Stephenson and Debrix, *Cinema*).

42 I met Rod Serling at Antioch College in Yellow Springs, Ohio, on May 27, 1966.

I interviewed Mario Andretti on November 7, 1977; his quoted remarks throughout are from that session.

Erma Bombeck, listed as 5′2″ in *Current Biography,* 1979, wrote of surprising others with her shortness in the *Chicago Sun-Times,* April 4, 1979.

Jerry Stiller's wish appeared in *The New York Times Magazine,* May 15, 1977.

42–43 Frank Perdue's secretary confirmed for me that his unexpected tallness is often noted by people meeting him for the first time, as was mentioned in a June 17, 1979, *Philadelphia Inquirer* profile of Perdue.

43 Julia Child's experience was described to me on September 28, 1977, when I interviewed her and her husband, Paul; their comments throughout are from that meeting.

44 Except as noted, the "Smaller and Taller than You Might Imagine" lists are based on comments and observations that have appeared in print.

SMALLER THANS: Marlon Brando was assessed by Paul Williams in *Gallery,* November 1979, p. 31, and by Joe Hyams, who wrote "he's shorter than he appears on screen," in *Mislaid in Hollywood* (New York: Peter H. Wyden, 1973), p. 120; Charles Bronson was listed as being "of small stature" by Bill Davidson in *TV Guide,* July 15, 1978, p. 24.

Johnny Carson is noted as touchy about his relative shortness by Kenneth Tynan in *The New Yorker,* February 20, 1978, p. 47; Geraldine Chaplin is "barely 5-feet tall," according to *Current Biography,* 1979; Julie Christie appears "larger on screen than off," wrote Julia Cameron in *Rolling Stone,* April 10, 1975, p. 54; Robert Conrad was called "the feisty little TV star" by Bill Davidson, *TV Guide,* July 15, 1978, p. 24; Walter Cronkite seemed "so much shorter than I expected" to actress Linda Carlson, according to Bill O'Halloway in *TV Guide,* March 24, 1979, p. 18.

Bette Davis appeared "almost startlingly petite" to Gail Cameron in *McCall's,* November 1974, p. 24; Robert De Niro has been described to me as "short" by those who have met him and is listed among short actors in *People*, July 31, 1978, p. 94; Kirk Douglas has been mentioned to me more than once as "surprisingly short" by those who have met him; Peter Falk's shortness has been noted from time to time, as in *Time*, November 26, 1973, p. 120; Jack Anderson has called Jane Fonda "tiny" in *Parade*, March 16, 1975, and elsewhere; Buckminster Fuller was called "only an inch or two over 5-feet" by Barry Farrell in *Life*, February 26, 1971, p. 48.

Steve Garvey claimed to be 5'10" but was called "stumpy" by his wife (who claimed 5'7" for herself and looked little shorter than he in pictures) in *People*, July 10, 1978; Patty Hearst "stands five feet," according to Lacey Fosburgh, *The New York Times Magazine*, April 3, 1977, p. 19, and often startles others with her petiteness; Katharine Hepburn appeared surprisingly "tiny" to interviewer Julie Goldsmith Gilbert, according to Rod Townley in *Philadelphia*, September 1978, p. 69.

Reggie Jackson "somehow is smaller than you expect," according to *The Daily Illini*, August 25, 1977; Mick Jagger was noted for being "rather small" in *Mick Jagger* by J. Marks-Highwater (New York: Popular Library, 1973), p. 13; Paul Newman's surprising shortness is often noted (in chapter 11 I write about a 5'8" actress who had to go barefoot with him in love scenes); Jack Nicholson appeared "so much smaller than you expect" to Norman Dickens in *Jack Nicholson* (New York: New American Library, 1975), p. 88; in *Olivier* (New York: Coward-McCann, 1969), p. 40, Virginia Fairweather notes that being "shorter than one imagines" helps Lord Olivier walk about in public unrecognized.

Burt Reynolds is "far smaller than his screen image suggests," according to Julia Cameron in *Rolling Stone*, April 10, 1975, p. 58; "Even at a distance [Suzanne] Somers seems smaller than she does on TV," wrote Bill Gladstone in the *Philadelphia Daily News*, August 20, 1978; Sylvester Stallone seemed "surprisingly short" to Roger Ebert writing in *Us*, October 18, 1977, p. 30; Ringo Starr was found "surprisingly slight" by Bill Davidson in *TV Guide*, April 22, 1978, p. 15.

Elizabeth Taylor is "much smaller than her screen image," writes Susan Margolis in *Fame* (San Francisco: San Francisco Book, 1977), pp. 165–166; Andy Warhol is referred to as a "leprechaun" in *This Fabulous Century* (New York: Time-Life, Vol. 7, 1970), p. 168; Raquel Welch "appears slighter in person than on screen," wrote Norm Goldstein in the *San Diego Union*, December 6, 1970; Henry Winkler told Barbara Walters about how often he's been told by others they expected him to be taller, on ABC-TV, December 3, 1977.

TALLER THANS: Warren Beatty was seen as "taller than he appears on screen" by Joan Drew in *Redbook*, May 1974, p. 101; Ingrid Bergman's tallness is discussed in chapter 11; H. Rap Brown is mentioned as "a bigger man than the newspapers and television filmclips had led me to believe, taller" by Clayton Riley in *Ms.*, March 1974, p. 96.

Fidel Castro is a 6-footer, according to *Current Biography*, 1970; Howard Cosell is called "a tall man" by Saul Braun in *TV Guide*, August 28, 1971, p. 22, "a shade over six feet tall," by *Playboy*, May 1972, p. 76, and "six-one and a half " by himself in *Cosell* (New York: Pocket Books, 1973), p. 132; although Jules Feiffer's point of view hardly seems "tall" and he himself has referred to the agony of growing up small (*People*, November 1, 1976), according to Jan Herman in the *Philadelphia Inquirer*, November 19, 1979, Feiffer is "tall and angular"; Bobby Fischer is called "a tall, burly fellow" by Robert Lindsey in *Us*, March 21, 1978, p. 74; Carey Winfrey wrote of David Frost: "In the flesh, he seems physically larger than he does on television," in the *New York Times*, March 28, 1979.

Boyish Jerry Lewis is regularly referred to as surprisingly tall — "six feet," according to *Current Biography*, 1962; Billy Martin, often called "little," appears relatively tall in photographs and is listed as 5'11" in both *Current Biography*, 1978, and the *New York Times*, June 5, 1978; although widely perceived as a little man, Richard Nixon is generally listed at 5'11" or 5'11½" (based on tailors' measurements, Madame Tussaud's concluded he was in the 6-foot range).

Gilda Radner was called "considerably taller and skinnier than she looks on television" by Tracy Young in *New Times*, August 19, 1977, p. 38; Ronald Reagan is "taller than one expects," according to Myra McPherson in the *Boston Globe*, December 26, 1977; Cybill Shepherd is "taller and generally bigger than her screen image suggests," wrote Julia Cameron in *Rolling Stone*, April 10, 1975, p. 54; Tom Snyder's 6'4" height, which I've observed myself, was mentioned by Mary Murphy in *Esquire*, March 28, 1978; Lowell Weicker told me of surprising people with his tallness during our interview, which is described in chapter 10.

GO BOTH WAYS: James Caan was characterized as "tall, tough, likable" by William Hall in the *Los Angeles Times* (*Calendar*), September 29, 1974, p. 26, and as "tall, handsome, and well-scrubbed" by John Simon in *Esquire*, June 1975, p. 62. But in *Genesis*, November 1974, p. 29, interviewer Bob Lardine told Caan: "I had the impression that you were a 200-pound six-footer. But looking at you now, I see that you're not that massive." According to *Celebrity Register*, p. 8, the actor is "just a shade over five feet ten and weigh[s] a mere 162 pounds."

Although Farrah Fawcett seemed "smallish" to Bill Davidson in *TV Guide*, May 21, 1977, p. 25, and was called a "small, athletic, smiling woman" by Arnold Hano, ibid., December 29, 1979, p. 20, Beverly Linet in *Celebrity*, April 1977, p. 9, advised that "at 5'6½" tall, there is little that is delicate about her."

That Joe Garagiola has been assessed as tall by one interviewer, small by another, was noted in *Current Biography*, 1976. Hugh Hefner was described as small in the *San Francisco Chronicle*, November 17, 1965, and tall in *Writer's Digest*, August 1955.

45–48 Jerry Parker told me about Mae West during a March 25, 1977, conversation in New York City. The actress's surprising petiteness is noted in: *The Philadelphia Record*, November 5, 1933; Alexander Walker, *Sex in the Movies* (Baltimore: Penguin, 1966), p. 65 (hereafter cited as Walker, *Sex*); the *Philadelphia Sunday Bulletin*, June 28, 1970; and David Hanna, *Come Up and See Me Sometime* (New York: Belmont Tower Books, 1976), p. 177. The *Philadelphia Daily News*, December 21, 1933, ran a feature describing in detail West's image-heightening strategies. Anita Loos wrote about her in *Kiss Hollywood Goodbye* (London: W. H. Allen, 1974), p. 170. Jon Tuska, author of *The Films of Mae West* (Secaucus, N.J.: Citadel, 1975), wrote me in a letter dated July 2, 1979, that when he told Miss West of his book, her height "was one of the things about which she was most 'sensitive.' "

49 Albert Meharabian wrote about movie sets in *Public Places and Private Spaces* (New York: Basic Books, 1976), pp. 206–207, as did Stephenson and Debrix in *Cinema*, p. 40. John Wayne's sets were discussed in *Current Biography*, 1951; and Mary Pickford's were described in Walker, *Sex*, p. 49, and in her autobiography, *Sunshine and Shadow* (New York: Doubleday, 1955), p. 147.

49–50 Seymour Fisher discusses people's relative sense of their own size in *Body Consciousness* (Englewood Cliffs, N.J.: Prentice-Hall, 1973), p. 108 (hereafter cited as Fisher, *Body Consciousness*); he refers to the Clark University Lilliputian-room experiments in *Body Experience in Fantasy and Behavior* (New York: Appleton-Century-Crofts, 1970), p. 31.

51 Thomas Wolfe wrote autobiographically about tallness in the story "Gulliver," which is included in *From Death to Morning* (1935; reprint ed., New York: Charles Scribner's Sons, 1963), pp. 137–138 (hereafter cited as Wolfe, "Gulliver").

Dick Cavett's rejoinder was quoted in *Look,* July 15, 1969.

52 Larry Csonka's comment appeared in *The Sporting News,* July 8, 1978.

Stephen Jay Gould's remarks here and throughout, unless otherwise specified, are from my interview with him at Harvard on September 28, 1977, or from his responses to my questionnaire.

Although much research has been done in recent years on the psychology of eye contact, relative height is seldom considered as a variable in such research. The *Los Angeles Times,* November 24, 1977, surveyed this field, and Michael Argyle and Mark Cook, *Gaze and Mutual Gaze* (Cambridge: Cambridge University Press, 1976) synthesizes such research done up to that time.

52–53 Desmond Morris discussed ritualistic evaluation and prostration in *Manwatching* (New York: Harry N. Abrams, 1977), pp. 142–152.

53 Bill Russell wrote about meeting Haile Selassie on p. 151 of the Berkeley ed. (New York, 1966) of *Go Up for Glory* (New York: Coward, McCann & Geoghegan, 1966).

Susan Berman made the comment about Myerson in *New York,* November 14, 1977, p. 45. A similar point was made in *Us,* October 18, 1977, p. 22.

56 Robert Sommer described his wheelchair experiment in a letter to me dated January 28, 1977.

57 The first 82 students I polled on Carter's height were enrolled at Cedar Crest College, Allentown, Pa., in the fall of 1977. The group of 47 students I subsequently polled, in the spring of 1978, were enrolled in a library science class at Kutztown State College, Kutztown, Pa.

The LBJ observer is quoted by Richard Harwood and Haynes Johnson in *Lyndon* (New York: Praeger, 1973), pp. 160–161.

Kids' drawings of Santa Claus were discussed in *Menninger Perspective* 12 (1958): 22–24, and by Roy Craddick in *Journal of Psychological Studies* 12 (1961): 121–125.

57–58 Voters' estimates of candidate size are reported by Harold H. Kassarjian in *Journal of Psychology* 56 (1963): 85–88.

58 On explorers' reports about Patagonians, see *Scientific American Supplement,* November 18, 1905. According to the *Guinness Book of World Records 1973* (New York: Bantam), p. 16, males among the Tehuelches of Patagonia who have been estimated to be as tall as 7'8" were in fact 5'10" on average, and at maximum were 6'6¾".

58–59 On Amazons, see: Guy Cadogan Rothery, *The Amazons* (London: Francis Griffiths, 1910); Helen Diner, *Mothers and Amazons* (New York: The Julian Press, 1965); Sara Weiss, "Oh, Those Amazon Women!" *Caribbean Review* 6 (July–September 1974): 11–17; the Oxford Unabridged Dictionary; and Phyllis Chesler, *Women and Madness* (New York: Doubleday, 1972). Although something of an Amazon fan, Phyllis Chesler is herself not tall — a fact she says many people note with surprise when first meeting her, and one about which she's apparently sensitive; she once asked a reporter if it was necessary to mention her shortness in print (*Human Behavior,* September 1978, p. 53).

59 Erving Goffman's analysis of human size in ads is in his article "Gender Advertisements" in *Studies in the Anthropology of Visual Communication* 3 (Fall 1976): 69–154, which was reprinted in 1979 as a hardbound book (Cambridge: Harvard University Press) and as a paperback (New York: Harper & Row).

59–60 Terence Young was quoted on Amazons and Andress in *Calendar (Los Angeles Times),* July 8, 1973.

60 The Royal Canadian Mounted Police manual was described and quoted in the *Los Angeles Times,* March 27, 1975.

Tony Horn's protest was described to me by his mother, Pat Horn, in a 1977 conversation.

Saul Feldman's paper, presented at the ASA's 1971 meetings in Denver, was included in revised form in Saul D. Feldman and Gerald W. Thielbar, eds., *Life Styles: Diversity in American Society*, 2d ed. (Boston: Little, Brown, 1975).

61 Wendell Wagner's protest was described in the *Los Angeles Times*, November 28, 1971, and in his May 16, 1972, letter to me (which enclosed a copy of "The Short Student's Demands").

"Remarks of the Honorable Edwin S. Cohen, Assistant Secretary of the Treasury for Tax Policy," delivered to the Federal Tax Institute of New England in Boston on April 29, 1972, were reported by the *Los Angeles Times*, April 30, 1972.

Edmund Szymczyk's lawsuit was reported ibid., February 2, 1978.

61 *The Guardian*'s 1713 report was discussed in Edward Wood's *Giants and Dwarfs* (London: Richard Bently, 1868), pp. 315–317.

62 John Kenneth Galbraith's conversation with Charles de Gaulle was described by him in *Ambassador's Journal* (Boston: Houghton Mifflin, 1969), p. 598.

William Berkowitz described his study of friendship choice and height in *Psychological Reports* 24 (1969): 373–374, and during a conversation with me on September 21, 1977, in Arlington, Mass.

The Virginia Commonwealth study, conducted by John Hartnett, Kent Bailey, and Craig Hartley, was reported by them in *Journal of Psychology* 87 (1974): 129–136.

63–65 Sidney Portnoy talked with me in his Philadelphia office on June 7, 1978. The lines quoted are from his Ph.D. thesis (Temple University, 1972), pp. 56 and 49, respectively.

4 Talls

p. 67 Wilt Chamberlain's comment was reported by Fred Katz in *Today's Health*, September 1971.

68 Rod, Libby, Jesse, Muriel, and I saw San Diego lose to Philadelphia on April 29, 1978 (7–2, as Jesse recalls).

71–74 Francis Riggs's book was described in *Newsweek*, December 20, 1943.

74–75 Wolfe, "Gulliver," p. 141.

75 The Wilt Chamberlain episode is from his autobiography, *Wilt* (written with David Shaw; New York: Macmillan Co., 1973), p. 37 of the Warner ed. (New York, 1975; hereafter cited as *Wilt*).

75–77 I interviewed Peter Isacksen in Los Angeles on November 22, 1977; his comments here and elsewhere are from that meeting.

77 John Kenneth Galbraith's remark is from p. 53 of the New American Library ed. (New York, 1970) of his book *The Scotch* (Boston: Houghton Mifflin, 1964).

The two tall brothers, Francis and Walter Steegmuller, were described by the former in *The New Yorker*, December 26, 1959.

78 Russell Baker's comment is from a column of his that ran in the *New York Times* on January 31, 1978.

Jimmy Cagney described his approach in *Cagney by Cagney* (Garden City, N.Y.: Doubleday, 1976), pp. 56–57 (hereafter cited as Cagney, *Cagney*. Chuck Connors's experience was mentioned in *TV Guide Roundup* (New York: Popular Library, 1961), p. 66.

George Mikan included this story in his article "I Hope I Never Stop Growing," *American Magazine*, January 1954, p. 104.

79 Howard Mudd talked with me in February 1977 in Del Mar, Calif.

Gulliver's observations are from pp. 125 and 167 of the 1967 Penguin ed. (Middlesex, England, 1967) of Jonathan Swift's *Gulliver's Travels* (1726).

James Howell was quoted in *The Record* (American Institute of Actuaries) 29 (1940): 221 (hereafter cited as Actuaries, *Record*).

Nick Nolte's role in *The Deep* was characterized by John Lombardi in *Playboy*, August 1978, p. 36.

81–82 Albert Payson Terhune wrote about meeting a giant in "Troubles of a Big Guy," *American Magazine*, June 1926, p. 106 (hereafter cited as Terhune, "Troubles").

82 By extrapolation from statistics published in National Center, *Height* (p. 5), 0.01 percent of American men are 6'10" or taller.

82–85 Michael Crichton discussed his height with me in an interview in Culver City, Calif., on November 15, 1977.

5 Smalls

p. 87 The Colonel Meecham passage appeared in Pat Conroy's novel *The Great Santini* (Boston: Houghton Mifflin, 1976), pp. 165–166.

88 Randy Newman's early prediction about public response to "Short People" was quoted in *Us*, February 21, 1978. Steve Lawrence and Tim Conway, Gene Hughs of Gusto Records in Nashville, and Kevin O'Neill of WVBF-FM in Boston all composed songs called "Tall People," as reported in the *Los Angeles Times*, February 5, 1978, and February 11, 1978, and in the *Allentown* (Pa.) *Morning Call*, January 19, 1978. The Maryland state legislator was mentioned on a radio news broadcast I heard on WAEB-AM (Allentown, Pa.) on April 5, 1978. Newman's further comments appeared respectively in: *Rolling Stone*, November 17, 1977; *Circus*, January 5, 1978; *Champaign-Urbana* (Ill.) *News-Gazette*, January 13, 1978; *People*, January 30, 1978; and ibid. The *Wall Street Journal*, January 18, 1978, included a good roundup of reactions to "Short People."

89 The letter to *Playboy* ran in the November 1977 issue; the one in *People*, July 17, 1978.

89–90 De Toledano wrote of Robert Kennedy's size on p. 28 of the Signet ed. (New York, 1968) of *RFK: The Man Who Would Be President* (New York: Putnam's, 1967).

90 J. Anthony Lukas wrote of Julius Hoffman in *The New York Times Magazine*, March 29, 1970.

Erich Maria Remarque, *All Quiet on the Western Front* (Boston: Little, Brown, 1929), pp. 10–11 of the Fawcett Crest ed. (Greenwich, Conn., n.d.).

Ian Fleming's passage is from *Goldfinger* (New York: Macmillan Co., 1959), p. 25 of the Signet ed. (New York, n.d.).

91 Roth's letter in *British Medical Journal* ran February 3, 1968.

The RCMP manual was quoted in the *Los Angeles Times*, March 27, 1975.

The discussion of smaller-people's problems appeared in R. G. Barker, B. A. Wright, and M. R. Gonick, *Adjustment to Physical Handicap and Illness: A Survey of the Social Psychology of Physique and Disability* (New York: Social Science Research Council, 1946), quoted from p. 13.

91–92 The 1975 study is by Aleonso Prieto and Michael Robbins, reported in *Per-*

ceptual and Motor Skills 40 (1975): 395–398 (hereafter cited as Prieto and Robbins, *Perceptual Skills*).

92   David Rimoin's observation was made in our interview on February 23, 1977, in Torrance, Calif. *Time*'s article on his clinic ran on May 7, 1973. Rimoin coauthored (with James Brust and Charles Ford) the paper "Psychiatric Aspects of Dwarfism," *American Journal of Psychiatry* 133 (1976): 160–164.

John Money's comments were made October 10, 1977, when I interviewed him in his office at Johns Hopkins University, Baltimore, Md.; his remarks hereafter are from that session unless otherwise noted.

93   I wrote Col. MacCarthy on February 27, 1978, and received his reply dated March 7, 1978. (Both letters were ably translated by Andrea Herrmann.)

R. Frank Richardson, *Napoleon: Bisexual Emperor* (New York: Horizon Press, 1973), pp. 68–69 and 230, discusses errors in recording Napoleon's height (p. 69 quoted).

94   Alfred Adler's reference to Napoleon is in Heinz Ansbacher and Rowena Ansbacher, eds., *The Individual Psychology of Alfred Adler* (New York: Basic Books, 1956), p. 36.

94–97   I interviewed Mark Moore at Harvard on September 28, 1977.

99–101   David Landsberg's comments here and throughout were made during an interview with me in Los Angeles on November 22, 1977.

101   J. Edgar Hoover's instructions to FBI employees and his scaled furnishings are mentioned in Joseph Schott, *No Left Turns* (New York: Praeger, 1975), pp. 160, 198, 111–112; Norman Ollestad writes about Hoover's riser on p. 131 of the Lancer ed. (New York, 1968) of *Inside the FBI* (New York: Lyle Stuart, 1967).

101–102   I visited Richlee Shoe and Foot-Joy in Brockton on February 22, 1977.

105–107   Joel Grey's comments to me, here and throughout, are from a June 23, 1978, interview and a June 3, 1978, telephone conversation; his nightclub routines were reported by *Time*, November 26, 1973, and *Newsweek*, March 11, 1974.

6   Petites and Amazons

p. 109   George Will, *Newsweek*, June 26, 1978.

110   "Hello Twelve, Hello Thirteen, Hello Love" from *A Chorus Line;* music by Marvin Hamlisch, lyric by Edward Kleban, copyright © 1975.

111–113   I interviewed Janet Wong in New York City on March 9, 1978.

113–114   Suzi Quatro was quoted in the *Philadelphia Inquirer*, July 4, 1979, and Joan Didion in the *St. Louis Post-Dispatch*, June 19, 1979.

115   Joan Rivers's thoughts here and elsewhere are from her response to my questionnaire.

117   *Us* wrote about Colleen Dewhurst on November 15, 1977; Jack Anderson on Jane Fonda in the *Chicago Daily News*, May 12, 1972; the *Philadelphia Inquirer* on Veronica Porche, August 14, 1978; *The New Yorker* on Judith Cohen, May 30, 1977; *The New York Times Book Review* on Claire Bretécher, April 16, 1978; and *Life* on Rona Barrett, March 21, 1969.

118   *New Times* wrote about Mary Jo Peppler on March 7, 1975; *People* on Midge Costanza, December 26, 1977; *Newsweek* on Lucie Arnaz, February 26, 1979; the *Philadelphia Inquirer* on Françoise Sagan, January 8, 1979; *Current Biography* on Madeline McWhinney, 1976; and Lally Weymouth on Iphigene Sulzberger in *New York*, January 17, 1977.

119 Rudolph Valentino was quoted in praise of dainty women in *Photoplay Treasury* (New York: Crown Bonanza Books, 1972), p. 99.

120 Judith Wax, who died in a DC10 crash in Chicago, is quoted from her autobiographical *Starting in the Middle* (New York: Holt, Rinehart & Winston, 1979), pp. 127–128 and 132 (hereafter cited as Wax, *Starting*).

122–123 Marilee, Harriet, and Harold Marzoni are pseudonyms.

124 Virginia Spencer Carr wrote of McCullers's height in *The Lonely Hunter* (Garden City, N.Y.: Doubleday, 1975), p. 30. *The Heart is a Lonely Hunter* (Boston: Houghton Mifflin, 1940) is excerpted from p. 94 of the Bantam ed. (New York, 1977). Carr described the mother-daughter episode on p. 30 of her biography.

124–125 I met with Lynnie Greene in New York City on February 16, 1978.

125–126 Seymour Fisher's observation is from Fisher, *Body Consciousness*, p. 121.

126 Tatiana Kalatschova — considered the "perfect" model at 5'7", 117 pounds, size 8 — was profiled in *Parade*, July 2, 1978. Northern Illinois University statisticians George L. Miller and Chipei P. Tseng discussed their analysis of the heights of Miss America contestants and other considerations in their report to the American Statistical Association on "The Anatomy of Miss America" (mimeographed, 17 pp., 1979; hereafter cited as Miller and Tseng, "Anatomy"); their findings were summarized in the *Philadelphia Bulletin*, August 14, 1979, and the *New York Times*, September 4, 1979. The White Rock soda label lady's evolution is illustrated in Peter Farb, *Humankind* (Boston: Houghton Mifflin, 1978), p. 242.

127 Allan Katcher and Max Levin describe the four- and five-year-olds' drawings of themselves in *Child Development* 26 (1955): 103–110 (pp. 108–109 are quoted). Juliet Popper Shaffer reports on fifth- to eighth-grade girls underestimating their height in *Genetic Psychology Monographs* 70 (1964): 97–134, p. 122.

Jerome Kagan described his results in *Journal of Personality* 34 (1964): 118–128 (pp. 124–125 quoted). Avrum Miller's research was for his M.A. thesis "Height as a Variable in Social Perception" (University of Guelph [Ontario], 1973).

127–128 Abe Arkoff and Herbert Weaver reported the results of their study of Japanese-American and Caucasian-American women in *Journal of Social Psychology* 68 (1966): 323–330 (p. 325 quoted).

129 The experiences of early- and late-maturing girls were reported by Mary Cover Jones and Paul Henry Mussen in *Child Development* 29 (1958): 491–501.

129–130 The case studies were described by Jean MacFarlane in *Physical and Behavioral Growth* (Ross Pediatric Research Center), "Report of an October 30–31, 1957, Conference," pp. 74–76.

7   Height Between the Sexes, Sex Between the Heights

p. 135 Hugh Morris's *The Art of Kissing* (Philadelphia: Franklin Publishing Co., 1936; New York: Doubleday, 1977) was discussed in *The New York Times Book Review*, March 20, 1977.

136 Jeanne Brooks and Michael Lewis discussed their experiment and those leading up to it in *Child Development* 47 (1976): 323–332 (p. 330 quoted in part).

137 The men's and the women's height statistics are taken from National Center, *Height*, p. 2.

138 Sylvester Stallone's comment appeared in *Today* (*Philadelphia Inquirer*), April 30, 1978.

The manikin experiment is described by John Spiegel and Pavel Machotka in *Messages of the Body* (New York: The Free Press, 1974; p. 311 quoted).

The London social worker's comment was quoted in the *London Evening Standard,* December 20, 1977.

138–139 Sally Kellerman's comments appeared, respectively, in *The National Enquirer,* June 21, 1977, and *People,* March 10, 1975.

139 Carson McCullers, *The Ballad of the Sad Cafe* (Boston: Houghton Mifflin, 1951).

Barbara Jefferis, *The Tall One* (New York: William Morrow, 1977).

141 William Stini's data is adapted from his contribution to Elizabeth Watts, Francis Johnston, and Gabriel Lasker, eds., *Biosocial Interrelations in Population Adaptation* (The Hague: Mouton Publishers, 1975), p. 30.

142 On girls' muscles, see Tanner, *Daedalus,* p. 911.

142–143 On baboons' and gibbons' size, see: M. Kay Martin and Barbara Voorhis, *Female of the Species* (New York: Columbia University Press, 1975), pp. 121–143; and Walter Leutenneger and James Kelly in *Primates* 18 (1977): 117–136 (hereafter cited as Leutenneger and Kelly, *Primates*).

143 The size increase of terrestrial man is discussed by William Stini in *American Anthropologist* 73 (1971): 1019–1030 (p. 1023 quoted).

On primate size differences, see Leutenneger and Kelly, *Primates* (p. 132 quoted).

J. M. Tanner's comment is from Tanner, *Daedalus,* p. 907.

143–144 Charles Darwin first suggested in 1871 that increased body size conferred an advantage among males competing for females; recent evidence confirming this hypothesis is reported in *Nature,* October 27, 1977, pp. 797–800, and ibid., November 10, 1977, pp. 99–100.

144 Leutenneger and Kelly, *Primates,* p. 133, is quoted (on female availability).

Richard Leakey's thoughts are from his and Roger Lewin's *People of the Lake* (Garden City, N.Y.: Anchor Press/Doubleday, 1978), pp. 237, 234, 36–37.

145 A. M. Thomson reported his findings in *The Eugenics Review* 51 (1959): 157–162 (p. 161 quoted).

Marvin Harris wrote in *The New York Times Magazine,* November 13, 1977; Thomson notes that tall women are more likely to migrate, ibid., p. 162, and in Thomson, *Growth,* p. 197.

145–146 Janet Saltzman Chafetz, *Masculine/Feminine or Human?* (Itasca, Ill.: F. E. Peacock Publishers, 1974), p. 23.

146 Frank Ward's comment is cited in Helen Beal Woodward, *The Bold Women* (New York: Farrar, Straus & Young, 1953), pp. 339–340. Weston La Barre is quoted from his book *The Human Animal* (Chicago: University of Chicago Press, Phoenix Books, 1954), p. 108.

Mary Wollstonecraft scolds her sisters in *A Vindication of The Rights of Women* (1792; reprint ed., New York: W. W. Norton, 1976), p. 76. Elizabeth Gould Davis, who died in 1974, wrote about woman's "downfall" in *The First Sex* (New York: Putnam's, 1971); p. 96 of the Penguin ed. (Baltimore, 1972) is quoted here.

147 Irwin Shaw's story "Small Saturday" appeared in *Playboy,* September 1971 (p. 100 excerpted here).

Ellen Berscheid, Elaine Walster, and George Bohrnstedt reported their study of body image in *Psychology Today,* November 1973 (p. 126 quoted).

148 The Cedar Crest survey was conducted in the fall of 1977.

148–149 William Graziano, Thomas Brothen, and Ellen Berscheid, "Height and Attraction: Do Men and Women See Eye-to-Eye?" *Journal of Personality* 46 (1978): 128–145 (p. 143 quoted).

149 The University of Minnesota study, conducted by Elaine Walster, Vera Aronson, and Darcy Abrahams, is reported by them in *Journal of Personality and Social Psychology* 4 (1966): 508–516 (p. 510 quoted).

149–150 Christopher Smart's complaint is anthologized in Norman Callan, ed., *The Collected Poems of Christopher Smart* (London: Routledge & Kegan Paul, 1949), pp. 112–113.

151 Dustin Hoffman's comment was made to Beverly Sills on her television program broadcast May 7, 1978, on WNBC-TV in New York City.

151–153 Sammy Davis, Jr.'s, tall partner, Azizi Johari, described their act in *Playboy,* June 1975, and in *Black Stars,* August 1976.

153 The further Irwin Shaw excerpt is from *Playboy,* September 1971, p. 122.

156 I interviewed Richard Clopper in his Johns Hopkins University office on October 10, 1977.

G. A. Piersol, *Human Anatomy* (Philadelphia: J. B. Lippincott, 1907), p. 1972.

156–157 William Masters and Virginia Johnson's confirmation of Piersol's finding is from *Human Sexual Response* (Boston: Little, Brown, 1966), p. 193.

157–158 Hugo Beigel's 1954 study "Body Height in Mate Selection" was published in *Journal of Social Psychology* 39 (1954): 257–268 (p. 263 quoted). Seymour Fisher's "Power Orientation and Concept of Self Height in Men: Preliminary Note" was published in *Perceptual and Motor Skills* 18 (1964): 732.

158–159 Sandy Allen is listed as 7'7¼", the world's tallest living woman, in *Guinness Book of World Records 1979* (New York: Bantam), pp. 15–16; she was quoted about marriage by Leslie Bennets in the *Philadelphia Evening Bulletin,* January 10, 1978.

8   At the Ends of the Spectrum

p. 161 Abe Lincoln's comment is from Frederick Drimmer, *Very Special People* (New York: Amjon Publishers, 1973), p. 178 of the Bantam ed. (New York, 1976).

162–168 Sandy Allen appeared at the Downingtown (Pa.) Farmer's Market, where I interviewed her, on January 7, 1978.

170–174 The smaller-people's workshop took place at the Human Growth Foundation's annual meeting held in Pittsburgh on May 21, 1977; the later gathering was the Short Stature Symposium VI of the Moore Clinic, Johns Hopkins University, Baltimore, Md., took place June 18, 1978.

175–176 My interview with Lee Kitchens took place at the Pittsburgh meeting on May 21, 1977; *People's* interview with him appeared in the November 21, 1977, issue.

9   Big Bucks in the Boardroom

p. 177 Gerard R. Roche was quoted by Milton Rockmore in *The American Way,* January 1978, p. 49.

178–179 Leland Deck's story and comments are from our June 1972 telephone conversation; his study is reported in *Journal of the College and University Personnel Asso-*

ciation 19 (1968): 33–37 (hereafter cited as Deck, *Personnel*); the two-page follow-up "Supplemental Study," in photocopied form, is dated 1971 (hereafter cited as Deck, "Study").

179–180 The Provident Mutual study was published in Actuaries, *Record,* pp. 211–223.

180–181 Adam J. Boxer described his study for me on July 21, 1978. Previous analysis of the Air Corps cadet data (though not by height) is reported in Robert Thorndike and Elizabeth Hagen, *Ten Thousand Careers* (New York: John Wiley & Sons, 1959) and in Paul Taubman and Terence Wales, *Higher Education and Earnings* (New York: McGraw-Hill, 1974).

181 The Canadian poll, conducted in thirty-two urban centers by Montreal's Data Laboratories Research Consultants, was reported in *Weekend Magazine* (a supplement to various Canadian newspapers), September 30, 1978, p. 3.

David Kurtz's study was reported by him in *Personnel Journal* 48 (1969): 981–983; he told me about response to it during a telephone conversation in June 1972.

181–182 John Kenneth Galbraith's comment is from the *Christian Science Monitor,* May 18, 1977.

182 Leland Deck's remark is from Deck, *Personnel,* p. 35.

The *U.S. News and World Report* article, "Short People — Are They Being Discriminated Against?" ran in the March 28, 1977, issue.

182–183 Harry Scharlatt described his seminars for me in his Union Carbide office in Manhattan on July 21, 1978; his subsequent remarks are also from that interview.

183 Robert Half's comments here and throughout were made to me by phone, April 19, 1978.

184 David Chambers's thoughts were expressed when I interviewed him in his Manhattan office on April 21, 1978; the episode involving a 5'10" candidate was also mentioned in the *Wall Street Journal,* November 24, 1976.

184–185 Tom Mechling's comments were made to me over the phone on June 12, 1978; T. Vincent Learson is described in William Rodgers, *Think* (New York: Stein & Day, 1969), p. 250.

186 Joseph Murrey's Ph.D. thesis, "The Role of Height and Weight in the Sales Performance of Salesmen of Ordinary Life Insurance," was completed at North Texas State University (Denton) in 1976 (p. 2 quoted; hereafter cited as Murrey, "Salesmen").

David Kurtz's comment appeared in *U.S. News and World Report,* March 28, 1977.

186–187 John T. Molloy describes his experiment in *Dress for Success* (New York: Peter Wyden, 1975), pp. 123–125 of the Warner Books ed. (New York, 1976).

187–188 Robert Stevens reported the shorter of 37 salesmen selling more insurance in *Carroll Business Bulletin* 14 (Winter 1975): 15–16. Ben Feldman is profiled in *The New York Times Magazine,* April 2, 1978.

188 The Police Foundation's study is *Police Officer Height and Selected Aspects of Performance* (Washington, D.C., 1975), done in conjunction with the International Association of Chiefs of Police and the Urban Institute (p. 1 quoted).

188–190 *Smith* v. *City of East Cleveland,* 363 F. Supp. 1131 (N.D. Ohio 1973).

190 Judge J. Marsh noted Bill Klem's size (and renown) in his decision striking down professional umpires' size requirements in *New York State Division of Human Rights* v. *New York–Pennsylvania Professional Baseball League,* 36 App. Div. 2d 364 (1971). The Supreme Court's decision on Alabama prison guards is *Dothard* v. *Rawlinson,* 433 U.S. 321 (1977).

190–191 *Boyd* v. *Ozark Air Lines, Inc.* is in 419 F. Supp. 1061 (E.D. Mo. 1976).

191 Carol Wagner's case was reported extensively in the New York press; her comment here is from the *New York Times,* October 31, 1976.

Leland Deck's hypothesis is from Deck, "Study," p. 1.

192 Shirley Chisholm described her job hunt in *Unbought and Unbossed* (Boston: Houghton Mifflin, 1970), pp. 39–40 of the Avon ed. (New York, 1971).

193 Judith Wax's comment is from Wax, *Starting,* p. 131. The survey of Scottish working women is reported in Thomson, *Growth,* pp. 197–198.

Joseph Murrey's finding is reported in Murrey, "Salesmen," pp. 2, 115, and 127–128.

194 Francine Gomez was described in *Newsweek,* April 9, 1973.

194–195 Letitia Baldrige was quoted by Fred Katz in *Today's Health,* September 1971.

195 Nancy Marchand's comment is from *The National Enquirer,* April 3, 1979.

196 Terry Smith made these comments during an interview with me in Coopersburg, Pa., on May 29, 1978.

198 Harry Johnson reported his finding in an undated letter to me received in May 1978.

199–200 TALL JOBS: *Pond* v. *Braniff Airways, Inc.,* 500 F. 2d 161 (5th Cir. 1974). The call for chorus girls appeared in *Back Stage,* August 4, 1978; the Lido ad ran in the *San Diego Union,* May 7, 1979. The Texas Department of Safety's 1974 report (prepared by C. A. Dempsey), "A Study of Police Height Requirements," p. 34, indicated that of 1,000 fugitives sought by the FBI, 96.7 percent were males who averaged 5'10", as did a sample of 3,796 Texas felons, 74 percent of whom were between 5'8" and 6'2"; Ernest Hooton, *The American Criminal* (New York: Greenwood Press, 1939) reported that thieves and murderers were tall.

Psychologist A. T. Poffenberger made the point about doormen in *Applied Psychology* (London: D. Appleton, 1927), p. 261. The study of Finnish lumberjacks by O. Eränkö and M. J. Karvonen appeared in *American Journal of Physical Anthropology* 13 (1955): 331–344. The statistical study of Miss Americas was Miller and Tseng, "Anatomy"; Cheryl Prewitt's height was listed in the *Philadelphia Inquirer,* September 9, 1979; the report quoted ran in *Parade,* September 2, 1973, p. 9. Eileen Ford's model standards are characterized by Rita Christopher in *Us,* September 20, 1977, p. 24; *Us,* May 31, 1977, p. 84, reported Ford's ideal-height range.

On Wall Street's ex-jocks, see *New York,* January 8, 1973, pp. 28–32; the prevalence of former athletes among his colleagues was confirmed for me by an ex–basketball player at a brokerage in New York. Enoch Gowin's occupational height data is reported in his book *The Executive and His Control of Men* (New York: Macmillan Co., 1916), p. 25 (hereafter cited as Gowin, *Executive*). Champion teamsters' heights were reported by Albert Damon and Ross McFarland in *American Journal of Physical Anthropology* 13 (1955): 711–742.

200–202 SMALL JOBS: On astronauts, see *U.S. News and World Report,* March 28, 1977; on the Pole, see the *Washington Post,* July 2, 1978, and *Information Please Almanac 1979,* p. 37. Ted Giannoulas was described in *People,* September 25, 1978. Blacksmith Jim Hall of Philadelphia was profiled by the *Philadelphia Inquirer,* August 22, 1979. The owner of Shorty's Bakery is quoted in *U.S. News and World Report,* March 28, 1977. Francis Galton's thought about small soldiers is from his book *Hereditary Genius* (1869; New York: Horizon Press, 1952), p. 139.

Short news photographer Maurice Sorrell cited his advantage in *Ebony,* October 1975; on Richard Avedon's impersonator, see *Newsweek,* September 19, 1977. The two psychologists, Jim Hassett and Gary Schwartz, noted their occupational stature in *The New York Times Magazine,* February 6, 1977. Dorothy Storck wrote about radio reporters' shortness in the *Philadelphia Inquirer,* July 5, 1976. Bill Davidson commented on the shortness of Darin and other singers in his book *New Types of Old Americans at Harvard* (Cambridge: Harvard University Press, 1932), p. 4.

Frederick Drimmer, *Very Special People* (New York: Amjon Publishers, 1973) mentions midget Egyptian gods and Gregory of Tours, pp. 191–192 of the Bantam ed. (New York, 1976); Karl Pearson's observation is from *Philosophical Transactions of the Royal Society, Series A* 192 (1899): 217; Pope John Paul I's comment was widely quoted, as in the *Allentown* (Pa.) *Morning Call,* August 28, 1978. The shortness of William Morris's agents was referred to as the rule of Tom Thumb in the *New York Times,* September 9, 1973; the agency was compared to Lilliput by Stanley Ralph Ross (quoted by Burt Prelutsky) in *West* (*Los Angeles Times*), May 7, 1972.

10 Voting by the Inch

p. 203 The "news item" is from *Newsweek,* December 24, 1979, p. 19.

204 Kandy Stroud quoted Gloria Carter Spann on her brother Jimmy Carter in *How Jimmy Won* (New York: Morrow, 1977), p. 128 (hereafter cited as Stroud, *Jimmy*). *People,* January 23, 1978, quoted the President's delight at his White House popularity. Carter's autobiography, *Why Not The Best?* (Nashville: Broadman Press, 1975) includes some of his size recollections — e.g., being smaller than his younger sister (p. 12 of the Bantam ed.; New York, 1976) and being small when he entered Annapolis (ibid., p. 45).

The Georgia newsman who recalled Carter — Bill Robinson — was quoted in *The National Enquirer,* July 12, 1977.

205 Robert Ellis Smith's comment was made during a conversation I had with him in Washington on January 23, 1977.

Ed Muskie's "height problem" was noted in the *Los Angeles Times,* July 14, 1976, and elsewhere; Peter Bourne confirmed Carter staff uneasiness about the Maine senator's 6'4″ height.

205–206 The summary of Jimmy Carter's problems debating Gerald Ford is from my own observation, plus: Stroud, *Jimmy,* p. 364; *Newsweek,* September 27, 1976; Martin Schram, *Running for President* (New York: Stein & Day, 1977), p. 296 (hereafter cited as Schram, *President*); and the personal recollection of Peter Bourne, as well as Ford staffers Peter Kaye, Stuart Spencer, and Richard Cheney, who spoke to me by phone on February 24, 1977, September 29, 1977, and September 30, 1977, respectively.

206 The 305 questionnaires include 200 in general (see Appendix A) and 105 filled out by students at Cedar Crest College and Kutztown State College.

207 Jimmy Carter was quoted about Peter Bourne in *New Times,* August 21, 1978, p. 14.

208–209 John Adams is quoted on George Washington (from a letter to Benjamin Rush) in Rudolph Marx, *The Health of the Presidents* (New York: Putnam, 1960), p. 35; Madison's problems are described in that work — which includes the quotes from Washington Irving (p. 67) and Dolley Madison (p. 69) — and in Bess Furman, *White House Profile* (New York: Bobbs-Merrill, 1951), p. 55, where the contemporary — Mrs. William Seaton — is quoted.

209 Thomas Dewey's shoes are discussed by William Manchester in *The Glory and the Dream* (Boston: Little, Brown, 1974), p. 452.

Robert Kennedy's shoe problem was reported by the *New York Times*, April 13, 1978; the picture-taking episode is described in William Honan, *Ted Kennedy* (New York: Quadrangle, 1972), p. 132 of the Manor Books ed. (New York, 1972).

209–210 William Kruskal has described his search in various letters to me and in a phone conversation in mid-1978. The *This Week* article appeared on July 10, 1960. He is quoted from his October 13, 1971, letter to Saul Feldman.

210 The Ales Hrdlicka information is from his work *The Old Americans* (Baltimore: Williams & Wilkins, 1925), pp. 5–6 of the Arno Press ed. (New York, 1970).

Frank Cormier's experience was described in his book *LBJ: The Way He Was* (Garden City, N.Y.: Doubleday, 1977), pp. 180–181.

214 Ernest Furgurson wrote of LBJ's ''6'3'' style of leadership''-in the *Los Angeles Times*, May 16, 1971; Robert Sherrill's observation is from *The Accidental President* (New York: Grossman, 1967), p. 10 of the Pyramid ed. (New York, 1968).

The semifacetious commentator on Big Jim Thompson, Michael Kilian, wrote in the *Chicago Tribune*, June 15, 1978; Thompson's comments are from his letter to me dated June 23, 1978, in response to my questionnaire.

The television commentators discussed Bill Bradley on Philadelphia's KYW-TV on June 7, 1978.

214–215 Daniel Moynihan's advance man, Jim Levy, was quoted in the *New York Times*, October 5, 1976.

215 The finagling of Morris Udall's assistant is described in Schram, *President*, p. 67.

215–216 On Herman Badillo and Abe Beame, see especially *The New Yorker*, July 23, 1973, p. 60.

216 Gloria Schaffer's experience and observations are from her telephone conversation with my associate David Berry on March 29, 1978.

217–218 Lowell Weicker's comments are from my June 22, 1978, interview with him.

218 Howard Baker's remark during the Watergate hearing was televised June 28, 1973; the comment was paraphrased in the next day's *Los Angeles Times*.

The 1866 survey was reported in U.S. Department of Agriculture, Agricultural Research Service, *Home Economics Research Report #10*, August 1960, Washington, D.C., p. 5. Enoch Gowin's survey data is from Gowin, *Executive*, pp. 23, 28.

220 Howard Baker's letter to me was dated July 20, 1973.

223 William Berkowitz's study was reported in American Psychological Association, *Proceedings* (of the Seventy-ninth Annual Convention), 1971, p. 282, and during our conversation.

Jimmy Breslin's essay appeared in *New York*, July 28, 1969 (p. 25 quoted).

224 J. James Exon's comments are replies from his questionnaire.

Louie Welch talked of getting into politics in *U.S. News and World Report*, March 28, 1977. Ed Koch's problems with La Guardia's desk were reported in the *New York Times*, April 12, 1978.

225 Shirley Chisholm's first quote is from *The New York Times Magazine*, June 25, 1978; the second is from p. 85 of the Bantam ed. (New York, 1974) of her book *The Good Fight* (New York: Harper & Row, 1973).

Harold H. Kassajarian in *Journal of Psychology* 56 (1963): 85–88 found voters perceiving their preferred presidential candidate as taller, as, to a lesser degree, did Charles D. Ward in *Journal of Personality* 35 (1967): 381–401.

227 William Safire called Jimmy Carter ''smaller than life'' in the *New York Times*, August 3, 1978.

The late George Meany's little joke ran in *Time*, November 27, 1978.

An official physical profile of the President, reported by the *Philadelphia Inquirer*, April 4, 1979, gave his height as 5'9½".

Carter's response to visitor Annie Duitscher, 106 years old, was reported by the *Los Angeles Times*, November 22, 1977.

11 Casting to Size

p. 229 Billy Wilder's thought about Humphrey Bogart and Audrey Hepburn is quoted by Ezra Goodman in *The Fifty-Year Decline and Fall of Hollywood* (New York: Simon & Schuster, 1961), p. 263 of the McFadden ed. (New York, 1962).

230–232 Scott Rudin's comments used here and subsequently were made in my interview with him on July 21, 1978. The Al Pacino movie he was casting, *Born on the Fourth of July,* was subsequently postponed indefinitely.

232 James Arness's casting problems have been widely discussed, most completely by Favius Friedman in *Motion Picture,* July 1958.

George Kennedy's comment is from the *Philadelphia Inquirer,* January 5, 1979; he made a similar observation in *Home* (*Los Angeles Times*), April 25, 1976.

233 Jane Feinberg discussed casting with my colleague Jane Weisman Stein in Los Angeles, February 1978.

David Hartman's recollection is from *Today's Health,* September 1971.

233–234 Bonnie Franklin's comment is from *People,* May 16, 1977.

234 Beverly Sills reprinted her poem in *Bubbles: A Self Portrait* (New York: Bobbs-Merrill, 1976), p. 62.

234–235 John Houseman described his problems with Alan Ladd in his introduction to Raymond Chandler's screenplay of *The Blue Dahlia* (Carbondale, Ill.: Southern Illinois University Press, 1976), p. xiii, reprinted there from *Harper's,* August 1965. A good summary of Ladd's career was done by Julian Fox in *Films and Filming,* June 1972 and July 1972; Beverly Linet, *Ladd* (New York: Arbor House, 1979) elaborates to some degree on the actor's height difficulties. On his problems with Sophia Loren, see ibid., pp. 204–206, and p. 91 of the Pinnacle ed. (New York, 1976) of Donald Zec, *Sophia* (New York: David McKay, 1975). James Robert Parish, *Hollywood's Great Love Teams* (New Rochelle, N.Y.: Arlington, 1974), p. 595, mentions the Ladd-Loren joke; *Mad*'s parody of the situation ran in the November 1958 issue.

236 James Cagney wrote of standing on a box in Cagney, *Cagney,* p. 56. Humphrey Bogart is quoted about wearing lifts on p. 48 of the Signet ed. (New York, n.d.) of Joe Hyams, *Bogie* (New York: New American Library, 1966).

236–237 Dwight Ott used Sylvester Stallone as a metaphor for bigness in the *Philadelphia Inquirer,* August 20, 1978. Stallone's height-oriented casting is common gossip in the movie industry, and was mentioned by *People,* May 8, 1978. He himself wrote about preferring Carl Weathers to Ken Norton in *Sylvester Stallone's Official Rocky Scrapbook* (New York: Tempo, 1977), p. 37. Robert Hatch called Stallone "a big man" in *The Nation,* June 3, 1978. Stallone talked of being considered too small to play Rocky in his *Playboy* interview, September 1978, p. 82.

237 After reading the *New York Post*'s April 18, 1979, report about Mac Davis having to stand on a crate for huddle scenes with Nick Nolte in *North Dallas Forty,* I watched that movie carefully and noticed the boots, camera angles, and disappearing feet.

The custom shoemaker, Pasquale Di Fabrizio, was chronicled in *The National Enquirer,* December 24, 1972.

Viewers can sometimes catch a glimpse of Burt Reynolds's impressive heels in his movies; his comment about 6-foot actors was reported by Roger Ebert in the *New York Times,* March 26, 1972.

238   Alexis Smith discussed her casting problems with Robert Berkvist in the *New York Times,* November 12, 1978, and with Julia Lawlor in the *Philadelphia Daily News,* September 8, 1978.

Melanie Griffith was quoted about going barefoot with Paul Newman in the *San Diego Evening Tribune,* August 19, 1975.

Ingrid Bergman's first meeting with David Selznick is described on p. 184 of the Pocket Book ed. (New York, 1972) of Bob Thomas, *Selznick* (Garden City, N.Y.: Doubleday, 1970), and in the *Philadelphia Evening Bulletin,* June 8, 1969; Selznick's cable is reprinted in Rudy Behlmer, ed., *Memo from David O. Selznick* (New York: Viking, 1972), p. 127, 130; Bergman's height problems in general are surveyed by *The National Enquirer,* December 23, 1973.

240   Maureen Silliman told me of the soap opera experience in an interview in New York on July 21, 1978.

240–241   Patty Weaver's remarks are from a February 1977 interview I had with her in Los Angeles. She appeared with Ron Howard in "Huckleberry Finn" on ABC-TV, March 25, 1975.

241–242   The casting calls are from: *Back Stage,* August 4, 1978; *Variety,* August 9, 1978; and *Drama-Logue,* November 11–12, 1977.

242–243   Richard Dreyfuss's comments were made to Roderick Mann, *Philadelphia Inquirer,* October 8, 1978; Meyer Mishkin's experiences with Dreyfuss were described by him to my associate Jane Weisman Stein in Los Angeles, February 1978; Dreyfuss mentioned his interest in playing Napoleon to Michael Goodwin in *The New York Times Magazine,* January 15, 1978, p. 15; Rex Reed's comment about the actor is from the *Philadelphia Inquirer,* May 4, 1975.

243   Katharine Ross's reaction to Dustin Hoffman was noted by *Life,* November 24, 1967.

244   Lee Majors's agent was quoted in *People,* July 31, 1978; the suggestion about Sally Field was made by Molly Haskell in *New York,* November 14, 1977.

12   Choosing Up Sizes

p. 247   Perry Chappas's comment is quoted by Larry Keith in *Sports Illustrated,* March 19, 1979, p. 26. This cover story on Harry Chappas touches on the controversy surrounding his height — 5'3", according to publicity-minded White Sox owner Bill Veeck; 5'5", according to other reports. Chappas himself is vague on the subject. I chose the average.

249   Janet Guthrie talked of driving, not carrying cars in the *New York Times,* April 16, 1978.

250   Nate Archibald's problems are discussed in Larry Fox, *The Giant Killers* (New York: Tempo, 1974), pp. 70–78, as are Larry Bowa's in the *Philadelphia Inquirer,* July 10, 1978; Hank Aaron's in the *Los Angeles Times,* April 5, 1974; and Joe Morgan's in Fox's book, pp. 19–25.

251   Randy Jones's comments were made to me in an interview on February 18, 1977, in San Diego.

252 Paul Gardner's thoughts are from his book *Nice Guys Finish Last* (New York: Universe Books, 1975), pp. 58–59 (hereafter cited as Gardner, *Nice Guys*).

The Sporting News, June 3, 1978; the *New York Times,* May 7, 1978.

252–253 Women intercollegiate athletes were reported taller than other coeds by Eldon Snyder and Joseph Kivlin, *Research Quarterly* 46 (1975): 191–199 (on p. 195).

253 The UCLA experiment was "A Study of Stature in Relation to Physical Performance," by Frederick W. Cozens, ibid. 1 (1930): 38–45.

Larry Hinson's complaint was reported in the *Los Angeles Times,* August 19, 1971.

254 The volleyball promotion ran in the *New York Times,* August 6, 1978.

On soccer, see John Allen, *Soccer for Americans* (New York: Grosset & Dunlap, 1967), and Paul Gardner, "Soccer, American Style," in *The New York Times Magazine,* May 4, 1975. The Yugoslav study, "Body Height and Predisposition for Certain Sports," by Radovan Medved, is in *Journal of Sports Medicine and Physical Fitness* 6 (1966): 89–91 (hereafter cited as Medved, "Height"). Kin-Itsu Hirata, "Physique and Age of Tokyo Olympic Champions," ibid. 6 (1960): 207–222 is quoted from p. 212 (hereafter cited as Hirata, "Physique"). The coach quoted is Jim Lennox of Hartwick College in *The Sporting News,* January 14, 1978.

254–255 On basketball's evolution, see: Gardner, *Nice Guys,* pp. 126–133; Leonard Koppett, *24 Seconds to Shoot* (New York: Macmillan Co., 1968); and Bob Rubin, *Basketball's Big Men* (New York: Scholastic Book Services, 1975).

255–256 The Kentucky study is reported by Ernst Jokl in *Journal of Health, Physical Education and Recreation,* 40 (1969): 65–68; the 1978 study is in the *New York Times,* December 11, 1978; that of Harvard crew team members is noted in Francis Riggs, *Tall Men Have Their Problems Too* (privately published, 1943), pp. 21–24; and that of Robert Malina is recorded in *American Journal of Physical Anthropology* 37 (1972): 135–142.

256 On height changes among foreign athletes, see Ernst Jokl et al., *Annals of the New York Academy of Sciences* 143 (1966): 908–937 (p. 919 especially).

256–257 On cycling, see: ibid.; *Bicycle Racing at the Trexlertown* (Pa.) *Velodrome,* 1978 souvenir program; *Racing '78* (*Velonews*), Brattleboro, Vt., 1978; and J. E. Lindsay Carter in *Human Biology* 42 (1970): 535–569 (p. 536).

258 Joe Morgan explained why he signed with the Astros in the *San Diego Evening Tribune,* November 19, 1975; Dave Twardzik's intention was noted in *The Sporting News,* January 7, 1978; the news report on tykes is from the *San Diego Union/Evening Tribune,* November 16, 1974.

259 Howard Cosell's comment was made on ABC-TV, April 18, 1977, Jim Palmer's on the same network during the 1978 World Series, and Jim Healy's on KLAC-AM (Los Angeles) on May 24, 1973.

260 Among suggestions for creating size categories in sports is that of T. Khosla in "Unfairness of Certain Events in the Olympic Games," *British Medical Journal* 4 (1968): 111–113.

The testing of Navy recruits was reported in *Research Quarterly* 23 (1952): 347–355.

260–261 On tall vs. small athletic virtues in general, see: Hirata, "Physique"; Medved, "Height"; and Tanner, *Athlete;* as well as Allan Ryan and Fred Allman, *Sports Medicine* (New York: Academic Press, 1974) and Behnke and Wilmore, *Body.*

261 The size of Boston Marathoners is reported by N. C. Lumian and V. F. Krumdick in *Athletic Journal* 45 (1965): 68, cited by David Costill, *What Research Tells the Coach about Distance Running* (Washington, D.C.: American Alliance for Health, Physical Education, & Recreation, 1968; hereafter cited as Costill, *Running*).

The 1970 text on physical performance is Astrand and Rodahl, *Physiology,* p. 326.

262 I talked by phone with Jerry Levine on September 20, 1979.

Woody Allen is quoted as being too short for chess in Bill Adler and Jerry Feinman, *Woody Allen* (New York: Pinnacle, 1975), p. 7; the Karpov-Korchnoi rivalry was reported by the *New York Times,* July 30, 1978.

Fencer Bob Yarrison, 6'6", discussed reach and target size in relation to his stature in the *Boston Herald-American,* December 26, 1977; Muriel Fischer in the *New York Times,* June 5, 1978, suggested fencing as ideal for man-woman competition.

263 Champion skiers were found shorter in Medved, "Height," p. 89.

265 On track and field, see: Tanner, *Athlete; Astrand and Rodahl, *Physiology;* Hirata, "Physique"; Costill, *Running;* and George Dintiman, *What Research Tells the Coach about Sprinting* (Washington, D.C.: American Alliance for Health, Physical Education, & Recreation, 1974).

The study of volleying ability and size was reported by Dorothy Mohr and Martha Haverstick in *Research Quarterly* 27 (1956): 74.

266 Wilt Chamberlain was quoted in *Today's Health,* September 1971, and Kareem Abdul-Jabbar in the *New York Times,* April 2, 1978, and in *Sports Illustrated,* October 30, 1978.

267–268 On Kurt Thomas, see *Life,* March 1979.

268 Billy Gazonas, 5'5", who went from College Player of the Year to the Tulsa Roughnecks, is written about in *Time,* May 1, 1978, p. 81. On Charlotte's athletic program, see *Sports Illustrated,* August 14, 1978, p. 14.

13   Putting Height in Perspective

p. 269 The children's talk show, "America after Lunch," hosted by Gary Coleman, was featured on "America 2-Night," televised May 4, 1978, on WKBS-TV in Philadelphia.

270 Erik Erikson's comment is from his book *Childhood and Society* (1950; New York: W. W. Norton, 1963), p. 404.

271 Layne Longfellow's comment here and those appearing later are from a tape he sent me in mid-1977 in response to my questionnaire.

272 Allan Katcher and Max Levin's comment is from *Child Development* 26 (1955): 103–110 (pp. 103–104 quoted).

273 Martha Wolfenstein writes of kids' jokes in her book *Children's Humor* (Glencoe, Ill.: The Free Press, 1954), pp. 23–61.

The Hopi's threat is mentioned in Wayne Dennis, *The Hopi Child* (New York: John Wiley & Sons, 1940), p. 78.

273–274 Berkeley youths are mentioned in *Dear Doctor Hip Pocrates* (New York: Grove Press, 1969), p. 28.

274 Seymour Fisher's thought is from Fisher, *Body Consciousness,* p. 125.

275–276 Ann Landers's first exchange, from her syndicated column, appeared in the *Champaign-Urbana* (Ill.) *Morning Courier,* May 1, 1977; the second letter ran ibid., May 11, 1978.

276–277 Ruth Gordon's dialogue is from p. 347 of the Dell ed. (New York, 1972) of her autobiography, *Myself among Others* (New York: Atheneum, 1971).

277 Alexis Smith made her comments (to Julia Lawlor) in the *Philadelphia Daily*

News, September 8, 1978, and (to Dorothy Storck) in the *Philadelphia Inquirer,* September 20, 1978.

278   John Money's comment is from p. 137 of his article "Dwarfism: Questions and Answers in Counseling" in *Rehabilitation Literature* 28 (1967): 134–138 (hereafter cited as Money, "Dwarfism").

Kareem Abdul-Jabbar's carrying his birth certificate is mentioned in Joel Cohen, *Big A: The Story of Lew Alcindor* (New York: Scholastic Book Services, 1971), p. 11.

279   King-Size's booklet "Taller than Our Fathers" (1976) is by Deborah Natansohn.

Albert Payson Terhune's comment is from Terhune, "Troubles," p. 103.

280   The thalidomide girl's problems were described in the *Los Angeles Times,* June 22, 1972, where her mother is quoted ("Joanne" is a pseudonym).

282   Michael Crichton's comment is from *Today's Health,* September 1971, p. 26.

J. M. Tanner makes the one-century-plus estimate frequently in his writings on growth trends — e.g., Tanner, *Daedalus,* p. 928; *Scientific American,* September 1972, p. 42.

284   Jeanne Parr described her sixth-grade experience in a conversation with me in New York City on February 16, 1978.

285   Billy Martin was called "the fiery little man" in the *San Diego Evening Tribune,* June 18, 1979, and "the feisty little manager" in the *New York Times,* August 7, 1978.

286   John Money talked about triggering mechanisms in our interview and wrote of them (with Ernesto Pollitt) in *Pediatrics* 68 (1966): 381–390 (p. 389 quoted).

286–287   Sylvia Plath's excerpt is from p. 8 of the Bantam ed. (New York, 1972) of *The Bell Jar* (New York: Harper & Row, 1971).

287   Seymour Fisher and Sidney Cleveland say body awareness may begin as early as six months in their book *Body Image and Personality* (Princeton, N.J.: D. Van Nostrand, 1959), p. 263.

287–288   Boyd McCandless's comments are from his book *Adolescents* (Hinsdale, Ill.: The Dryden Press, 1970), p. 92.

288   Prieto and Robbins, *Perceptual Skills,* p. 397.

Paul Williams made this comment in an interview in *Gallery,* November 1977, p. 33.

289   Charles Schulz is described in: *Saturday Evening Post,* January 12, 1957; *Los Angeles Times,* August 28, 1973; and p. 19 of the Signet ed. (New York, 1971) of Lee Mendelson (in association with Charles Schulz), *Charlie Brown and Charlie Schulz* (Cleveland: World, 1970).

Ron Fimrite wrote about Pete Rose in *Sports Illustrated,* May 15, 1978. Rose's choice of Robert Blake is mentioned in *Today* (*Philadelphia Inquirer*), October 15, 1978.

290   Carol Burnett was described by Lacey Fosburgh in *Ladies' Home Journal,* September 1977.

290–291   Helen Hayes mentioned not liking her small size in *Modern Screen,* December 1934, p. 79, and on p. 114 of the Fawcett Crest ed. (New York, 1969) of her autobiography, *On Reflection* (New York: M. Evans, 1968). Discussions of reactions to her portrayal of Cleopatra appeared in *Colliers,* March 30, 1929. Her performance as Mary Queen of Scots was evaluated by Irene Kuhn in the *New York World-Telegram,* January 16, 1934. Hayes discussed playing Mary in an undated *Philadelphia Ledger* clipping on file at the Philadelphia Free Library's Theater Collection.

292   On depressive reactions to stimulated growth, see Maria Kusalic, Claire Fortin, and Yvon Gauthier, "Psychodynamic Aspects of Dwarfism: Response to Growth Hormone Treatment," *Canadian Psychiatric Association Journal* 17 (1972): 29–33, and the subsequent paper by Kusalic and Fortin, ibid. 20 (1975): 325–331. Also see John Money's contribution to L. I. Gardner, ed., *Endocrine and Genetic Diseases of Childhood,* 2d ed. (Philadelphia: W. B. Saunders, 1975), pp. 1218–1227; and Money, "Dwarfism," from which his comment is excerpted (p. 134).

293 Albert Payson Terhune's list appears in Terhune, "Troubles," p. 104 (which is quoted).

Joel Grey made reference to smallness's universality in his interview; Wilt Chamberlain did so in *Wilt,* p. 40.

294–295 John Eichenlaub's thoughts are from *Today's Health,* July 1954.

295 William Graziano et al., "Height and Attraction," *Journal of Personality* 46 (1978): 128–145 (p. 144 quoted).

Abe Beame's observation appeared (in an article on Paul Williams) in the *Toronto Globe and Mail,* May 29, 1978; Calvin Murphy's, in *Sports Illustrated,* November 16, 1970, p. 26; John Cassavettes's, in his *Playboy* interview, July 1971, p. 64.

295–296 Mel Brooks's comment is from his *Playboy* interview, February 1975, p. 48.

Illustration Credits